A
BIOGRAPHY
OF
BILLY STRAYHORN

LUSH
LIFE

DAVID HAJDU

NORTH POINT PRESS

FARRAR STRAUS GIROUX

NEW YORK

North Point Press
A division of Farrar, Straus and Giroux
19 Union Square West / New York 10003

Copyright © 1996 by David Hajdu
All rights reserved
Published simultaneously in Canada by HarperCollins*CanadaLtd*
Printed in the United States of America
Designed by Abby Kagan
First published in 1996 by Farrar, Straus and Giroux
First North Point paperback edition, 1997

The Library of Congress has catalogued the hardcover edition as follows:

Hajdu, David.
    Lush life / a biography of Billy Strayhorn / David Hajdu.
        p.   cm.
    Includes bibliographical references and index.
    ISBN 0-374-19438-6
    1. Strayhorn, Billy.   2. Jazz musicians—United States—Biography.
I. Title.
ML410.S9325H35   1996
781.65'092—dc20
[B]   95-44707
                                             CIP
                                             MN

FOR ROY HEMMING

CONTENTS

PREFACE

Interviewer: How do you collaborate?

DUKE ELLINGTON: Sometimes, you know, I get an idea or somebody gives me an idea or we have a job to do, you know, and it has to be done. And sometimes I may need a little help, you know. *He* never needs any help. And so I'll call him from wherever I am, if I'm in another city, and say, "Now, this thing is going to be in four parts," or something like that, and, "You know, I mean, I think you would enjoy doing, say, for instance, the second movement, or the third movement—or the first, second, and third, and fourth movements. I will do the fifth movement." You know.

BILLY STRAYHORN: Yeah—you just *did* the fifth movement. I did the first four.

DUKE ELLINGTON: Well, I have a tremendous responsibility, you know. After all, if we're going to do a suite of four parts, I mean, I think Billy should do three of the movements, and I should only do one, because I have the responsibility of presenting it and being on stage when it's premiered. And, you know, I mean, I'm the one who's going to catch it, no matter whether, what it is, you know. If it's a big success, I have the tremendous responsibility of having to *bow*.

(Laughter)

BILLY STRAYHORN: He bows magnificently.

DUKE ELLINGTON: Oh, listen—it's the greatest thing. It's a wonderful thing, I mean, to bow after a Billy Strayhorn orchestration. This is one of the things I do *best*.

Duke Ellington was teasing, of course. But what if, behind the ironic hipster repartee, there was at least a hint of revelation in his talk of composing less than all of the work associated with him?

In a triumphant, celebrated career spanning five decades, Edward Kennedy Ellington transcended his origins as a dance-band leader to achieve international renown as one of the most original and enduring composers of the twentieth century. His stature has grown markedly in the years since his death in 1974. The perpetually expanding catalog of music recorded under his direction—more than 1,500 releases on compact disc worldwide—has become the largest in jazz and among the largest in all genres. Repertory orchestras such as the Smithsonian Jazz Masterworks Orchestra in Washington, DC, and the Lincoln Center Jazz Orchestra and the Carnegie Hall Jazz Band in New York perform Ellington with all the formal reverence granted the classical canon. Musicologists, educators, and historians have made Ellington inquiry an expanding field of study. What, then, would it mean if at least a portion of that "Ellingtonia" had been created in a manner far more complex and collaborative than many of Ellington's listeners may know? What if Duke Ellington wasn't just kidding and if, to an extent, sometimes, he really was taking bows for another composer?

What about Billy Strayhorn?

That's the question I began seeking to answer in the spring of 1984. I first heard Strayhorn praised with an almost evangelical fervor (a phenomenon that soon grew familiar as I asked more musicians about him) when I interviewed Gil Evans, the composer and arranger best known for his collaborations with Miles Davis, which produced the hybrid of improvisational pensiveness and orchestral sophistication labeled "cool jazz." "All I did—that's all I ever did—[was] try to do what Billy Strayhorn did," Evans told me.

What exactly did Billy Strayhorn do? And if he was so great, why wasn't he better known? I found a few basic facts a matter of record: William Thomas Strayhorn, born 1915, served as Duke Ellington's arranger for nearly three decades. He composed the Ellington Orchestra's theme, "Take the 'A' Train," and was the co-composer, with Ellington, of "Satin Doll" and other jazz standards introduced by Ellington's orchestra. Beyond that and such particulars as his birthplace (Dayton, Ohio), city of residence (New York), and various jazz-magazine awards he won (the *Down Beat* Jazz Critics' Poll for Best Arranger, 1946 and 1948, etc.), the absence of historical material on Strayhorn seemed conspicuous. From 1939, when Strayhorn began his association with Ellington, to his death from cancer in 1967, *The Readers' Guide to Periodical Literature* listed precisely one article on the subject of Billy Strayhorn. Moreover, in the first stages of my research, as I conducted exploratory interviews with musicians and Ellington specialists, I encountered a preponderance of riddles and contradictions.

A variety of assumptions about and perceptions of Strayhorn had settled into conventional wisdom within jazz circles. Among the most pervasive: Strayhorn was a raw talent with no professional experience until Ellington discovered him and groomed him in his own image. Strayhorn dedicated his entire professional life to the service of Duke Ellington and did virtually nothing outside Ellington's orbit. Strayhorn's role in the Ellington organization was, essentially, to assist Ellington in executing Ellington's ideas as Ellington wanted. Strayhorn was Ellington's alter ego and wrote in a style so akin to Ellington's that few people could distinguish their work.

Meanwhile, I found, an embittered subculture of Strayhorn devotees had long been clinging to equally reductive mirror views: Ellington was just a glamorous figurehead. Strayhorn really wrote all of his music of worth.

Promulgated for years, none of this turned out to be so simple. Much of it proved dead wrong.

Indeed, illusion emerged as one of the central themes of Billy Strayhorn's life. Through interviews with hundreds of musicians, performing artists, and other colleagues, as well as with Strayhorn's friends and family members (more than three thousand hours of conversations over the course of eleven years), unrestricted study of Strayhorn's personal papers, music, and artifacts (protected by his estate since his death), and research at the Smithsonian Institution, the Library of Congress, and various collections of jazz materials, I found that Strayhorn led an extraordinarily active and influential life despite his near anonymity. In time, it became evident that Strayhorn composed far more music than the listening public knows—hit songs, jazz pieces, concert works, film scores, music for a Broadway show. Urbane and a bon vivant, he lived well and hard. Strayhorn was homosexual, and he never seemed to care who knew. He lived in Harlem and loved Paris, where he collaborated on a musical drama with Orson Welles. His dearest friend was Lena Horne, who considered him her "soul mate" and "true love." He worked for the civil rights movement, often closely with the Reverend Dr. Martin Luther King, Jr. Strayhorn suffered demons, and he smoked and drank until the effects killed him.

This book is an effort to extricate Billy Strayhorn from the world of myth, to see who Billy Strayhorn was, how he came to create what he did the way he did it, and what *he* was doing during the applause.

1

SOMETHING

TO

LIVE

FOR

From the first, he was nameless. Lillian Strayhorn, twenty-three years old, had already had three children by the time she delivered her third boy in the early hours of November 29, 1915, and she had buried two of them. Sadie, the firstborn, had been premature and never could build her strength; she was "a coo baby," Lillian said. James Jr., a hearty boy born in 1912, was still faring well. Leslie, a second son, had been fine until he started walking and fell a few times, then went into convulsions; Lillian and her husband were told their child had brain fever. (As his mother often pointed out later, Leslie would have made a handsome man, which anyone could tell from the portrait she had taken of him in his coffin.) The newborn, unfortunately, was also sickly, despite being the first of Lillian's babies to be delivered by a doctor and in a hospital, the Miami Valley facility in Dayton, Ohio; he had rickets, and his parents decided not to name him. On the birth certificate filed four days after his birth, the tiny child was referred to as Baby Boy Strayhorn.

To heal him, the Strayhorns rejected professional advice—a doctor recommended cracking, straightening, and resetting the boy's bones, a surgical procedure fairly common at the time—in favor of a less traumatic home cure. Lillian followed the instructions of a neighbor woman and, after washing the dishes each evening, saved the water, which tended to be swirling with fat from the family's typical diet of fried meats. Standing her baby up in the water, Lillian massaged the greasy, soapy mixture into his skin; in time, his legs did begin to straighten and strengthen, whatever the reasons.

The rest of the Strayhorn family's problems had no such simple remedy. Married in a Baptist church ceremony on March 10, 1910, eighteen-year-old Lillian Young and twenty-year-old James Nathaniel Strayhorn had set out to lead an easier life together than the fates—and white-dominated early-century society—seemed to allow a black couple. The only child of Alice Young, a single mother from a comfortable working family in wooded Mars Hill, North Carolina, Lillian was attentively raised and well educated. She graduated from a two-year program for women at Shaw University, a Baptist school whose curriculum stressed ladylike manners and social skills. Poised and soft-spoken, with an eye for modest, womanly clothes and an ear for elegiac language ("I see the rain is slackening"), she earned a lifelong reputation for formality. James, a descendant of the founder of the first whiskey distillery established in the South after the Civil War, was also raised in relative comfort and style, in his case with four siblings (sisters Julia and Georgia—both graduates of finishing school—and brothers Joseph and William) in a roomy Prairie Victorian house in the black section of Hillsborough, North Carolina. Though James quit school to work after completing the eighth grade, his parents, Lizzie (Elizabeth) and Jobe Strayhorn—particularly his mother, an amateur pianist and art buff—had taken pride in exposing their children to music and culture. A firecracker of a man, James seemed a perfect counterbalance to Lillian, as ebullient as she was sedate, as spontaneous as she was doctrinal, as adventurous as she was restrained. They made an exquisite-looking couple: willowy, elegant Lillian, with her curly, pulled-up hair, her clear, open eyes, and a soft smile that nudged two sets of double dimples on her cheeks; and thick-set, towering James, with his glistening liquid eyes and broad, sly, cocksure grin.

In their second year of marriage, they left North Carolina for Dayton—electricity was the business of the future, and the Ohio Valley had emerged as a manufacturing center for the electric-supply industry. James was hired at a plant as a wire-puller: a team of men using handgrips would pull a roll of nearly molten copper until it stretched to wire thinness. Little more than a Northern industrial version of Carolina fieldwork, wire-pulling was considered a good job for a young black man; James didn't last long, though he never said why. He tried his hand at shipping goods for another plant but was let go because he couldn't drive. By the time his nameless son was born, three years after the move to Dayton, James was working as a janitor. Life at home was a struggle: Lillian, James, three-year-old Jimmy, and the baby all lived in one room of a boardinghouse on Norwood Avenue, a labor-housing district unequipped with the electricity that its residents were employed to supply for others, including the white working families just a few blocks to the west. Frustrated, the Strayhorns abandoned their electric-age ambitions in early 1916 and sought comfort in familiar arms. They moved again, this time to live with James's older sister Julia in Montclair, New Jersey. Then fairly rural—Julia warned her family that ghosts lived in the fields near the multifamily house she shared on New Street—the area was low on big-company job opportunities for James. To worsen matters, word came from North Carolina that Lillian's mother had died of an intestinal obstruction in a hospital in New Haven, Connecticut, where she worked from time to time as a relatively well-paid domestic to help support her extended family in North Carolina. In 1920, faced with disappointment after disenchantment, the family moved yet again, this time south to Braddock, Pennsylvania, outside of Pittsburgh, where the mills virtually guaranteed work to men willing to lend their bodies to the production of steel.

By now, Baby Boy Strayhorn was a five-year-old; smallish, round-faced, and cheeky, having inherited his mother's double dimples, he looked a year or two younger than his age. His parents hadn't yet filed a legal name for him, though they were saying he was William, named for James's eldest brother. Most everybody called him Bill. Unlike his older brother, Jimmy, a tall, reedy rascal who relished playing roughhouse with his father, Bill gravitated toward quiet, creative play. He liked to read—or pretend to, before he learned how; when guests came to the Strayhorns', Bill would pick out a book, trace the words with his eyes, and theatrically turn each page as he improvised a story. And he demonstrated an ear for music. The Strayhorns' first home in Braddock was a mixed-race boarding-house on the misleadingly named Willow Way, where a middle-aged black woman named Mame Pyle ran a discreet brothel. Since she worked at home and was generally respected by the other women in the building (including Lillian, who told her children that Mame Pyle's independence was honorable), the madam would occasionally baby-sit for neighborhood children. Bill was among them, and when he was in Mame Pyle's parlor, which was equipped with a bar and an equally well-stocked Victrola, he would watch the records as they played. Evidently, he could retain songs so well by ear that he quickly developed the ability to find any record anyone requested, although he couldn't read the labels. Of course, most of the records Mame Pyle had on hand for her business were ones most young people rarely got to hear: "race records," including early jazz.

The Strayhorns bounced around the Pittsburgh area, always struggling. In 1925, after five years in the borough of Braddock, they moved to neighboring Rankin, sharing space in a big corner building on Fifth and Harriet Streets. Finally, in 1926, they settled in a single-family house in the Homewood district of Pittsburgh proper. This would be the first place Bill would know as a permanent home—a 1,600-acre patchwork of blocks housing some 42,000 working-class people, 15 percent of them black. In front of the Strayhorns' house lived a large Italian family with a son who had blond hair; he came back home from the navy and ran the numbers. Next to them were the Hickenbottoms, a black family with lots of kids. Laterally adjacent to the Strayhorns, across a vacant lot, lived Harry Collins, who had an enormous stomach and very short, thin legs; he was a bootlegger and operated a small-time speakeasy in his back room. Next to him, there was a tin-roof shed where two older black men lived together. They had a fondness, late in the evening after a few drinks, for doing the buck dance—indoors. The neighbors could tell they were dancing because of all their hooting and hollering, as well as bumping into things; once one of them kicked over their potbelly stove and burned down part of their shed. A few doors down, there was a Presbyterian church, all white, although the pastor would invite the black kids in when they climbed up the outside walls to watch the services through the tilted-open stained-glass windows. Behind the Strayhorns, at first, lived the Moskendrics, an Italian family with five children, who in time moved to Susquehanna Street, a nicer block in the neighborhood.

This fairly typical urban outgrowth of the industrial era was scarcely a melting pot, despite its diversity and intimacy. "Blacks and whites lived next door to each other, and if you didn't like what your mother made for dinner, you'd eat what you had to and go next door to the Italians, walk right in and sit down with them. But this only went so far," remembered James "Steve" Stevens, a lifelong resident of Homewood who lived near the Strayhorns. "The white people had a definite superior attitude, even though they lived next door to you. You knew to hold your tongue with the white people— even the kids your own age—and let them have their way, because they didn't treat you as an equal. Whenever there was a skirmish, the police would side with the whites without asking us a question." To prevent matters from reaching that point, one old black woman rocked on a Hermitage Street porch and watched the children play, keeping a special eye out for the safety of the white children and warning a wayward one with a cry: "Get out of the street before you kill yourself, you little white devil!" As thanks for this peacekeeping service, neighbors would bring her tins of Five Brothers pipe tobacco.

Housing in Homewood was racially configured to some degree. The whites generally occupied the residences on the main streets— good-sized and well-equipped two-story row houses—and the black families those in the alleys behind them—low-hanging, unpainted shelters with no electricity. The Strayhorns lived at 7212 Tioga Street Rear, a dirt-and-gravel road named for the bigger, tree-lined and paved street in front of it. Lillian tried to train her children to refer to their address as "Tioga Street, the zenith way." The location's shortcomings weren't entirely semantic, however. "The landlords who owned these properties didn't want to keep them up, although they still wanted to make money off them. So they would let a black person move into them, and that's how the neighborhood was integrated," recounted Robert Conaway, a boyhood friend of Billy Strayhorn's who worked with him musically in Pittsburgh (and eventually married one of his sisters). "Billy lived on a little side street where they had a little shack," said Conaway. "He lived in a four-room shack there—actually, that's what it was, a shack. They [later] tore it down. It was an eyesore, actually." At best, the house was spartan: a box, flat-roofed and made of wood, with two rooms on each floor. Facing the front door, stairs led up to two bedrooms; the toilet was in the basement. The largest room in the house was the kitchen, at the rear of the main floor, and it had a wood-burning stove, a round table, and press-back chairs arranged on an apple-green painted floor. In the front room, two folding chairs faced the heater (wood-burning) that handled the whole house. There were plain pipe-and-globe gas light fixtures, unpainted walls, and no pictures hanging.

By now, James's ambitions, already pulled to wire thinness, were beginning to disintegrate. Drifting from the steel mills to lower-paying labor, he ended up working as a hod carrier. His job was to heap plaster onto a handled metal plate (the hod) and to carry it on his shoulder to masons working on construction sites. He didn't mix the plaster and he didn't apply it; he carried it and could prove he did by the hump on one shoulder that hod carriers wore as a badge of duty. After an especially grueling period, a hod carrier's hump would tend to crack open, abscessed. Unlike many others at this work, however, James didn't lose the hair on one side of his head from the exposure to lye, although he was hospitalized twice for chemical damage to his eyes. Much the same, Lillian found her own dreams of leading a society life degenerating to a routine of survival. The family kept growing: after Bill came the first girl who lived, Georgia, in 1921; another healthy boy, John, in 1924; another, Theodore, in 1926; then premature twins, Samuel and Harry, both of whom died shortly after their birth in 1928. Lillian carried the responsibility of rearing the five children with few labor-saving devices—she sewed their clothes by hand—and with progressively less help from James; after working long days, he was spending more and longer evenings at Harry Collins's place.

"He became a bitter person and a drinker," explained Lillian Strayhorn Dicks, Lillian and James's last child, born in 1930. "My father shouldn't have been born when he was born—that was his first mistake. I think the fact that he was born out of his time was the cause of a lot of his unhappiness, the frustration or whatever. He was bright and had a lot of personality, and he probably would have done very well years later. But back then, who needed a bright black man with personality? That goes a little against the grain when you have to put your head down and you have a family to raise. So, being blessed with a sharp tongue and a temper, he became a bitter person—a bitter person with a lot of responsibility and a lot of frustration." Volatile and envenomed by drink, James released his frustrations on his family. The least of his attacks were verbal: when his son John came down with a case of eczema, James razzed him with the nickname Johnny Blaze Face. Most were physical: he would routinely beat one of the boys for ostensible infractions he wouldn't explain. Bill seemed to trigger the worst in him, perhaps because the boy was so small and quiet, the easiest prey, so different from James—and so much like Lillian. With few exceptions, James treated him dismissively, and the exceptions were often ugly. Bill started wearing eyeglasses and once laid them on the floor while he was reading; when James entered the room, he stomped on them and walked away laughing. "He traumatized his children, especially Billy, because of the kind of mistreatment that he would subject them to. He was very cruel to them," said Robert Conaway. "The children, when they were young, were frightened of him." As Lillian Strayhorn Dicks recalled, "Oh, he was abusive. He would say things that would hurt you. He would hit. You learned to be fast with the side step."

Like many parents who nurture sick babies to health, especially parents who have lost earlier offspring, Bill's mother always seemed uniquely connected to her "miracle baby." "They were extremely close—to the exclusion of everyone, I think," said Lillian Strayhorn Dicks. If that closeness provoked his father's wrath, his mother was quick to intercede in his defense. "She would deflect [James's] anger away from Billy and bear the burden of that," one member of the Strayhorn family said. "She would stand up there and challenge him. She would basically interpose herself and protect Billy from his rage. I think that's part of what shaped her and her relationship with Billy." Her own aspirations may have faded ("I know she wanted more in life," said Lillian Strayhorn Dicks, "and I think she felt, If only Jim had done things differently . . .") but she clearly saw hope in Bill, still just a grade school boy without much direction or evident sense of himself. She took extreme measures to insulate him from his father as well as from his older brother, Jimmy, and indeed from all of Homewood, sending him on a series of long visits to his grandparents in North Carolina.

Bill had first spent time in Hillsborough with his mother at the age of five or so, and the two of them, sometimes with other family members, had visited occasionally since. But from age eight to eleven, he stayed in Hillsborough during school vacations for weeks at a time. Hillsborough was literally his second home—and spiritually, it seems, his first. "His sister Georgia used to say that he was different when he came back from Hillsborough, that something good happened to him down there," a Strayhorn family member confided. "It's almost as if that's where he found himself. I know he got a lot of attention down there and had the run of the place, pretty much, and that couldn't be further from the situation in Homewood, where he really didn't have the room to hear himself think." Space and leisure time were abundant in and around Lizzie and Jobe Strayhorn's house on the corner of Hillsborough Avenue and West Margaret Lane. It was an airy place, surrounded by a wide plank porch and, at its perimeter, greenery in the summer. Lizzie had a special affection for flowers, and she'd spend hours discussing them with Bill. The inside of her house was friendly: pictures decorated the walls, and the Victrola was well-used, usually to play spirituals. The thoroughly furnished parlor was arranged around the piano, a symbol of cultured gentility rare on Tioga Street Rear. In the evenings, Lizzie, who served as pianist for her church, played often and prettily, as neighbors would recall years later. Apparently she also made an impression on her grandson, whom she guided and encouraged until the piano eventually became central to his life in Hillsborough. "My grandmother played the piano, and I used to kind of, you know, waddle over to the piano—toddle, shall I say?—" Strayhorn recalled, "and pick out little things that sounded good to me." Experimenting at the keyboard, he approximated a few tunes he had heard in church, among them "When the Roll Is Called Up Yonder, I'll Be There," a favorite of his mother's. "In Hillsborough, he was able to live more like our mother wanted him to live in Homewood," Lillian Strayhorn Dicks said. Bill would disappear for hours and take long walks by himself, wandering through the old slave cemetery catty-corner from Lizzie and Jobe's house, following the squirrely bank of the Eno River, a few hundred yards to the south, or roaming the trails of the woods to the west, where people liked to pick scuppernong grapes.

Back on Tioga Street Rear, where the focal point of the living room generated heat rather than warmth, Bill's budding interest in music and flowers had few outlets. The family's weekly household budget of fifteen to twenty dollars left no extra money for music lessons, let alone an instrument: when he entered the fifth grade of Homewood Elementary School in his brother's hand-me-downs, his classmates teased him because the toes of his shoes were curled up like pixie boots. His parents had at last filed an amendment to his birth certificate, legally naming him William Thomas Strayhorn; establishing his own identity was another matter. As he would recall in later years, "During grade [school], I had no music, except what one ordinarily gets in grade school—you know, group singing and that's about all. One thing I wanted was to play the piano, and I wanted that badly. But my family didn't have a piano. You can't learn to play one if you haven't got one."

Bill set out to buy himself a piano. "I started selling papers. On the same corner as that on which I sold my papers was a drugstore, and occasionally I would do errands for the druggists—you know, deliver medicines and things like that," he told an interviewer. This drugstore was the Pennfield Pharmacy, a busy shop on the corner of Penn Avenue and Carnegie Place, an upper-middle-class district called Point Breeze. "Well, eventually, being the neighborhood paper-boy as it were, I got to know everyone in the district, so the druggist hired me because I was so familiar with all his potential customers. He took me as a sort of, well, a kind of soda fountain and delivery boy. But I worked things up until I was practically a clerk. Of course, during all this time I was going to grade school and selling papers as well. So I finally bought myself a piano and started to play it. I started to study, and the more I learned, the more I wanted to learn. My family was kind of large and so couldn't indulge me in all my wishes, so I had to do this for myself. It wasn't all that easy, but I guess if you want something hard enough it just gets done. Directly I got that piano."

What he bought was an upright player piano with a broken roll mechanism, and it became the new centerpiece of the parlor on Tioga Street Rear, much to his mother's pleasure; his father was rarely home long enough to react one way or another. Lillian's only objection was to her son's repetition of piano exercises. As Lillian Strayhorn Dicks said, "There would be times when Mama would say, 'Okay—I can't take another! Play a song through, won't you?' " (Long after this, his mother would delight in recalling the first song she ever heard Bill play, the spiritual "Brighten the Corner Where You Are.") He paid for his own sheet music and lessons, which he took from Charlotte Catlin, a black teacher associated with Volkwein's, a music store that was a hub of musical activity in Pittsburgh. As Robert Conaway recalled, "All the money he could get a hold of, he bought music. He had so much music that the house was swamped with music—all kinds of music, novelty music and everything. He had music stacked up everywhere, in the corners and places. It was orderly but all stacked up. He had it stacked this high." (Conaway gestured to his chest, about four and a half feet from the floor.)

Most eleven-year-olds in Homewood gravitated toward the streets. In good weather, boys and girls together played One-Two-Three-Dropkick in the alleys or roller-skated back and forth on Penn Avenue till dark—on Saturdays, they might race all the way to Sharpsburg and back, a good five miles. Bill Strayhorn didn't join them. If his Hillsborough experiences represented a certain enlightenment in repose, he seemed to seek some kind of continuity at home: after school, he walked around the closest thing to the woods, Frick Park, a 340-acre patch of trees (135 varieties) and man-made ponds, and he found solidarity in one good friend, Harry Herforth, a kindred spirit from a white street in Homewood. The two had much in common: small and soft-featured, Herforth was one of nine children raised by a single mother who worked as a three-dollar-a-day domestic, and both boys were developing an interest in music. (Though Herforth hadn't begun playing an instrument when he and Strayhorn became friends, he soon took up the trumpet; as an adult, he played assistant first chair with the Boston Symphony.) "We were scrabbling to keep body and soul together," Herforth recalled. "Billy and I were both in about the same straits, it seemed to me. But we had a bond that was memorable. We gravitated together because of our artistic sensibility. He was well-read. He was an egghead as a kid. He talked about books, and I talked about books that we had read—*Treasure Island,* short stories by Jack London—and we didn't talk about much else. Other kids were talking about girls and sports. Directly across from our grade school was the Homewood library, and it was a place of hallowed sanctity to each of us. We would go there, and as soon as you go into the door, to me it was like going into a temple, a cathedral, because of the books—the books were just full of wonderment. When I mentioned this [to Strayhorn], I discovered that Billy, too, felt that the library was a cathedral of learning. That was what brought us together."

Strayhorn introduced Herforth to his outdoor sanctuary. "When we had time, we would go to Frick Park, and we would walk and talk—we walked and talked and walked and talked. As I recall quite clearly, we never talked about kids, other people. We talked about composers, authors, playwrights—not esoteric ones, but ones that were esoteric to us at the time. He would ask me if I had heard of Cesar Franck. 'Did you hear this?' 'Have you heard that?' That was 90 percent of our conversation. Looking back on my whole life, that was one of the outstanding things: taking a walk with Billy Strayhorn. I went to his house frequently, but only to pick him up on our way somewhere. I would sit in the living room. I never talked to any member of his family aside from his mother, and that was just 'Hello.' His father would pass by, but he wouldn't even look at me or Billy. There was no conversation whatsoever, not with me and not with his son."

For the next five years, Strayhorn and Herforth attended Westinghouse High, a public school endowed by George Westinghouse, the electrical industrialist whose local factory then employed some thirty-five thousand workers in the Pittsburgh area; the company logo hung over the auditorium stage. Within its two city blocks of austere white-granite walls, Westinghouse had an enrollment of four hundred, about 20 percent black, and was well known for its gym team, which from the late 1920s to the late 1930s won the city finals ten years straight. In 1927, Carl McVicker, a young Carnegie Tech graduate, joined the Westinghouse faculty as an instrumental-music teacher and instituted a music program considered so radical that two teachers left the school over it. (It helped McVicker's cause that his oldest friend was superintendent of schools.) He accepted and encouraged students of all backgrounds and races to play all instruments. "Mr. McVicker instilled self-respect in those of us who were his students, because he respected us regardless of our background," said pianist Ahmad Jamal (once Fritz Jones), a student of McVicker's who made his professional debut while still attending Westinghouse. In addition, McVicker started a school swing band as a (then-controversial) alternative to the concert orchestra and marching band. Under McVicker, music-hungry students like Strayhorn thrived. "We were a factory-town school, so we had a lot of kids like Billy, kids who needed an outlet of one kind or another but had a hard time because they were black," explained McVicker, a gangly six-foot-three man with open, deep-pooled eyes and a Chaplin mustache; he looked like the music teacher of a student's doodle. "I wanted any kid in my program who was serious, and Billy was about as serious as they get. Earnest, hardworking, wanted to get ahead in music. As a matter of fact, I would say he was much different from most high school musicians. He was an intellectual. He had a broad base of knowledge of academics, although he learned everything we could teach him about music—and more. You know, he didn't play in the swing band. He wasn't interested. He was a serious pianist and concentrated strictly on the concert repertoire."

For high school piano and harmony instruction, Strayhorn had Jane Patton Alexander, a middle-aged musical conservative who stressed rules and discipline. Strayhorn would remember her with begrudging gratitude. "She did a wonderful thing for me: she taught me a basic progression, and I did that for two years," he said in a 1962 interview. "Couldn't vary. Had to do it in all kinds of ways. Of course, I hated it. But it was invaluable training." Alexander must have held him in high regard: when she had to leave the classroom, she put Strayhorn in charge of teaching his own class. "He would get up from his little chair and go up in front of the class and proceed to teach the class—oh, for a good forty, forty-five minutes," says Frank Spangler, one of Strayhorn's music-theory classmates. "He was just a kid like the rest of us, but he was already like a professor."

Bit by bit, from classroom to auditorium and then to ballroom, Strayhorn began taking his musical ambitions public. In school he worked his way up the scale of academic orchestras, eventually assuming the role of first pianist for the forty-nine-piece Senior Orchestra, which performed concert scores of lenient pieces like Grieg's "Sigurd Jorsalfar" and Karl Goldmark's "Sakuntala Overture." Strayhorn joined the orchestra for an hour of rehearsal every day at noon, the fourth period, and performed with it at school assemblies and the annual commencement exercises. The culmination of his experience with the orchestra came on the evening of March 1, 1934, when he was featured in a performance of Edvard Grieg's Piano Concerto in A minor, op. 16. "I never heard a student play that way before or after," said Carl McVicker more than fifty years later. "The orchestra may have been a group of students, but Billy Strayhorn was a professional artist."

Outside of school, meanwhile, Strayhorn started to test the local music waters. As Harry Herforth began to master the trumpet, he and Strayhorn worked up some duets, including W. Paris Chambers's "Commodore Polka"—pleasant and gently impressive diversions, exactly the sort of thing civic groups had clean-scrubbed students perform as entertainment interludes at meetings. The duo of Herforth and Strayhorn filled this bill at several high school assemblies, at a few PTA meetings, and once for the Pittsburgh Board of Education. "I don't know how many of the people who heard us were expecting a mixed-race duo, but we certainly were subjected to a lot of glares. We were nervous enough without that," said Herforth. "I do think it softened the blow that Billy was perceived as my accompanist, though that's not at all how we wanted to be seen." Under McVicker's direction, Westinghouse High provided Pittsburgh organizations an alternative to the Herforth-Strayhorn duo: the Orchestra Club, a twenty-five-piece classical ensemble selected by audition from the top ranks of the larger school orchestra. Strayhorn, the pianist, was the only black member. The group performed frequently at social events around Pittsburgh, including banquets at both of the city's major hotels, the Schenley and the William Penn.

The club's first trombonist, John Stitt, would remember Strayhorn as "pretty quiet—he kept to himself, since there weren't too many black fellows in classical music back then." Frank Raucci, the bass violinist, would recall something more unusual: "He had a book full of music, which he played when the club met. It was beautiful, I remember. We found out later that he had been playing his own compositions—he was writing all this time. But we could never tell. They sounded just like works by a classical composer."

From all evidence, one piece the Orchestra Club probably heard was a piano waltz titled "Valse" that Strayhorn composed while he was in his teens. A fully developed short composition (three pages), it derives expressive force from purling melodic lines and graceful modulations. Its mood is warmly impassioned, and it moves languidly (marked *lento sostenuto* for tempo). Harmonically, the piece owes something to Chopin, shifting among flat keys, primarily B-flat minor, and it remains something of a prodigy's exploration. But in its emotional lucidity and sheer loveliness, it bears the unmistakable mark of Billy Strayhorn.

He tackled a far more ambitious task in composing a hybrid of classical and vernacular music titled Concerto for Piano and Percussion. Like his piano waltz, the short piece is "through-composed": it develops organically, with knowing use of music theory; it is no innocent's experiment. Unlike the waltz, however, Strayhorn's Concerto for Piano and Percussion was performed before an audience. Huddling inside against the record cold, more than six hundred family members and friends of the winter 1934 graduating class heard the piece at commencement exercises in the Westinghouse High auditorium. (There were two graduating classes each year, one in late January or February, and one in June.) The composer was one of seventeen black students in the class of 145. "Oh man, it was great," said the percussionist Michael (Mickey) Scrima, for whom the piece was composed. A high-energy kid with huge dark eyes and a sharp nose, Scrima became music buddies with Strayhorn in the band room. (In adulthood, he would become a respected swing-band drummer best known for a stint with Harry James in the 1940s.) "It was something that he worked up just for us—a classical piece, all written down, including all my parts. I had a xylophone and timpanis all tuned up to a certain note. I even had to go out and get a set of bells just to play one part. It was all just so, just perfect. The audience loved it—it was a lot of fun, a whole lot of fun. I don't know how much they understood it, mind you—if they realized how sophisticated this piece was, and how extraordinary it was that this kid in their school had written it."

Years later, some Westinghouse students would swear they had heard Billy Strayhorn play *Rhapsody in Blue* that day, and they weren't far wrong: there is quite a bit of Gershwin in this early Strayhorn effort. Rhythmically vibrant and catchy, it applies variations of jaunty popular-music-style phrases over chromatic harmonies and syncopated rhythms in much the way that Gershwin had popularized, by way of black jazz, European concert music and Yiddish theater songs. Strayhorn's composition is the work of a musical sophisticate: his manuscript includes fastidious tempo markings and "enharmonic" note spellings (to distinguish between F-sharp and G-flat, technically different notes, but the same key on the piano). Moreover, for all its Gershwin influence, the piece has distinctive Strayhorn touches (the E-flat-minor chord with a major seventh early in the piece would appear recurrently in his later work) and is, as a whole, a work of stylish charm.

As a skilled musician, Strayhorn gained a certain kind of high school celebrity, which is not quite to say popularity. He was often invited to the big parties held in both white and black circles, but there always seemed to be a piano and he was inevitably asked to perform. Similarly, groups of classmates would sometimes drop by his house, prompt him to play for a while, then leave together as they had come. "Everybody was in awe of Billy, you know, because of his music," said Beatrice Wright Westbrooks, one of his schoolmates and a Homewood neighbor. "We all thought he was really something special—everybody talked about him." What his peers said, however, was often laced with unease. "Well, Strayhorn—he was just like, you'd say, a genius. He was very much to himself. Some might have called him like a little oddball or something, because he didn't socialize much. But he was too busy with his work and his creations and things like that," said his classmate Dorothy Ford Gardin. "Talent. Talent. Talent. That was Billy. But he didn't hang around much, because he was into his own musical creative type of thing, his own niche, so to speak," Fred Staton recalled. "He was like Einstein. He was an unusual guy, very unusual," agreed William Brown. Below his senior-class picture in the yearbook, the inscription reads: "It's hard to express our opinion of you . . ."

"I think my brother really dove with full force into everything my mother always wanted for him—music, books, art, the whole world of culture," explained Lillian Strayhorn Dicks. "I don't know if she wanted him to live the life she always wanted, or if he wanted to be like her, or if they both wanted Bill to be the opposite of his father. But he dedicated himself to all the finer things in life." Strayhorn, that is, embraced all the era's standard symbols of refinement. He studied French, joining the high school's Cercle Français; when his brothers and sisters riled him at home, he would strike back with a casual *"Taisez-vous."* He kept his clothes impeccably clean and pressed; when practicing piano at home, he neatly hung up his pants first, then played in his shirt, socks, shoes, and underwear. President of the Westinghouse Pen Club, he took out a subscription to the *New Yorker* and acquired a grand vocabulary, which he employed with conscientious diction; his classmates nicknamed him Dictionary. "He had a hard time, man," said Mickey Scrima. "It's no wonder he was timid. He was in a *shell*. You got to remember, those Pittsburghers were tough. How can I say this? He had a hard time making friends. To tell you the truth, people used to call him a sissy. That's what everybody said. The thing is, he had bigger fish to fry. All he did day and night was concentrate on the only thing he cared about, the one thing he wanted—to go on doing what he did on the day of our graduation: be a classical concert pianist."

Along with the announcement of a performance of William Strayhorn's Concerto for Piano and Percussion, the program for the commencement exercises for the class of winter 1934 included the class motto, "Let success by virtue be our goal."

2

PASSION

FLOWER

High school graduation was the time for young Homewood men to follow their fathers into adult induration; most (like Jimmy Stray-horn, who found work in construction) entered a trade. Escapees were rare; a few (like Harry Herforth, who won a scholarship to the New England Conservatory) followed rarefied pursuits. What could Billy Strayhorn do? "Billy looked into colleges but was discouraged because of his race and could not get the necessary financial aid," said Herforth. "The very idea of a black concert pianist was consid-ered unthinkable. It had nothing to do with Billy's considerable talent." Strayhorn resolved to continue working as a soda jerk and delivery boy at Pennfield Drugs and eventually pay his own way through a school that would accept him. (His fountain specialty: an original recipe using lemon juice and various other ingredients to simulate coconut flavor.) He kept musically active at Westinghouse High, returning frequently to play piano for music classes and assemblies, and around Homewood, occasionally playing a few songs for a neighbor's family gathering.

A few months out of high school, Strayhorn connected with a fellow Homewood musician, Ray Wood. Born John Raymond Wood in Kentucky six years before Strayhorn, he had had some minor success in Pittsburgh as a section player in several "sweet" bands formed of part-time musicians for weddings and civic functions. His instrument was the C-melody saxophone, and he composed a bit. For a living, Wood, the oldest of eight children, helped his mother run a small catering business out of their two-family house on Cassina Way, a few blocks from Strayhorn's house. (Wood's father had died a few years earlier of heart failure related to alcohol abuse.) Although his association with Strayhorn was brief, Wood would seem to have been an object of some emulation to the younger musician: an ambitious young black man striving to rise above his hardscrabble background through music and a self-styled cosmopolitanism. Tall, olive-skinned, and stunningly handsome, Wood wore a manicured mustache and a porkpie hat. His friends nicknamed him Mr. Dignity. As his mother's chef (he took pride in his knowledge of food and his skill in preparing impressive dishes) and a photo buff (he built a darkroom in his mother's basement), Wood was dabbling in several arts with some degree of success. He may not have been homosexual, but Wood probably represented the closest Strayhorn had come to a gay sensibility among Homewood's black men.

In the autumn of 1934, the two musicians worked together on a pair of songs of the type Wood was performing in society orchestras: "You Lovely Little Devil" (music by Strayhorn, lyrics by Wood) and "I'm Still Begging You" (music by Strayhorn and Wood, lyrics by Wood). A tuneful up-tempo number, "Devil" dared a tone of sly naughtiness with sassy lyrics and melodic phrases reminiscent of schoolyard taunts. A formulaic ballad, "I'm Still Begging You" mimicked the commercial laments of the late 1920s deftly, although not especially imaginatively. Its opening words are "Queer how we first met."* Whatever the roots of, the

---

* In common usage at the time, *queer* meant "unusual" or "eccentric." As early as the eighteenth century, however, the term had also been used to suggest homosexuality, according to C. A. Tripp (*The Homosexual Matrix*, New American Library, 1975).

intricacies of, or the problems in the fleeting partnership with Wood, Strayhorn would never discuss any aspect of it with his friends or family members; he kept Wood and their work a secret, and Wood was never known to speak of his association with Strayhorn. On October 12, 1934, Wood registered copyrights for "You Lovely Little Devil" and "I'm Still Begging You" (in both writers' names) with the Library of Congress, where the music would languish unperformed and unknown, except to the partners who left their work together behind them.

It was a Westinghouse High School tradition for the graduating class to put together a program of four or five songs and skits in a forum of official insurgency called Stunt Day. Since Strayhorn had played piano for portions of both the 1933 and 1934 editions—including, in 1933, a spoof of a Cab Calloway performance by a student in a mop wig—a few members of the 1935 class asked him to return and help with their event. The ringleader was Oliver Fowler, a sharp-looking, pencil-mustached ladies' man and itinerant baritone sax-ophonist with show-business aspirations; he went by the nickname Boggy (or Boggie, but pronounced like Bogie) and had done the Cab Calloway impersonation. "I was organizing the show's activities, and some different people told me about Billy and recommended for me to go and meet him and so forth," Fowler said. "He had graduated, but then when I got in touch with Billy and told him about all the talent we had available, he got to thinking that he could do something along the lines of his objectives, and he joined up. He offered to write the whole show, all the songs and every-thing." For Strayhorn, this small-scale student project must have seemed a reasonable exercise. Seeking a standard to make music that bridged the classical and vernacular idioms, he had turned to George Gershwin for his Concerto for Piano and Percussion. Gershwin wrote theater music while he worked to be taken seriously as a con-cert artist; Strayhorn would try the same route. "Billy really idolized Gershwin and wrote that Stunt Day music in a Gershwin spirit, although it was very original. Billy was very clever," said Robert Conaway, who served as rehearsal pianist for the production. Per-formed for students in the Westinghouse auditorium on May 23,

1935, the approximately twenty-minute presentation featured about two dozen students, all black, including a chorus of dancing girls and a small band led by Strayhorn. Its title—the Gershwinian *Fantastic Rhythm*.

"For something that was expected to be a little high school production, it made quite an impact. Everybody you saw seemed to know about it," said Conaway. "The music Billy wrote for it really was as sophisticated as anything you would hear in a major theatrical production in that day." Agreeing, Fowler tethered his ambitions to Strayhorn's talent and set out to expand *Fantastic Rhythm* into a full-scale professional production. "Boggy was always an out-front kind of person, a big show-off," remarked Fred Staton, a tenor saxophonist who had played with both Strayhorn and Fowler in the Westinghouse orchestra. Athletically built and smoothly confident, Staton led the Moonlight Harbor Band, a fixture at one of black Pittsburgh's hottest spots for dancing, the Savory Ballroom (and soon to be the orchestra for the full-scale *Fantastic Rhythm*). "The minute Boggy saw the impact *Fantastic Rhythm* had in school, he figured, Hey—this is a good thing. I'd better keep it going," said Staton.

In the weeks between Stunt Day and the June 1935 Westinghouse High commencement, Strayhorn was busy, at Carl McVicker's request, preparing a duet to perform at the graduation exercises with a senior-class clarinetist, Jerome Eisner. "I wanted to do something that was serious and accessible at the same time, so Strayhorn suggested 'Song of India,' and we did it before Tommy Dorsey did the same number," said Eisner, a bean of a youngster with a quick grin and a striped head of slicked-back, deep-waved hair. "He did an original arrangement, and he was sure generous about it. I had the introduction—what he wrote for me, it was beautiful, man—and I had the ending, which was just as nice." They rehearsed a few times at Eisner's house, where there was a grand piano that his mother had won by entering her daughter in a beauty contest, and then, according to Eisner, "We did it in front of the school, and the number went over very well. We could have done any stock piece, you know, but Billy wanted to do exactly what I was comfortable with, even if he had to write a special arrangement. He seemed to do it with no effort at all."

Shortly, Boggy Fowler found a pair of would-be entrepreneurs willing to back a full-scale production of *Fantastic Rhythm*, Al Wess and Jess Williams, young partners of indeterminate profession; their investment was about five hundred dollars. Fowler handled the organizational duties, including booking the theaters, arranging for any necessary permits and licenses, and lining up the rest of the production staff and performers. For choreography, he sought Harold Belcher, an established professional tap dancer from the Hill, Pittsburgh's black social center, who had taught himself dance while selling newspapers on the street, to increase tips. "Most of the choreography in the show was with the chorus line," Belcher recalled. "The girls were just glad to be in the show and get a chance to get in front of the people and throw theirself around a little, because they were more or less what they call society-type girls, and they wasn't allowed to get out and act up and whatnot. And for them to get in the show and learn a little dancing and get up and dance—why, you see, that would take away that shyness their parents had on them. 'Oh, she's dancing now—it's all right.' " To handle the costumes, Fowler signed up Dorothy Ford, a tall (and somewhat bowlegged) chorus girl. "I had to make them without patterns and [with] whatever material we could afford or find at home," she said. "I more or less copied everything from things I saw, pictures in magazines and the like. One I'm proud of was a see-through dress with a bodysuit underneath—there was a moon in one of the sets, and it looked like it was shining through the dress, so the girl looked like she was naked." Harold Strange, a star Westinghouse art student, doubled as set designer and comedian. "I always painted—drew pictures, you know? No big nothin'," he said. "We did go all out for some of the sets. For one number, we built a whole room with a bay window and a landscape behind it. That was Strayhorn's idea. Him and the music gave us most of the ideas for the sets." For publicity, Fowler enlisted Ralph Koger, a reporter at the *Pittsburgh Courier*, the black newspaper; Koger was well enough known locally that Fowler put his name and photograph on posters for the show. "After work, I'd put up signs—we had signs printed up, and we'd put them up all over the streets, telling people that the show was going to be there," he said. "The radio stations did a few things, and all the newspapers covered it.

I have to say, it got quite a lot of attention for a while there." Marie Pleasant, a wispy, light-skinned singer who had been performing at the Waldorf in Pittsburgh's genteel East End, got the part of the female lead. "One of my big numbers in *Fantastic Rhythm* was 'My Little Brown Book,' which later became so famous, of course," she said. "Well, Billy used to tell me, 'You inspired me to write this.' It was because I was so shy. I was so quiet, and the song is about a person like that. He used the word *peruse* in the song, and it has stuck with me ever since. I always use it. *Peruse*." For comedy, there was a troupe of young beginners, including featured comedian Henry Lee, who created a pantomime bit accompanied by a Strayhorn instrumental. " 'The Silent Fight,' we called it, although it wasn't silent—Billy had music in the background," said Lee. "We wore thug clothes, caps slung along the sides of our heads, and we carried on something terrible with little antics. It was quite funny—amusing, I do believe."

The poster for an early production of the new, full-scale show proclaimed, "Songs and Entire Book Written By Billy Strayhorne." "I'd say he used that spelling because it was suggestive of the Hornes [a prominent black family in Pittsburgh, one of whose members was Lena Horne, a rising figure in black society]. And perhaps to distance himself from his own family," said Robert Conaway. The sheer scale of Strayhorn(e)'s participation in *Fantastic Rhythm* almost justified the affectation. In addition to all the dialogue scenes—a revue-style series of sequences about urban life, the business world, and problematic love, slackly connected by a story thread involving newspaper reporters on a big-city beat—Strayhorn wrote ten original songs, accompaniment to dances and comedy skits, and incidental music; he also composed full arrangements for all the music to be performed by a twelve-piece orchestra (three saxes, one clarinet, two trumpets, two trombones, guitar, bass, drums, and Strayhorn on piano). "I was in demand, so I became involved in this show and did indeed become deeply involved," Strayhorn would recall. "Actually, even in those early days, what I was doing was arranging, composing and lyric writing, but I thought nothing of it—I was just doing it to try and make the show a success." He worked diligently but, it seemed, effortlessly. "To put it in one word, the kid was a genius," said Fred Staton, who handed out the band parts Strayhorn composed. "Any time you take a teenage kid, and he would sit down and write music like he was writing a letter—whoo! Whole scores! We would just *look* at him. Whoo!" Clyde Broadus recalled a similar experience: "He'd create a song out of *nothing*. Just like that, he'd create a song and write it out and then play it. I watched him. I sat at his home, watched him, how he'd write music. He'd just sit down there—dit, dit, dit, dit—right there. I asked him, 'How do you do that?' He said, 'I don't know. It just comes to me.' "

The ten songs with words and music that Strayhorn wrote for *Fantastic Rhythm* range from typical 1930s razzmatazz to inventive recitative, with several quirky stops—including an arch take on misogyny and a hymn to silent submission—between them. A precurtain overture interweaves the show's major musical themes, arranged with sophisticated voicings for the Moonlight Harbor Band; Strayhorn's classically oriented harmonic sensibility was so uncommon for the milieu that he wrote instructions to the musicians on the eighth bar of the music manuscript: "This chord is correct." The first several scenes, greatly revised from the Stunt Day presentation, establish characters and advance the show's story with a combination of spoken dialogue, leitmotifs, and complete songs—a fairly advanced approach for a regional production in 1935. The opening number, "We Are the Reporters," introduces three newspapermen, a chorus of secretaries, and their editor, who crows:

> *I'm the boss*
> *My employees say that I'm a pest*
> *But I can buy them, every one*
> *Because I'm the boss.*

Harold Strange, who handled the editor's role, remembered Strayhorn's attitude toward the character. "The idea was that the boss is somebody who can buy and sell people. He owns them," said Strange. In the following number, "The Sob Sisters," the paper's three female human-interest columnists compare notes with an investigative reporter and a food columnist:

(woman)
I'm that awful creature
That the daily tabloids feature
As a sob, sob sister
(man)
I'm that scribbling felon
Who exposes guys like Mellon
And I make them blister

Melodically, both early numbers have simple conversational melodic lines for the benefit of limited singers. "I played one of the Sob Sisters, and I couldn't sing what Billy originally wrote," said Dorothy Ford. "So he changed it for me to something I could practically just talk." The third musical sequence, "Don't Mess Around with the Women," goes further in this direction; it's a pure recitative, spoken above an instrumental backing. The Sob Sisters attend a Women Haters' Convention, where several members are debating the merits and liabilities of misogyny. The head of the group pronounces:

I fell in love with a woman once
She called me Sugar Pie
I overheard her say one day
She'd be glad if I should suddenly die
So I don't mess around with the women
They don't mean you any good

Like "Don't Mess Around with the Women," the four ballads that constitute *Fantastic Rhythm*'s romantic core are all shaded with a skeptical, often ironic, attitude toward romance. A cynical ode to sexual surrender, "Let Nature Take Its Course" could easily be the theme song of a man haters' club:

When you've been around you'll find
That men like to have their way
They all have a one-track mind
So don't let your tongue betray you
And if my child

> *He likes your smile*
> *And wants to hang around for a while*
> *Don't use any force*
> *Let nature take its course*

The song flows easily and has a lilting melody that belies the lyrics' unusual celebration of acquiescence:

> *Nature has a certain way*
> *Of making golden silence seem to say*
> *Much more than a persuasive voice*
> *Didn't you know?*

A slow-tempo minor-key vehicle for Dorothy Ford—it was the number sung in front of a prop moon—"It Must Be a Dream" is a lament of untempered despair:

> *I've got the blues in my love song*
> *I'm in the dumps on up on the eightieth floor*
> *Ho-hum!*
> *It must be a dream*
> *It just doesn't seem*
> *That there's no you beside me*
> *To be my excuse for living*

Later in the show, after Ford's character finds her love, she sings a follow-up number, "I'll Never Have to Dream Again." But here again, romance has a dark side. The sentimental, almost childish lyrics are vapidly unconvincing:

> *I'll never have to dream again*
> *Dreams that always die*
> *I'll never have to sigh again*
> *Never have to cry*

Strayhorn set the tune to a brooding minor-key melody in waltz time; the piece is like a grade school valentine set to the music of an Eastern European dirge. The only song in *Fantastic Rhythm* to be published and recorded in later years is "My Little Brown Book," which also deals with loneliness. Thematically an old-fashioned heart tugger, the song is noteworthy for a single chord change, a chromatic modulation in the last stave that foreshadows the contours of dozens of pieces associated with the 1940s.

While not as emotionally complex as the rest of the show's music, the three major dance tunes demonstrate their composer's versatility. Both "The Rhythm Man" and "Harlem Rumba" (the latter a showcase for the peroxide-blond Tioga Street native Delores Gomez, Boggy Fowler's girlfriend) are subtly jazz-infused songs related to the "rhythm" theme. The title number, the show's big closer, is ideal for a massive group tap dance. The lyrics simply mark the beat:

> When you shake your hip
> Till it starts to slip
> And you rock your soul
> Till it seems to roll
> They call that Fantastic Rhythm!

It all ends, unusually for this sort of song, on a ninth chord, a warm Strayhorn harmonic touch.

Working in small groups at first, the cast of more than fifty began to run through material in June 1935; their rehearsal hall was Strayhorn's living room on Tioga Street Rear. "All that could get in there got in there. All that couldn't get in there got out," said Clyde Broadus. By fall, as the sets, the costumes, and the lighting started coming together, the whole group began gathering for rehearsals at Westinghouse High. As Strayhorn would recall, "We were all out of high school, but the only auditorium we knew, of course, was the auditorium in the high school. So we went back to the school, hired the auditorium, put out publicity and put on this show for a grand total of two nights [at that location]. Oh, that was really something." Advance tickets, available through businesses such as the Lincoln Drug Store and Ramsey's barbershop, cost twenty-six cents; reserved seats, forty-seven cents; children's tickets, sixteen cents. Presented on November 6 and 7, 1935, *Fantastic Rhythm* made a notable impression, largely but not exclusively in Pittsburgh's black community. All three major Pittsburgh papers covered the performance, the *Courier* proclaiming in its headline, " 'FANTASTIC RHYTHM' HIGHLIGHT OF WEEK'S ENJOYABLE EVENTS," and praising (in an article probably written by Koger) "ten new snappy, lively tunes, from fox-trots to rhumbas, by Billy Strayhorne, budding young musical genius."

Appealing to a young mixed-race audience and building on the show's success at Westinghouse, Fowler immediately booked a string of Pittsburgh high schools—Schenley, Baxter, Allderdice, and others—for performances over the next few months. The show's ongoing success was such that in mid-1936 it was booked for a run at the Roosevelt Theater, one of the most prestigious venues for black culture in Pittsburgh. "See, back in them days, you couldn't go but certain different theaters, because they didn't allow colored," said Boggy Fowler. "So we went to all the colored theaters—we'd go to all the colored places that you could go." Indeed, from 1936 through 1938, *Fantastic Rhythm* played in major black theaters throughout southwestern Pennsylvania, including Rankin, Braddock, Homestead, East Liberty, and Orangetown. The cast changed somewhat, as higher-profile performances called for better performers; in 1937, Billy Eckstine, a promising young Pittsburgh vocalist, joined the show. "It was a big break for me to do *Fantastic Rhythm*," he said. "That really was the big time, and mostly due to that music by Billy. That's what made it truly professional." The show's composer, however, was missing; after the first few performances, he pulled out from active participation and another acclaimed young Pittsburgh pianist, Erroll Garner, took over. "After writing it, Billy didn't seem to have any interest in the show," Ralph Koger speculated. "He made it known that he intended to do greater things. This was nothing to him, and he moved on."

While Strayhorn was proving deft at a variety of musical assignments, his ambitions remained focused on the classical world. "His dream was still to pursue classical piano," said Harry Herforth, who discussed the future with Strayhorn while home from the New England Conservatory. "His difficulty was finding the means to do it." After six years of soda jerking, Strayhorn had saved enough money to afford classes at the Pittsburgh Musical Institute, a private conservatory founded in 1915 and housed in a graceful wooden Victorian building on Bellefield Avenue, an easy streetcar ride from Homewood. PMI was small (enrollment in the 1936–37 year was under sixty) but reputable; it offered a bachelor of music degree in association with the University of Pittsburgh. Strayhorn was accepted in 1936 and began piano and music-theory classes that fall; he was one of two black students enrolled that term. "I remember, he was a very serious student," said Roy Shoemaker, a music-theory instructor. "We accepted anybody—boy, girl, white, colored, or striped—as long as the student was serious about the music, and he was." For piano, Strayhorn studied privately under PMI's founder, Charles N. Boyd, a tweedy, charismatic middle-aged man highly regarded by students for his intellect and cultivation; Boyd was a friend of Albert Schweitzer, who had once played organ for PMI students. "I felt bad for the other teachers who taught the same subjects [as Boyd]," declared his daughter, Muriel Boyd Albitz. "When the semester started, the line to get in Daddy's class was a block long, and the others would get two or three [students]. I would know people who ordinarily would cuss a little bit. When they talked with him, they talked differently, they became different. They became better people, if just for the time they were with him." As one of Strayhorn's classmates, Bruno Salvaterra, recalled, "He always searched out your strong points and would build on them. I was in awe of him, truly. Everybody was."

Boyd was playing organ for friends in his home on April 24, 1937, when he died of a heart attack at age sixty-two, and Strayhorn, in his second term of study, lost the incentive to return. "I went to the Pittsburgh Musical Institute for a short time," Strayhorn recalled. "And it was only short because the man who taught me died shortly after I went to study with him. He was so wonderful that I didn't think there was anyone else there who could teach me. So I didn't stay."

Urbane, worldly, empathetic, stimulating, Boyd seemed everything that would appeal to Strayhorn in a mentor and role model— that is, he was the antithesis of Strayhorn's father. By the mid-1930s, James Strayhorn had slipped further into a pattern of alcohol abuse and rage. The children, fearful of his wrath, kept their distance on the rare occasions when he drank at home rather than at Harry Collins's place or, on payday, at the bigger, rowdier Bucket of Blood.

Latching onto his son Johnny for some reason, he once pulled the boy down into the basement and literally crucified him, tying him with wire to nails on the rock walls; it took his wife's intervention with a skillet to settle James down for the night. Lillian, now sleeping in her daughters' room, maintained her dignity with a dedication to refined behavior in defiant contrast with her world. "Papa would be in one of his moods, raising hell," said Lillian Strayhorn Dicks. "We kids would be hustling to get out of the house, and as we were throwing on our coats, Mama would tell us, 'Now remember, ladies and gentlemen do not put their hands in their pockets.' Billy Strayhorn provided his mother respite, as well as hope. "I'd wake up sometimes in the middle of the night to the sound of laughter downstairs," said Lillian Strayhorn Dicks. "And the next morning, I'd go down to the kitchen and I'd see an empty box of ice cream in the garbage. I'd know Bill and Mama had been up all night. He would bring ice cream home for her—she loved it—and the two of them would sit up at the kitchen table all night, talking and laughing." Increasingly, though, Strayhorn kept away from Tioga Street Rear, except to sleep and play some piano. "After a while, he was barely around anymore," said Lillian Strayhorn Dicks. "When he wasn't working at the drug store, he was out with his friends, doing something in music."

With Harry Herforth away at college, Strayhorn drew closer to his old piano-and-percussion partner Mickey Scrima and Scrima's circle of friends, especially his neighbor Bill Esch, who played guitar. Scrima and Esch were as determined as Strayhorn was to build careers in music, and they would rendezvous with Strayhorn at Pop Lesher's, a soda shop in Homewood known for its jukebox filled with jazz and pop hits. On Sundays, they'd take in an amateur ball game in the park; wherever they were, they talked music. Slim and blue-eyed, with longish dirty-blond hair and a curlicue smile that hid teeth needing some work, Bill Esch was a "walking musical encyclopedia who lived, breathed, and sweated music," according to Esch's older brother Ray. As Scrima said, "He was the kind of guy that, if you wanted to know about any band in the country, he knew about every, every band that ever played a note of music. He went on and on with Strayhorn about a bandleader, Joe Haymes, because Haymes used parallel ninths in his arrangements.

He would buy every record that he could possibly buy. He'd have his radio on all night, and he'd call me when I was sleeping and say, 'Hey, turn on station so-and-so. Benny Goodman is coming in from Chicago.' We couldn't call Strayhorn, because his family didn't have a phone, so we'd save all this up to tell him the next day."

It was Esch, along with Scrima, who fanned Strayhorn's developing fascination with jazz into ardor. Together, Esch and Scrima pitched in to buy Strayhorn his first jazz record, a 78 rpm Art Tatum solo. "He literally wore it out and had to buy another one," said Scrima. "When we first started palling together, Billy wasn't into jazz at all—he was a classical piano player. We would get all these records and sit down, in Esch's house usually, and listen to them for hours. Tatum, Teddy Wilson, Duke Ellington, Earl Hines, Benny Goodman—they were the big ones we listened to. Billy was all ears, man, and he was hooked in a minute. He really loved Tatum and Teddy Wilson best of all of them. What he realized, we talked about, was that everything he loved about classical music was there, in one form or another, in jazz—and here was a place he could apply himself. Art Tatum was black. Teddy Wilson was black. And they were serious musicians, like Strayhorn saw himself."

Since Esch was primarily interested in arranging (regarded as a so-so guitarist, he was writing charts for a local swing band, the Buddy Malone Orchestra, for which Scrima was playing drums) and since Strayhorn had had experience orchestrating *Fantastic Rhythm,* much of their conversation together often centered on arrangements and orchestrating technique. "He was a fine arranger," Strayhorn would say, "and I learned a good deal from him." (Jack Purcell, a longtime Pittsburgh bandleader who used Esch's charts as early as the 1930s, described Esch's work at the time as "methodical—he had very unusual, attractive voicings, and he always had something to say; there was always a point to what he wrote.") Evidently the self-taught Esch was also influenced by his classically trained compeer: according to Veronica Heffernan Esch, Bill Esch's girlfriend during the period of his friendship with Strayhorn (and later Esch's wife), "My husband had no musical training other than what he learned from Billy Strayhorn. I don't want to take anything away from my own husband, but I was with them when they studied together in the house, and my husband was really learning just as much from Strayhorn as Strayhorn was learning from him." ("By the way, Billy wasn't one of those ones who only know music," said Veronica Esch. "He and I went shopping once in Horne's department store for a suit for Bill—he had wonderful taste in clothes— and you should have seen the looks we got. The manager came over and was just about to throw us out, but we were finished, and we were leaving anyway.")

Strayhorn himself had no girlfriend at the time, or at any point earlier in his life, by all accounts. He is not known to have so much as danced with a girl. At the parties he attended, he often played piano; otherwise he talked casually to young women and men but wasn't one to flirt (with members of either sex). He never attended a prom or other school social event except to perform. His closest known friends, all male and heterosexual, generally thought of him as asexual but at some point speculated that he might be homosexual. "The topic of sex just never came up with us," noted Harry Herforth. "Considering that we were best friends during adolescence, I suppose that fact in itself is significant. I myself was a very late bloomer and didn't start dating until my late teens, but looking back after a while, I could see clearly that Billy was probably always homosexual." Mickey Scrima was a bit more prescient: "To be perfectly honest, a lot of us suspected that Billy was gay, by simple virtue of the fact that he never talked about girls, for god's sake. But I never heard anything about him being with a guy either, and he never came on to any of us."

There was a quiet, insular gay social scene in Pittsburgh in the 1930s, and a gay black member of the *Fantastic Rhythm* cast—Michael Phelan, who danced Strayhorn's "Harlem Rumba"—was part of it during the period when Strayhorn lived in the city. "There were very few public places where we could meet," he said. "On Saturday night only, there was a private club on Liberty Street. You paid five dollars and walked down steps into the basement. It wasn't much. Most of the gay socializing took place at private homes where there were parties. Now, they always wanted me to do a dance, so I knew practically everybody who was gay in town. And I certainly knew everybody who was black and gay. I met Billy, strictly businesswise, from doing *Fantastic Rhythm*. But I never saw him *any-where*." There is no evidence that Strayhorn was involved in gay relationships in his youth, but one thing is clear: he was never known to engage in a heterosexual relationship, not even to test the experience or for appearances' sake.

One of Strayhorn's youthful compositions is so steeped in cynicism about romance that it implies some depth of experience with love, unrequited and perhaps gay. Begun some time earlier, according to Strayhorn, but completed in 1936, the song was entitled "Life Is Lonely" but later renamed with a lyric phrase that lingered with those who heard it: "Lush Life." It is a masterpiece of fatalist sophistication that belies its author's youth but betrays years of ferment. His friends heard versions of the song as early as 1933, when Strayhorn sang some of it a cappella for Harry Herforth. "I had the idea for this, and I started it," Strayhorn later explained. "And every now and then I'd go back to it, and add a little more to it—you know, a problem would come up, how it would end and how to work it out. You couldn't solve it then, you had to go on to other things, and you keep coming back to it. So that's how it was done." From its opening lines, "Lush Life" can easily be interpreted as an evocation of a homosexual experience: "I used to visit all the very gay places, / Those come what may places . . ." Strayhorn himself would be cryptic about its meaning. "It's a song most persons have to listen to twice before they understand it, and then lots of them don't know what it's about," he hinted. Even so, a seventeen- or eighteen-year-old Homewood kid would not have been likely to use the word *gay* to signify same-sex romance in 1933; the usage had scarcely begun to seep beyond homosexual circles to which Strayhorn wasn't known to belong. In any case, the lyrics of "Lush Life" are wishful, not literal; dreaming of a week in Paris, Strayhorn rarely walked past Frick Park. "Lush Life" is a prayer:

> *I used to visit all the very gay places,*
> *Those come what may places*
> *Where one relaxes on the axis*
> *Of the wheel of life*
> *To get the feel of life*
> *From jazz and cocktails.*

The girls I knew had sad and sullen gray faces
With distingué traces
That used to be there, you could see where
They'd been washed away
By too many through the day
Twelve o'clock tales.

Then you came along with your siren song
To tempt me to madness.
I thought for a while that your poignant smile
Was tinged with the sadness of a great love for me.
Ah, yes, I was wrong,
Again I was wrong.

Life is lonely again
And only last year
Everything seemed so sure.
Now life is awful again,
A trough full of heart
Could only be a bore.

A week in Paris will ease the bite of it.
All I care is to smile in spite of it.
I'll forget you, I will
While yet you are still
Burning inside my brain.

Romance is mush
Stifling those who strive.
I'll live a lush life in some small dive
And there I'll be while I rot with the rest
Of those whose lives are lonely, too.

Good as its lyrics are, "Lush Life" can stand on its own musically as a full-composed work as clear and sharp as anything by, say, Jerome Kern. It is distinguished by a probing concerto-style exploration of its principal key (D-flat), some nicely surprising harmonic turns, melodic lines of often odd yet utterly natural-seeming duration, and virtually no repetition. Most impressively, the piece exquisitely weds words and music: A key change on "everything seemed so sure" suddenly suggests optimism, and stress notes—for instance, the "blue note" E-natural on the word *jazz*—fall precisely on the lyrics' points of drama. Though darkly majestic as a whole, "Lush Life" does have moments of gawky ostentation. Between its scathing high points of protest—submitting to passion is mad, great love comes with sadness, romance is mush—there are bits of ersatz–Cole Porter pretense: the strained internal rhyme of "too many through the day," the awkward "trough full of heart." Then, so suffers many a prayer.

Somewhere around June 1937, Jerry Eisner, the clarinetist for whom Strayhorn had arranged "Song of India," heard from him for the first time in two years. In the meanwhile, Eisner, through subbing in local "territory" bands, had begun building a reputation as an up-and-coming Goodman-style instrumentalist. Like most other musicians who had played with Strayhorn in high school, he had no idea that Strayhorn had grown to write music on the level of "Lush Life." "Jerome, this is Billy Strayhorn. I want you to come up to the drugstore to meet somebody. Come up before we close at five," Eisner recalled Strayhorn saying. Eisner showed up to find Strayhorn waiting with Calvin Dort, a snazzily dressed, thirtyish son of a prosperous white Pittsburgh family. "Expensive clothes, but he was a schlump," said Eisner. "Fixed teeth, but never kept himself neat." They all walked to Dort's house a few blocks away, where Dort had an elaborate new, green-sparkled Ludwig drum kit set up in the living room. No piano. Dort spun a few records, playing along on the drums—strictly with the brushes, in the style of Ray Bauduc of Bob Crosby's Bobcats—then poured a round of beers while Strayhorn started talking about forming a band. "That was it," said Eisner, "and we had a trio": piano, clarinet, and drums, the same configuration—racially too—as the Benny Goodman Trio.

Within weeks, the as-yet-unnamed group began rehearsing regularly, prompted by another terse phone call from Strayhorn. "Jerome, we're going to pick you up in fifteen minutes," Eisner remembered Strayhorn saying at around eleven one night. The new band mates gathered in a closed-down shoe store in a building in

East Liberty that Dort's family owned; Dort had his drum kit and an upright piano set up in the empty storefront. "We went at it all night," said Eisner. "What songs we all didn't already know, Strayhorn knew or could figure out in his head on the spot." A few days later, Strayhorn formalized the group's repertoire and handed out sixty-page spiral music-manuscript books in which he had penciled out lead sheets (indicating the chord changes and melody lines) for dozens of tunes. Taking the initiative as de facto musical director, Strayhorn not only chose the band's material—mostly jazz and pop hits, many drawn from the Goodman catalog, including "Body and Soul," "Diga-Diga-Doo," "Oh, Lady Be Good," and "Lullaby in Rhythm"—but also included stern instructions for achieving the precise sound he wanted: "If you use the Ab9 in the 2nd measure be sure and use Gb (the 7th) in your lick," "No fast licks on this one," "Play this as straight as possible. It will come off better."

Mingled with the expected standards were a few surprises, Strayhorn originals, all romantic ballads in the melancholy vein. Since Strayhorn would occasionally sing in rehearsals, a few songs in the book were complete with lyrics, including the original "If You Were There" (never to be recorded or published). Sweetly tuneful, the piece is charming despite the awkward naïveté of its lyrics:

> I'd like a houseboat on the Hudson River,
> I'd tour the Rockies in the oldest flivver,
> And even troubles would be fun to share
> If you were there.
>
> A penthouse would be
> A prison to me
> Unless I could share it with you,
> And even the stars above lover's lane
> Would be as tasteless as a glass of stale champagne.

The band also had words and music for a superior Strayhorn torch song, "Your Love Has Faded." A teary elegy of rejection, the song has a memorable pop-ballad melody and functionally melancholy lyrics.

Your love has faded,
It's not what it used to be,
You don't belong to me completely.
Your kiss is colder,
There's none of that old desire,
None of that burning fire that thrilled me.

I don't know what has changed you,
I've never been untrue,
Someone has rearranged you,
And all I get for being true is just a frozen kiss or two.

Your loved has faded,
The flame that once burned so bright
Has faded into the night.

More impressively, the book included a Strayhorn composition that embodies the whole of his youthful frustration in a masterstroke of yearning, "Something to Live For." Its melody is an outright cry; its modulations ache. As in "Lush Life," the use of *gay* hints, possibly, at homosexual romance; only with "Something to Live For," however, does Strayhorn speak directly from feeling rather than fantasy. Here, he puts his social climbing in compellingly personal, emotional terms:

I have almost everything a human could desire,
Cars and houses, bearskin rugs
To lie before my fire,
But there's something missing,
Something isn't there,
It seems I'm never kissing
The one whom I could care for.

I want something to live for,
Someone to make my life an adventurous dream.
Oh, what wouldn't I give for

Someone who'd take my life and make it seem
Gay as they say it ought to be.
Why can't I have love like that brought to me?

My eye is watching the noon crowd,
Searching the promenade,
Seeking a clue
To the one who will someday be
My something to live for.

The Pittsburgh jazz world was essentially segregated. On the Hill, the black section and the high point of the city's music scene, more than twenty nightspots, bars with music, and private clubs in residential homes were open every night; its smaller-scale but higher-profile white counterpart, East Liberty, had five or six legitimate clubs and as many after-hours places. "Billy could easily have played the Hill every night of the week and made enough money to never go back to the drugstore," said Jerry Eisner. "He wanted to play the East Liberty clubs, because they attracted the more legitimate musicians and the wealthier patrons—they represented success and prominence. But the racism there could have eaten him up." Using Calvin Dort's family pull, Strayhorn got his mixed-race trio its first gig in East Liberty, though in one of the district's less genteel establishments, a semilegal joint on the second floor of the Triangle Theater building on Station Street called Charlie Ray's. A former prizefighter with whispered mob connections, Charlie Ray was constructed like a small safe; he wore a six-inch cigar on his lower lip and evidently never lit it. His club, an airtight box with a low pressed-tin ceiling, attracted hustlers, show-business people, and miscellaneous nocturnals. Ray called Strayhorn Jasper, a racist slur, though he liked the trio, or at least his customers' response to it, and he kept it booked on Fridays and Saturdays for nearly a year. "We'd play till the morning, but we'd break on Saturday nights when the Benny Goodman *Camel Caravan* show came on the radio," said Eisner. "We'd all listen intently. Teddy Wilson would play something, and we'd go back up on the bandstand, and Strayhorn would play what he just heard, perfectly, calling out the chord changes. The people really liked us—I know, because one customer turned the jukebox on while we were playing, and somebody else threw him down the stairs." Billy May, then a Pittsburgh trumpet player, became a fan of the band and sat in with them. "They were a fine, professional little band, no amateur act," he recalled. Linton Garner, Erroll's older brother and a well-regarded modern pianist in his own right, was struck by Strayhorn's musicianship. "He could play straight-ahead jazz," said Garner. "But he was really an explorer, quite avant-garde to some extent."

Spurred by Strayhorn's adventurous playing and his long-held interest in arrangements, the group progressed in the Goodman mode and became a quintet in early 1938, expanding to include bassist Bob Yagella and vibraphonist Charles "Buzzy" Mayer. (Goodman added vibraharpist Lionel Hampton for his quartet.) Yagella, who was husky and about ten years older than Strayhorn and Eisner, was part of a musical family of boys trained to play violin. "He played the bass like a string instrument, more like a cello, than like a percussion instrument as so many jazz musicians did in those days," recalled his brother Leo, a Pittsburgh-area bandleader for many years. Bob Yagella joined Strayhorn's group on the coattails of his friend Mayer, whom Strayhorn got to know in late 1937 through Volkwein's music store, where Mayer was giving drum lessons. Lean and raffish, the twenty-four-year-old Mayer had already played in a successful Pittsburgh sweet band, the Billy Catizone Orchestra, and led his own swing ensemble, Buzz Mayer and His Pirates, by the time he became friends with Strayhorn. "He was a damn fine xylophone player," said Billy Catizone, "but he was frustrated in my band, which was a society orchestra. He went with Strayhorn because the word was spreading that Strayhorn was a great musician." According to alto saxophonist Ray Leavy, who played with Mayer, "Our band just didn't have enough players of Buzz's quality, so we couldn't make it. He was more serious. His mind never stopped working—he was like an engineer. He had that kind of mind." Compatible in temperament, taste, and ambition, Strayhorn and Mayer experimented as a duo before Strayhorn brought him into his group. They worked out a few duets, combining tunes at Strayhorn's suggestion, and took their work together seriously enough to try it out in the recording studio.

In March 1938, Strayhorn and Mayer booked time in the economical George Hyde Studio and recorded demonstration records of three pieces: "I Surrender, Dear," and two medleys, one of "I Never Knew" and "Diga-Diga-Doo," the other of "I Got Rhythm" and "China Boy." All are predominantly Mayer showcases; the tunes were all best known for their performances by the vibraharpists Lionel Hampton and Red Norvo. Strayhorn still shines through with a hip, casual sense of time and some quirky touches: he skips and adds a few beats here and there in the medley of "I Got Rhythm" and "China Boy," toying with his idol's work. For Strayhorn's group, a bonus of adding Mayer was one guaranteed booking: Mayer's mother owned an amusement park about fourteen miles southwest of the Pittsburgh city limits, between the towns of Bridgeville and Canonsburg. (Mayer's father had died of pneumonia in 1927 shortly after being severely burned in a gas explosion while constructing the park.) Set on fifteen acres and catering mainly to an affluent white clientele, the park consisted of a small lake with some fifteen rowboats, a carousel, and some spin-around rides for children; five or six octagon-shaped cottages designed in a faux-Japanese style; and an outdoor bandstand that couples could use for ten cents a dance. All through the summer of 1938, Strayhorn's group was the entertainment at Rakuen Lakes, and Billy Strayhorn lived there, sharing cottages with the Mayer family. "During the day, Buzz and Billy would help out a bit with any chores, carrying supplies, whatever," remembered Lois Hill, a Mayer niece who lived with them that summer. "At night, they'd play music, and anybody who thought they were the help was suddenly in for a shock." Ray Leavy drove out to hear the group once, with the idea of sitting in. "I had my sax with me, but when I heard those guys play I kept it zippered up," he said.

As well as the group may have jelled as a quintet, it had to revert to a trio at summer's end; Mayer was studying for his pilot's license, and Yagella kept a day job in Pittsburgh that he wasn't willing to give up. The group was offered steady work—four hours a night, six nights a week—at a new nightclub that two friends of a friend of

Calvin Dort's were about to open in Winchester, Virginia, a wheat-farming town of about ten thousand people. It was to be a long-term engagement, advertised and promoted, so the group was told it needed a name. They chose the Mad Hatters, inspired by a drawing Eisner had seen in one of Strayhorn's issues of the *New Yorker*. When the group arrived at the club, a sign in front boldly announced the Mad Hatters. But the place was still being built. "We had to pitch in and paint the walls and everything," said Jerry Eisner. "What a scene. To make matters worse, much worse, this is the South now, and Billy wasn't allowed to stay in the boardinghouse where we were set up. He had to sleep in a cot in the back room of the club, and he did it, because the band was the priority." The club opened shortly, and the band's run was a success for several weeks. "I don't know if people thought we were a big act from the North or what, but we did real well," said Eisner. They did well, that is, until a patron in front made a remark about "that nigger on piano." Calvin Dort kicked his whole drum kit at the man, and as a ruckus ensued, the band fled out the back way. Outside, Dort somehow commandeered a truck, and he drove it north with the two white band members in the cab, Strayhorn alone in the dark in the back, until they reached the Pennsylvania border. "Although Billy was certainly no stranger to prejudice, that incident made quite a big impression on him," said Eisner. "It didn't make him give up, though—just the opposite. He was even more thoughtful and determined than usual. That's when he started talking about different ways to pursue his music."

When he settled back in Pittsburgh, Strayhorn took the trio into the recording studio at Volkwein's, where the Mad Hatters laid down four demo sides, including two Goodman Trio numbers famous for their Teddy Wilson solos: "Body and Soul" and "Sweet Sue" (the other two titles are lost and forgotten). The tracks capture a vibrant, polished group deeply influenced by Goodman and Wilson. Eisner has a mature tone and a tidy way with a phrase; Strayhorn displays a striking rhythmic sense and harmonic command, in addition to Tatumesque speed. On "Body and Soul," the original record of which included one of Wilson's best-known solo breaks, Strayhorn's improvisation is more in the spirit of the daring early Wilson than Wilson's own playing was at that point. Dort kept time and a low profile. Now rendered in shellac, the Mad Hatters would never play again.

Scuffling for another musical challenge and, perhaps, a safer one, Strayhorn took a late-night job as bar pianist at one of the nicer joints on Apple Street, a busy club in East Liberty with a good piano and a small old dog that roamed among the customers as if it and not its master, Woogie Harris, a mid-level local numbers man, owned the place. Besides the tips, Strayhorn was drawn to Harris's because it was a hangout for members of both the white and black arms of the (then-segregated) Musicians Protective Union. "Strayhorn liked to go up there and run chords off," said Kenneth Hill of the Moonlight Harbor Band, an alto saxophonist who occasionally sat in with Strayhorn at Harris's. "He got to play, and other musicians got to hear him. He was quite a good musician, it was obvious."

At the same time, between his hours at Harris's and his shifts back at the Pennfield Pharmacy, Strayhorn was working to gain a reputation as an arranger. With Jerry Eisner providing entrée, Strayhorn offered to contribute arrangements to a local rehearsal band run by Bill Ludwig, a wealthy drummer friend of Eisner's whose family owned a floral business in Pittsburgh's exclusive Squirrel Hill district. In all, Strayhorn wrote five or six orchestrations for Ludwig's twelve-piece unit, according to Eisner. "Nice, swinging charts," said Eisner. Strayhorn was also drawing on Bill Esch's association with the Buddy Malone Orchestra; though Esch filled most of the band book, Strayhorn submitted several sophisticated dance charts that Malone used at society dates, according to Mickey Scrima. "Most of the other bands were using stocks [over-the-counter arrangements]. So between Esch and Strayhorn, the Malone group had a really nice, original sound," Scrima said. "Strayhorn had some great voicings, very advanced, more advanced than the band most of the time." (One of Strayhorn's big-band pieces was "Ugly Ducklin'," which he also called "Smoky City." It was composed at the time of *Fantastic Rhythm* for a group configured like the Moonlight Harbor Band, although none of that ensemble's musicians recall performing the piece. According to Scrima, the composition was probably performed by the Ludwig group. A modernist, somewhat modal work, it would resurface years later under the title "Smada.")

As word of his arrangements for Ludwig and Malone spread among musicians, Strayhorn was offered a slot as regular arranger and pianist for a dance band formed by nineteen-year-old drummer Anthony Edward D'Emilio in mid-1938. A child violin prodigy from a musical Italian family, D'Emilio had studied the contrabass at Peabody High School under its respected musical director, Wally Cross (a Trotsky double), taken a few drum lessons at Volkwein's (more than likely from Buzz Mayer, the store's percussion teacher at the time), and initially tried breaking into the band business with a ten-piece all-white utility group he called the Anthony Edwards Orchestra. It ran through store-bought stock arrangements at a few fraternity dances and stag parties, then disbanded for lack of return business, according to the group's trombonist, Orva Lee Ice. Wanting an upgrade geared for the swing ballroom circuit, D'Emilio formed a fifteen-piece group with a jazzier name, the Rex Edwards Orchestra. The two chief soloists, Strayhorn and the lead tenor saxophonist (his name now forgotten), were black, the rest of the group white—"absolutely unheard of, to everybody who saw it," said Ice, who rehearsed with the new band but was not invited to join permanently. "After failing with a knock-around band, Ed [D'Emilio] got serious," explained Ice. "He was a great classical musician. He had very high standards with this band. That's why he didn't take a lot of men from the first band—me included—and that's why he got Billy Strayhorn."

The Rex Edwards Orchestra developed a repertoire of more than 120 pieces, mostly stocks heavily revised by Strayhorn—"He showed the guys how to alter the harmony and the accents to improve the original chart," recalled Ice—as well as several dozen of Strayhorn's own arrangements and at least a few original Strayhorn compositions, including the band's theme song, the lovely ballad "Remember." While D'Emilio booked and fronted the band, Strayhorn shaped the Rex Edwards Orchestra's sound with terse authority. "At rehearsal, he was the one in charge," said Ice. "He heard every instrument and every note. He knew exactly what he wanted, and he would correct you—'Hey, let's do that again. You're not breathing correctly.' " Inhibited by its mixed-race membership from playing the segregated ballrooms in Pittsburgh, the Rex Edwards Orchestra rehearsed extensively and performed mainly at social functions and private parties—thirty to fifty dates in 1938, in the estimate of Fred Whitlinger, a musician friend of D'Emilio's who acted as the group's unofficial, unpaid manager. "It was a real smooth band. Very pretty," said Whitlinger. "It had what it took, as far as the music went."

Seemingly inexhaustible in musical energy as well as ambition, Strayhorn continued to play at Woogie Harris's late at night and, later still, at a no-name second-floor after-hours place on Wood Street in Homewood where D'Emilio and his musician friends would frequently rendezvous. "We would try to stump him," remembered Orva Ice. "I would ask him to play something out of a symphony, and he would know the tune. And he used to take the classical pieces and adapt them to jazz. Another thing, the most sensational thing—he used to be able to, within half an hour, play tunes, bits and pieces, so that you were listening to maybe twenty-four tunes in half an hour. He made a sort of rhapsody out of them. The man had a sense—from his brain to his fingers—what should be in what order and how to intertwine and interweave the tunes. We just stared at his fingers, which were always slipping under the cuffs of his shirtsleeves, by the way." Another musician of D'Emilio's acquaintance, James "Honey Boy" Minor, a drummer and leader of one of Pittsburgh's most-talked-about black bands, heard Strayhorn both at Woogie Harris's and in Homewood. After a session sitting in with the Rex Edwards Orchestra, Minor asked Strayhorn to write a few arrangements for his group, too. Mickey Scrima, a big fan of Minor's hard-driving style, heard Honey Boy Minor and His Buzzing Bees perform Strayhorn charts at a dance date on the Hill. "They were Fletcher Henderson–type things, real swing numbers," said Scrima, "but with that Strayhorn sophistication, which a lot of that real swinging dance music didn't have. The combination of the two was fantastic." Minor himself was delighted with Strayhorn—that is, with his work. "I liked his music," said Minor. "We were very happy to play his music. But he wasn't for us. I think he liked boys." No matter. "There was no stopping him," said Scrima. "He was doing so much that was so great that he was bound to put one of those bands into the big time. Or he would hit the big time himself, or something."

3

OVERTURE

TO A

JAM

SESSION

Music appreciation was a business booster for Pennfield Pharmacy. School-age kids like Helen Reis and Jack Farrell, who lived a few doors apart in a row of brick houses two blocks from Pennfield, phoned in orders for ice cream or pop to satisfy multiple appetites. "I told my mother I just *had* to have something for dessert, because I knew Billy would bring it and play the piano for us if we asked, which everybody did," said Reis, whose parents would usually tip Strayhorn a dime. "So many people did the same that he got very well known in the area." Through this reputation for music-to-go, Strayhorn picked up some less demeaning and better-paying work performing at cocktail parties and business-related social events in the Point Breeze area. As Lillian Strayhorn Dicks recalled, "He got to spending a lot of time every night around the drugstore neighborhood. It was a white world where we weren't accepted, but Billy was, because of his talent. He was invited into people's homes. He was going to parties and playing the piano, which is what he wanted to do. He was doing whatever he thought he had to do to find success with his music, and he obviously presumed that whatever break he was going to get was going to come out of the white world, through a white music publisher or a white entrepreneur he might meet somehow." As it happened, it was a white acquaintance from the drugstore—David Perelman, a young, bushy-haired intern from the University of Pittsburgh's College of Pharmacy—who offered Strayhorn a more direct course, one into the era's center of black power.

Perelman's next-desk friend at school was twenty-year-old George Greenlee, said to be the first Negro admitted to the institution. Smartly groomed and intensely bright—he had a contained smile that stopped just short of a smirk—Greenlee had grown up in a moneyed stratum of black society, first in South Carolina and then in western Pennsylvania; his uncle William Augustus "Gus" Greenlee was an imperial force in black Pittsburgh. With seed money supposedly made hijacking beer trucks, the elder Greenlee built a numbers racket on a reputation for playing straight and paying up. Bulky and strong-featured, he liked looking the part of a racketeer and wore custom-made white suits and white ties with black shirts and white shoes. By the late 1930s, Greenlee's empire of sports, entertainment, and real-estate holdings included a stable of boxers (among them, the light heavyweight champion John Henry Lewis); Pittsburgh's Negro League baseball team, the Crawfords (whose ballpark, Greenlee Field, was the only black-owned stadium in the country); and the city's two most prosperous nightclubs, Crawford Grill One and Crawford Grill Two. In the hope that Gus Greenlee could open entertainment-career doors for a gifted black musician, David Perelman implored his classmate to exert some kindred influence. "David came to me one day and said, 'George, we have a delivery boy who's one of the finest musicians I've ever heard, and he doesn't seem to be able to get a break. Your uncle knows all the big musicians. Why don't you introduce him to somebody?' But I had never met this fellow Billy or heard him play. So I said, 'David, are you sure this guy is that good?' He said, 'Believe me.' " Greenlee proceeded on faith. "David was one of the first whites that accepted me as a friend and not as an oddball," Greenlee explained, "so I decided to go out on a limb for him. Besides, I didn't have time to meet this piano player. Turned out that my uncle was having a big party that night for the band that was opening in town the following evening. I could set everything up at the party for this guy to meet the incoming bandleader, Duke Ellington. Otherwise, I'd wait a week and introduce him to the next bandleader, Basie. But I thought I might as well get this over with and introduce this fellow to whomever was there first."

Shortly after midnight on December 1, 1938, George Greenlee nodded and back-patted his way through the ground-floor Rumpus Room of Crawford Grill One (running from Townsend Street to Fullerton Avenue on Wylie Avenue, the place was nearly a block long) and headed up the stairs at the center of the club. He passed the second floor, which was the main floor, where bands played on a revolving stage facing an elongated glass-topped bar and Ray Wood, now a hustling photographer, offered to take pictures of the patrons for fifty cents. Greenlee hit the third floor, the Club Crawford (insiders only), and spotted his uncle with Duke Ellington, who was engaged to begin a week-long run at the Stanley Theatre the following day. "As soon as my uncle introduced us," said Greenlee, "I turned to Duke and I said, 'Duke, a good friend of mine has written some songs, and we'd like for you to hear them.' I lied, but I trusted David. I knew Duke couldn't say no with my uncle standing there. So Duke said, 'Well, why don't you come backstage tomorrow, after the first show?' It was all set."

The next morning, Greenlee arranged (through Perelman) to meet Strayhorn for the first time in front of the Stanley Theatre before the 1:00 p.m. opening matinee. The day was chilly but still, and a light snow fell on and off. Strayhorn was collected, Greenlee would recall, and looked properly ascetic—"He was wearing his Sunday best, but they were pretty well worn." They watched the first show, a long set of Ellington Orchestra numbers peppered with a tap-dance act (Flash and Dash) and a comedy team (the Two Zephyrs), then found their way through the baroque old Stanley, eight stories high, with thirty-five hundred seats and three full floors of dressing rooms. Ellington's dressing room was the size of a large dining room and, in fact, was set up like one: several place settings were arranged on a table, and there was an upright piano along one wall. Ellington, alone with his valet, lay on a reclining chair in an embroidered robe, getting his hair conked, eyes closed.

"I introduced Billy, and we stood there," said Greenlee. "Duke didn't get up. He didn't even open his eyes. He just said, 'Sit down at the piano, and let me hear what you can do.' " Strayhorn lowered himself onto the bench with calibrated grace and turned toward Ellington, who was lying still. "Mr. Ellington, this is the way you played this number in the show," Strayhorn announced and began to perform his host's melancholy ballad "Sophisticated Lady," one of a few Ellington tunes Strayhorn knew from his days with the Mad Hatters; as a trio, the group used to play a version inspired by Art Tatum's arabesque 1933 recording. "The amazing thing was," explained Greenlee, "Billy played it *exactly* like Duke had just played it on stage. He copied him to perfection." Ellington stayed silent and prone, though his hair work was over. "Now, this is the way *I* would play it," continued Strayhorn. Changing keys and upping the tempo slightly, he shifted into an adaptation Greenlee described as "pretty hip-sounding and further and further 'out there' as he went on."

At the end of the number, Strayhorn turned to Ellington, now standing right behind him, glaring at the keyboard over his shoulders. "Go get Harry," Ellington ordered his valet. (Harry Carney, Ellington's closest intimate among the members of his entourage in this period, had played baritone saxophone for the orchestra since 1926, when he was sixteen years old, and the two frequently traveled together to engagements.) "Wellll . . ." proceeded Ellington dramatically as he faced Strayhorn eye to eye for the first time, Ellington gazing down, Strayhorn peering up. "Can you do that again?" "Yes," Strayhorn replied matter-of-factly, and began Ellington's ruminative "Solitude," once more emulating the composer's piano style. When Harry Carney entered the room, Ellington stage-whispered, "Listen to this kid play." Again Strayhorn declared, "This is the way I would play it," and reharmonized the Ellington song as a personal showcase. Brazenly (or naively) the twenty-three-year-old artist demonstrated both a crafty facility with his renowned elder's idiom and a spirited capacity to expand it through his own sensibility. The potency struck Ellington, Greenlee recounted: "Billy was playing. Duke stood there behind him beaming, and he put his hands on his shoulders, like he wanted to feel Billy playing his song." Carney hustled out and returned with two more members of Ellington's musical inner circle: alto saxophonist Johnny Hodges, thirty-two, a premier Ellington soloist since he joined the band in 1928, and Ivie Anderson, thirty-three, who became Ellington's first full-time vocalist in 1931.

As this group gathered around Strayhorn, "Things got hectic," said Greenlee. "Duke fired off a million questions about Billy's background and training and so forth. Billy kept playing from then on, mostly his own things—'Something to Live For,' which he sang, and a few others" (including a piece so new he hadn't given it a title yet). Recalling the occasion in later years, Ellington focused on that moment: "When Stray first came to see me in the Stanley Theatre, I asked him the name of a tune he'd played for me, and he just laughed. I caught that laugh. It was that laugh that first got me." However impressed he may have been by Strayhorn's musical skills, Ellington was also struck by something visceral.

Uncertain how best to use him—Ellington's orchestra already had a pianist—Ellington left Strayhorn with an initial assignment to write lyrics to an instrumental piece. As Strayhorn recalled, "I know how *something-or-other* it must have been to meet a young man in a town like Pittsburgh. I played for him. I played and sang. Uh, he, uh, he was—he liked me very much, and he said, 'Well, you come back tomorrow,' and he gave me an assignment. He had an idea for a lyric. He said, 'You go home and write a lyric for this,' and I did. I rushed home and I wrote this lyric." (The title of the song and the lyrics are unknown.) Strayhorn returned to see Ellington the following evening and submitted his work but found that the frantic events of late had taken a visible toll on him. "Everybody was just so wonderful to me—Ivie Anderson particularly, because she was worried," he said. "She said, 'Lookit, you go out and get yourself a sandwich or something, because you're not eating.' I must have looked a little peaked." Invited back, he visited Ellington again at the Stanley three days later, when he was given a second assignment, this time to apply his evident skill at harmonization to a vocal selection for Ivie Anderson. As Robert Conaway remembered, "After the meeting, he said, 'He likes my work, and he gave me an arrangement to do.' "

The next evening, Strayhorn worked on his orchestration for Ellington, polishing it with the help of his friend Bill Esch rather than returning to the Stanley; Ellington left the theater early that night anyway and spent the after-show hours at the Loendi, a black social club in a rambling three-story brick house on the Hill. By the following evening, Ellington's last at the Stanley, Strayhorn was ready and returned with his work, and, sharing his good fortune, he brought along Esch. Ellington, who was between shows, wrapped up dinner in his dressing room with Thelma Spangler, a striking, soft-spoken young woman he had met the previous evening at the Loendi. The three musicians huddled together on their feet, poring over music paper for about five minutes, discussing aspects of the arrangement animatedly, Spangler recalled. A chime sounded and Ellington tucked the manuscript under his arm, pronouncing, "Time to go back on."

Spangler watched the show from the wings. Strayhorn and Esch stood behind the curtain, near Ellington's piano, while Ellington passed parts of Strayhorn's arrangement to the musicians on stage. "Duke gave some of the guys some tips," said Spangler. "Like, he'd hum something to one guy, or he'd say, 'You come in here.' A couple of times he asked Billy something, and Billy answered him, and then Duke explained it to the band. It all happened very quickly. Then Ivie came out on stage. Duke whispered to her and raised his hands, and they did the song, just like that." The arrangement was a slow-tempo version of "Two Sleepy People." "Oh God, it was pretty, like something in a dream," Spangler said. "Ellington smiled all over himself, and he told Billy after the show how happy he was with his music."

Clearly pleased, Ellington offered Strayhorn work. The kind of work, however, remained unclear. As Strayhorn recounted, "He said, 'Well, I would like to have you in my organization. I have to find some way of injecting you into it. I have to find out how I do this, after I go to New York.' He was on his way back east then. So I said, 'Well, all right.' " Ellington paid Strayhorn twenty dollars for his orchestration of "Two Sleepy People" and jotted down subway directions to his apartment on Edgecombe Avenue in Harlem. "They were packing up—Willy Manning was getting clothes together in trunks and everything," Strayhorn recalled. "And off they went, and off I went back home and back to the drugstore."

Single-minded about music since childhood, Strayhorn had pursued every opportunity he had been given, had found, or had been able to create for himself in classical, theatrical, and popular music as well as jazz, throughout both the black and the white worlds as he knew them—mostly separate musical states despite his own ability to cross their borders. "He said he would go with any of the major bands that asked him, black or white," recalls Robert Conaway. "It was only a matter of time until somebody important recognized his talent." Yet the prospect of working with Duke Ellington in particular had extraordinary advantages. Strayhorn may not have had any Ellington records in his collection or have talked him up as much as he did Stravinsky and Art Tatum, but he was scarcely oblivious to Ellington's significance. "He was hip to Duke," said Mickey Scrima.

By the end of 1938, the thirty-nine-year-old Ellington had been performing professionally for more than twenty years. The first of two children born to a worshipful mother who instilled in her son a sense of privilege and a father who on at least one occasion served as a butler at a catered function at the White House (a matter of great pride to his family), Edward Kennedy Ellington earned his lifelong nickname in his childhood neighborhood, a middle-class black section of Washington, where he role-played the part of a duke and instructed his playmates to address him accordingly. Ellington began private piano lessons at the age of eight or so, though he was largely self-taught as a composer and arranger. He had some artistic talent, enough for him to make some money painting signs and to earn a scholarship that he declined to Pratt Institute, the commercial-art conservatory in Brooklyn. Leading his own band, the Washingtonians, Ellington got his first high-profile exposure in the late 1920s, a few years into his second sojourn to New York, when he and the band were featured in radio broadcasts from the Hollywood, later the Kentucky Club, off Times Square. Drawing inspiration from his individualistic musicians (including, early on, trumpeter Bubber Miley and trombonist Joe Nanton, specialists in fanciful "jungle" sounds), Ellington developed a genuinely inimitable orchestral approach distinguished by startling tonal colors and idiosyncratic improvisations.

"As the band grew, there were new members coming into the band, and they injected their personality," said Harry Carney. "I think the personnel really was largely responsible for inspiring Duke to write, in that the fellas were creative and had a wealth of ideas. And one thing would suggest something else to him, and he managed to keep it pretty well organized." In little time, however, Ellington proved a gifted composer and arranger as well as a brilliant motivator and a resourceful editor of his musicians' ideas. Sometimes in collaboration with band members Miley, Barney Bigard, and others, sometimes writing alone, Ellington built an increasingly sophisticated repertoire of original pieces, including "Mood Indigo" (1930), "Solitude" (1933), "Sophisticated Lady" (1933), and "In a Sentimental Mood" (1935)—plus, to the pleasure of music critics and scholars, ambitious longer works such as "Creole Rhapsody" (1931) and "Reminiscing in Tempo" (1935). As early as 1933, open-eared critics such as the English composer and author Constant Lambert recognized in Ellington a black composer comparable to Ravel and Stravinsky in imagination and originality of vision. While Billy Strayhorn hoped to emulate Stravinsky, Duke Ellington was already seen in some informed circles as the celebrated modernist's peer. As a personality, too, Ellington projected an air of Continental polish that meshed exquisitely with Strayhorn's own infatuation with townhouse culture: jazz and cocktails in the very gay places on the wheel of life. Billy Strayhorn read the *New Yorker*; Duke Ellington *was* one, as Strayhorn could become by working with him.

"He called me, and we met over at Esch's house," said Mickey Scrima. "Billy wanted to talk about what to do about Duke. Should he pursue it? He really wasn't sure what he would do with Duke, and he wanted to write. Finally, he decided to give it a shot. Maybe Duke would play some of his songs and, at the very least, he'd get a name for himself. Esch and I both told him, 'Go ahead—it's an opportunity. If it doesn't work out, you can always leave.' "

At Tioga Street Rear, Strayhorn's decision came as an inevitability. "Mama knew that Bill would be going to New York someday," said Lillian Strayhorn Dicks, "and I think Papa hardly realized Bill was still home. We all knew it would be hard on Mama, because she and Bill were so close. But she wanted this for him as much as he wanted it, and if she had any misgivings or feelings of disappointment for herself, they never showed. She encouraged him greatly, and he assured her that he would come home to see us all. For another thing, we all knew this would mean a better life for Bill, and maybe for Mama." Lillian seemed to take additional comfort in the fact that James's sister Julia had moved from Montclair to Newark, New Jersey; should Strayhorn's plans with Ellington collapse, there was family nearby. For several weeks, however, no plans emerged at all. "Every day, people would come up and say, 'What happened?' " said Strayhorn, "and I'd say, 'Nothing happened. I went down and sang and played for the man, and he's gone to New York.' They'd say, 'What's he going to do?' And I'd say, 'I don't know what he's going to do,' and this went on for about a month. I got a little weary of this, and I hadn't heard from Duke." Determinedly, Strayhorn wrote Ellington's office, inquiring where the bandleader would be in mid-January. "Bill Esch had to come to New York, so he proposed that I go along with him and just see Duke and see what he was going to do about me. Bill decided we'd go on the train. I said, 'That's well and good, but I do not have enough money for the train.' So he said, 'Well, I'll loan you the money.' So he did."

To make an impression on Ellington, Strayhorn decided that not only would he find Ellington in New York by following the bandleader's subway directions but he would write a new composition using the directions as the theme. Ralph Koger, still a reporter for the *Pittsburgh Courier* (and later the paper's news editor), remembered Strayhorn's excitement. "We were together talking about his meeting with Duke and his plans to see him, and he played me the song he was writing to give Duke in New York. He said, 'Listen— Duke gave me directions, and I turned them into something. So he played me the tune, and, sure enough, it told you how to get to Harlem: 'Take the "A" Train.' " The composition, complete with lyrics, came more quickly than the actual A train, Strayhorn would explain: " ' "A" Train' was born without any effort—it was like writing a letter to a friend. It was composed in 1939, though it wasn't used right away. I put together all the ideas I had in my head and perfected them, then I sat down before the piano and I wrote the tune in a really short time. This is the way I like to work. All my most meaningful pieces were born like that." Mickey Scrima was palling with Strayhorn and Esch when the two of them fine-tuned the composition. "Billy was playing the thing, and Esch was offering a little pointer here or there," said Scrima. "I remember, because we all loved Fletcher Henderson, and Billy said he was trying to do a Henderson thing. As a matter of fact, he was afraid it sounded too much like Henderson. We all really liked the way it came out, but Billy wasn't sure it sounded enough like Duke."

In response to Strayhorn's letter, a member of Ellington's staff wrote that the orchestra would be performing at Nixon's Grand Theatre in Philadelphia in mid-January. "I said, 'Well, that's fine,'" said Strayhorn. "I had no idea of the distance between New York and Philadelphia. It was all east of Pittsburgh." Departing Pittsburgh early on January 19, Strayhorn and Esch arrived in Newark that evening. Strayhorn got off to visit his aunt before moving on to Philadelphia; Esch continued to New York City. Unfortunately, Strayhorn discovered that the Ellington Orchestra's engagement in Philadelphia was over. Its next stop, though, was Newark, where it was playing at the Adams Paramount Theatre, a top venue for Negro artists. "[In the] morning [January 23, the fourth day of the band's one-week engagement], I got up and took the streetcar ride to the Adams Theatre and went to the stage door," Strayhorn recounted. "There was Mr. Manning. He was a familiar face, and he said, 'Oh, hello—good morning, young man. Come on in.' So I went in, and the show was just gearing to go on. Mr. Ellington was standing in the wings with a pearl-gray suit on—I'll never forget it. And Mr. Manning said, 'Duke, here's that young man.' They couldn't remember my name. So it was—oh, he had about five or seven minutes before he went on, so we talked. Actually, he didn't say too much, and I didn't say too much. We were just kind of looking at each other. I was scared to death, and he wasn't, of course. We just kind of looked at each other. Finally, he said, 'Well, it's really something that you arrived at this moment. Yes, because I just sent Jack Boyd,' who was his manager, 'upstairs to look for your address and send for you.' " "You don't have to," Strayhorn said. "Here I am."

From that foundation of intuitive connectedness and mutual faith, Billy Strayhorn and Duke Ellington began working together; theirs was an uncommonly personal business relationship from the start. Strayhorn had no job description and no contract, not even a verbal understanding of general responsibilities and terms of compensation. "I don't have any position for you," remarked Ellington. "You'll do whatever you feel like doing." A flattering promise of laissez-faire empowerment, the arrangement was as much familial as it was professional: everything would take care of itself—that is, Ellington would take care of Strayhorn. Accordingly, the bandleader called on his nineteen-year old son, Mercer, a student at the Juilliard School of Music, to arrange for Strayhorn to move into the Harlem YMCA; Ellington would pay the rent of five dollars a night.

Strayhorn returned to Pittsburgh for a few days to prepare (his mother pressed and packed all his clothes) and say some good-byes. "He came back, and he called me on the phone at home and said, 'Guess what?' " said Ralph Koger. " 'I'm going to work for Duke. I played that tune " 'A' Train" for him, and he liked it. I'm moving to New York!' "

Strayhorn's first night in Manhattan, however, fell short of his penthouse visions. Located on busy 135th Street about half a mile from Ellington's Edgecombe Avenue apartment, the Harlem Y was popular among middle-class blacks as one of two or three hospitable rooming facilities open to them in Manhattan. Still, its 240 rooms were small and spare; there were communal rest rooms and hallway pay phones. On his second day in town, Strayhorn called Mercer Ellington, who lived in the Edgecombe Avenue apartment with Duke Ellington's sister, Ruth, who was Strayhorn's age; Ellington's lover, Mildred Dixon; and Ellington himself, when the bandleader was not on the road. "Strayhorn said that he would like to talk, because he wanted to know about Duke Ellington," said Mercer. "So he came to the house the night after he stayed at the Y and had dinner with my aunt and I. The result was that he stayed, and we chatted and played records and all that kind of stuff. And when the time came for us to go to bed, we said, 'Well, I guess we'll go to sleep.' And I got up to go to my room. And Strays said, 'Well, I'll just lay here,' and Ruth went to her room, and that was it. And he only went back to the Y from that time on to change clothes. So we said, 'What the hell are we paying all the rent for? Go get your shit and move it here.' "

The Ellingtons had relocated from 381 to 409 Edgecombe Avenue shortly after the death of Duke and Ruth's father, J. E. Ellington, who succumbed to pleurisy in October 1937, twenty-eight months after their mother, Daisy, died of cancer. "We had a lot of unhappiness there [at 381 Edgecombe]," said Ruth Ellington Boatwright, who was a biology major at Columbia's New College with aspirations for a medical career when Strayhorn moved into her home. "Our apartment at 409 was very uplifting." A broad, sunny, tree-lined street in Harlem's posh Sugar Hill district, Edgecombe Avenue stretched along a cliff seven stories above nearly a mile of blocks spreading toward Manhattan's Harlem River. The Ellingtons' seven-room apartment at 409—a courtly brick-and-stone building with a vast Art Deco lobby—hovered twelve stories higher still, on the street side of the top floor. Two days after his arrival in New York, Strayhorn was living in an actual penthouse. "It was very splendorous," Ruth Ellington Boatwright said proudly. "Mostly in the area there were theatrical celebrities, stars, and very well-to-do intellectuals. When you looked out the windows, you could see the downtown Manhattan skyline. Everything looked like toys." The apartment was professionally decorated all in white. "He called me right away," recalled George Greenlee, "and he said, 'You won't believe it—this place is completely white, even the rugs! I'm talking to you on a white telephone!' He couldn't get over it," Greenlee said.

Living in Ellington's home with family members his own age and with Ellington paying for his housing, his food, and his living expenses, Strayhorn soon seemed like an Ellington himself, especially to Mildred Dixon, the household matriarch, a dainty woman whose wardrobe of lacy silks was the envy of the neighborhood. "He was just like family to me and treated me with the utmost respect," she said. "He pitched in whenever I needed help, particularly in the kitchen. He was quite a good cook, which he learned from his mother in Pittsburgh." (Strayhorn made sweet potatoes covered with orange peels and wrapped in tin foil, baked through the afternoon.) To Ellington's sister, Billy was a brother too. Delicately framed and soft-featured, with long, wavy black-brown hair and a taste for loosely draping dresses, Ruth had a quiet grace that diffused her intellectual vigor and self-confidence. Above all, she was dedicated to her brother, whom she always called by his given name, Edward. Her pet name for Strayhorn was Billums. "We all loved Billums like he was our very own," she recalled. "Edward arranged it that way, and we thought that whatever he did was wonderful. That's the way we were trained." Ruth relished the company of an open-eyed young housemate like Strayhorn; together, they roamed the city museums on days when she had a light load of schoolwork. "The Metropolitan Museum was our favorite place in the world. We'd sit on the steps and talk into the evening about everything—art and artists and people—anything and everything. He got very analytical, very abstract. He was extremely profound."

Temperamental differences kept Strayhorn and Mercer Ellington a few degrees apart, as did Strayhorn's still undefined role with Mercer's father. Wiry and reflexive, with a roguish mustache and an eruptive grin, Mercer was as at home on the street as his father was on the stage. "I was born a street hustler, I guess," Mercer Ellington allowed. "I raised myself. I was just left to malinger, wherever I happened to be. In the house when Strayhorn was living with us, I might cook some southern food, whereas Strayhorn was really bourgeois. He was interested in the proper method of tasting wine, proper ways of storing it—temperature and all that stuff. We really didn't have that much in common, other than music. And even that— my mother gave me my musical education up to that point. Not my father. My mother taught me how to play piano when I was younger and I lived with her. My father didn't take me under his wing the way he did Strayhorn."

His new town was so absorbing—Fats Waller was playing the Apollo, Artie Shaw was playing the Strand, and *Gunga Din* was a smash at Radio City Music Hall—that Strayhorn could keep happily occupied without any musical duties, and he had none until February 26, when Ellington sent him the music for two songs, "Like a Ship in the Night," a popular ballad by Bob Cooper and Will Hudson, and "Savoy Strut," a light dance tune by Ellington and saxophonist Johnny Hodges. Ellington's instructions: "Arrange these for a recording tomorrow at ten o'clock." Hodges was scheduled to cut two sides for the Vocalion label with a small group of Ellingtonians (Hodges, trumpeter Cootie Williams, trombonist Lawrence Brown, baritone saxophonist Harry Carney, bassist Billy Taylor, drummer Sonny Greer, and Ellington himself on piano, along with singer Jean Eldridge for "Ship in the Night"), although neither Ellington nor Hodges had charts prepared for the band. The titular leader of a de facto Ellington session, Hodges never wrote any arrangements other than "head charts" expressed instrumentally or orally to the band. Strayhorn was certainly equipped for the task at hand, having done a wealth of orchestrations both for *Fantastic Rhythm* and for big bands back home. Still, he had never been called on to work so suddenly and for an unfamiliar group. "What could I do?" he commented. "I did it." Working at the Edgecombe Avenue dining table, he wrote all through (though not straight through) the night. "He fell asleep on the manuscript paper," said Ruth Ellington Boatwright, "then woke up and kept on working until he fell asleep on the paper again."

The results were recorded with a casual ease that belied the arranger's effort, according to producer Helen Oakley Dance. "The fellas put the music he wrote in front of them and played it through. It was smooth as silk," said Dance. "Ellington didn't change a thing, and he was delighted." Though neither arrangement is a notable departure from Ellingtonia, neither is an attempt to duplicate the Ellington style. "That's not the way Duke worked with Billy or the musicians on the session," said Dance. As Strayhorn explained, "He left me to my own devices. He never sat down and said, 'Well, this is the way you do this.' Never, never—*never*. He felt that there are many ways that one can do things but one way that *you* can do it, and you find it." Apparently pleased with Strayhorn's way of doing a thing for which the ever-industrious orchestra leader had relatively little time, Ellington consigned the small-band side of his operation to Strayhorn. "From then on, Duke did very little of the arranging for the small groups," recalled Strayhorn. "Oh, he did a little, but he turned almost all of them over to me. You could say I had inherited a phase of Duke's organization." This on the basis of two first-time arrangements written on one day's notice.

Timing allowed Strayhorn freedom to develop music in his new element with all the independence Ellington had promised. On March 23, Duke Ellington and his Famous Orchestra boarded the *Ile de France* for a spring tour of Europe, with engagements in France, Belgium, the Netherlands, Denmark, and Sweden. This schedule gave Strayhorn nearly seven weeks at Edgecombe to work on new compositions and arrangements, as well as to study Ellington's own scores for an essential understanding of his technique. "I stayed home," said Strayhorn, "and wrote a few things like 'Day Dream.'" (The piece would be recorded in a Johnny Hodges small-band session the next year.) Overhearing Strayhorn's new work, Mercer Ellington implored his housemate to share it with him in his father's absence; Mercer wanted to premiere the material in a band he was organizing with classmates at Juilliard. Strayhorn agreed, and the Mercer Ellington Orchestra gave rehearsal performances of Billy Strayhorn's first New York compositions, including "Day Dream" and "Passion Flower" (to be recorded by a Hodges-led group in 1941). Mercer rejected Strayhorn, however, as a prospect for band pianist: "Strayhorn wasn't good enough to play piano." When Ellington and his orchestra returned to New York on May 10, Strayhorn was fully prepared with original charts suitable for small bands and with a deeper knowledge of Ellington's approach, garnered through his study of Ellington's manuscripts. Strayhorn's next visible role would be an unexpected one. On July 24, he accompanied the band for two weeks at the open-air ballroom on the roof of the Ritz-Carlton Hotel in Boston. Watching from the sidelines several nights into the run, Strayhorn noticed Ellington frequently hopping up from the piano on the side of the stage to lead the orchestra from the front of the bandstand; at the end of the night, the bandleader grumbled that a cold breeze was threatening his health—Ellington was known to be susceptible to hypochondria—and instructed Strayhorn to take over on piano for the rest of the run. "The guys in the band had never heard me play," said Strayhorn, who proceeded to perform all of Ellington's parts as well as several solo pieces each night. "They were sort of like, 'Oooh!' I was very flattered."

The Boston stay also expanded Strayhorn's responsibilities as an arranger. While working at the Ritz-Carlton, Ivie Anderson pitched for a chance to sing the frolicsome swing tune "The Jumpin' Jive," a popular Cab Calloway number; Ellington assented and assigned Strayhorn to arrange the song for the full orchestra. Strayhorn delivered it promptly, despite having to write out the individual instrumental parts for each band member himself; this "copying" task was usually the duty of the orchestra's valve trombonist, Juan Tizol, thirty-nine, the Puerto Rican–born, classically trained composer of such atmospheric specialty numbers as "Caravan" and "Pyramid." Busy enough copying for the prolific Ellington (and perhaps wary of this curious initiate), Tizol refused to copy the scores, according to Strayhorn.

When the time came to try out Strayhorn's debut work for the Ellington Orchestra—the band was rehearsing on the rooftop bandstand during the day—the arranger was missing. "I walked across the Boston Common, and I sat down, and I was trying to take as much time as possible, because I didn't want to be there when they played it," said Strayhorn. "When I got to rehearsal and the music was all passed out and everything, I went down in one of our hotel rooms below the roof, and I *hid*." Strayhorn couldn't escape Jonesy (Richard B. Jones, the "band boy"), who virtually forced him to go hear his own work. "So I went up, and they went through the arrangement, and it turned out all right," Strayhorn allowed. Though the piece was never recorded, Strayhorn's original pencil score shows the young orchestrator introducing a warm, impressionistic touch (through the use of a minor triad with a major seventh), one of his favorite chord effects. "So I was greatly heartened," Strayhorn said. "As a result of that arrangement, he put me in charge of the singers. Now I was to do all the vocal arrangements." In fact, Ellington's newfound faith in Strayhorn's skill at big-band orchestrations for vocalists was so strong that he recommended his new associate for a freelance commission offered to him in Boston. Mary Martin, a young stage actress and singer who had just made both her Broadway debut in *Leave It to Me* and her first film, *The Rage of Paris*, had requested an arrangement, and Ellington urged her to hire Strayhorn, who took the job for five hundred dollars. First word of the fee came as a disappointment, however: on hearing he'd be paid "five" for the job, Strayhorn complained to Ellington, "I was getting five dollars an arrangement in Pittsburgh."

Zipping through his protégé's rites of jazz passage, Ellington soon gave Strayhorn an instrumental assignment for the full orchestra. Strayhorn took up the task of adapting composer Pete DeRose's mood piece "Deep Purple," an instrumental recorded by the Paul Whiteman Orchestra in 1934 but best known as a vocal number after Mitchell Parrish added lyrics and, in the process, streamlined the melody for performance by singers. For his orchestration, Strayhorn adhered to the original melody, which, to Ellington band members familiar with the vocal version, sounded incorrect. "I got into a little *thing* with members of the band," recounted Strayhorn. "I wrote it the way the man originally wrote it. So when the band played it, it sounded like a wrong note. Duke asked me, 'Is that a wrong note?' I said, 'No. That's the original note, the way the man wrote it.' And everyone else said, 'Oh, no—there's somethin' wrong.' Finally, Ellington called everybody to attention, and he said, 'Now, look: This young man—I will not have you embarrass this young man. This young man is a very bright young man, and if he says that's the right note, I will not have you embarrass him.'" As he spoke, the latest record by the Duke Ellington Orchestra was selling briskly nationwide: a vocal rendition by Jean Eldridge of "Something to Live For," Strayhorn's yearning ballad from the Mad Hatters' repertoire. If, through Duke Ellington's musical largesse, Billy Strayhorn was beginning to find something he'd long lived in hopes of, he could have easily overlooked the fact that Ellington's name had been added as co-composer of the song.

4

SO

THIS

IS

LOVE

In Pittsburgh, who he was had inhibited Billy Strayhorn from doing what he could do; in New York, what he could do enabled him to be who he was. Earlier, provincialism had encumbered Strayhorn's arrival as an artist; in the more inclusive, cosmopolitan atmosphere of Manhattan, Strayhorn's musical success spurred his coming-of-age as an individual. Twice, too, change came with a gracious introduction. This time it was an Ellington, Mercer, who introduced Billy Strayhorn to a friend of a friend. Aaron Bridgers was a twenty-one-year-old black pianist from North Carolina who had met Duke Ellington through a mutual acquaintance, a Dr. Hill, after an Ellington Orchestra dance at Pepper's Warehouse in Bridgers's hometown, Winston-Salem (in the dance hall, the white and colored sections were divided by a clothesline). Bridgers had recently moved up North and into a small single room at 555 Edgecombe Avenue, a dignified turn-of-the-century building as prestigious as 409, and had dropped by the Ellingtons' apartment, meeting Mercer briefly.

Soon after that, in the fall of 1939, the younger Ellington glanced out a window of his apartment and spotted Bridgers lounging on a park bench by the Edgecombe cliff walk, and he decided to bring Strayhorn downstairs to meet him. "I knew I had to introduce these guys," said Mercer Ellington. "Ruth and I knew Billy was sort of lonely—he didn't have anybody in New York except us. I didn't really know that much about Aaron. I just thought they'd like each other."

Strayhorn and Bridgers had more in common than either would disclose on the street with Mercer Ellington. Their principal differences were physical: tall and a bit thickly built, Bridgers was a strong presence; he had narrow, wide-set eyes that cooled off the effect of a readily generous smile—the top of his face seemed more serious than the bottom. He dressed well but quietly, and he had a silky brush-line mustache. Temperamentally, Strayhorn and Bridgers were compatible spirits. "We had everything in common, particularly music. We became very close right away," explained Bridgers, who was working as an elevator operator at the Kenmore Hall Hotel on Lexington Avenue in midtown while studying informally from time to time with jazz virtuoso Art Tatum, practicing evenings on his landlady's player piano. "We had the same favorite musicians, especially Tatum and Teddy Wilson. And we both loved the French classical composers. I had always had a love for all things French, and I discovered that Billy did too." (Strayhorn would take to pronouncing Bridgers's name "Ah-ron," with coy Gallic flair.) The men started going out nearly every night, trying ethnic restaurants (especially no-name pasta houses) all over town, gabbing away on the subway in French. "We used to love to do that, just to annoy people," admitted Bridgers, proud of his two years of French at Atkins High School. "The sight of two black men together then, speaking French, would confound people to no end." In the morning, they'd walk a few blocks to Ginny Lou's restaurant for skillet-scrambled omelettes. "We couldn't have been closer," said Bridgers. Within weeks, the two had become inseparable, and before the end of Strayhorn's first year in New York, they moved in together.

Bridgers found the apartment through his friend Haywood Williams, a playful boxer dog of a man whose whole body bounced when he was amused, which was frequently. Two years younger than Strayhorn, Williams had just moved to Manhattan from rural Lackawanna, New York, around the time Bridgers met him at a party; Bridgers got Williams a job as a bellman at the Kenmore Hall. In turn, Williams helped arrange for the owner of his building on 126th Street to rent Strayhorn and Bridgers the bottom floor of 315 Convent Avenue, a handsome three-story brownstone on a cozy block of small Tudor-style row houses in Sugar Hill. Jimmy Rushing, the bearish blues singer then with the Count Basie Orchestra, lived upstairs with his wife, Connie. "They were always fighting and made all kinds of noise, screaming and hollering and throwing things all day," said Bridgers. "And when they made up at night, they were even noisier." The new roommates had both privacy and comfort in what was essentially the basement: a private entrance underneath the main stoop gave way to a long hall leading to the bedroom; on the right were an eat-in kitchen and an ample living room. Strayhorn and Bridgers had part of the space rebuilt as a young cosmopolitans' dream pad. With the help of a group of Bridgers's hotel coworkers as well as some professional carpenters—"Aaron was pretty handy," said Williams, "but not Billy. Oh, no"—they had a long bar constructed in the living room; along it, they placed a row of tube-steel stools with red leather cushions. To complete the cocktail-hour ambience, they arranged a couple of round bar tables and chairs in the center of the room and brought in an upright piano (an old eighty-dollar player model whose mechanics had been removed) and a long couch that could be converted into a bed. Strayhorn hung some prints, including a blue-themed Monet floral, and he splurged for a music lover's extravagance that became the apartment's focal point: an amateur record-cutting machine to make recordings of their singing and playing. Behind the apartment, glass doors opened onto a patch of garden where Strayhorn planted some flower seeds. "Nobody had an apartment like Billy and Aaron's place," said Williams. "It was straight out of the pages of *Esquire* magazine." In place of Waspy Ivy Leaguers and their Vargas girls, however, there were two giddy young black men.

"Living with Billy was wonderful. It was a wonderful time of life for us," said Bridgers. "We were just coming into our own. We discovered everything together." On a typical day, Strayhorn might neaten up, perhaps rest for a while, and shop or spend some time with Ruth Ellington; he rarely worked traditional hours. Though Strayhorn and Bridgers hired a housekeeper, a middle-aged West Indian woman, Strayhorn left her little to do. "She was very motherly to us," said Bridgers, "but Billy had the place so spotless that all that was left was the laundry. He had quite a few very delicate silk shirts, and he had her wash them. It was quite an honor, because the only other person he ever allowed to touch his favorite clothing was his mother." (Strayhorn still shipped her his most precious garments for her to hand-launder, press, and mail back to him.) A few nights a week, Strayhorn would cook. "He had certain dishes that he'd prepare that were his specialties. He never made ordinary things," said Bridgers. "They were combinations of things that he created himself, like music, things with beans and greens and goodness knows what. Some of them didn't have names, also like his songs." When Bridgers came home, there were always empty glasses in the refrigerator ready for chilled cocktails (as *Esquire* recommended). If Bridgers played piano or listened to a record—Bartók and Hindemith were his favorites—Strayhorn might work. "Nothing I did ever seemed to bother him, even when he was writing music," said Bridgers. Conditioned to block out household distractions at Tioga Street Rear, Strayhorn could disappear in an internal world. "I could be playing one thing on the piano, and he could sit down with a piece of music paper and write the most intimate, complicated composition for a full orchestra," said Bridgers. "He could hear it all in his head, no matter what was going on around him." Most evenings, Strayhorn would come up with a plan to go out and would phone Bridgers, who in the mid-1940s took a new job as a guard at the United Nations. "He'd call, and all he'd say was, 'Such-and-such place. One o'clock.' And I'd meet him there." Their Monday-night haunt was the Hollywood, a bar for show-business insiders near Small's Paradise on Seventh Avenue in Harlem where pianists congregated each week and took turns at the keyboard; Strayhorn would occasionally knock out a Teddy Wilson number, but Bridgers, who had yet to perform professionally, sat out the sessions. Most other nights, Strayhorn and Bridgers would gravitate to either of the entrepreneur Barney Josephson's chichi cabarets, Cafe Society Uptown on the Upper East Side or Cafe Society Downtown in the Village. Both nightclubs, glitzy spots showcasing gifted young black singers like Hazel Scott and Sarah Vaughan, got to be known as exotic simply by welcoming a mixed-race clientele. "There weren't that many places below Harlem for blacks to go, and we weren't made to feel out of place at Cafe Society," said Bridgers. "Billy and I were never made to feel anything but completely at home there. Nobody looked at the two of us like we were strange because of who we were."

At home one night, Strayhorn and Bridgers invented a psychological experiment. They went to sleep with the radio on and, upon wakening, each sat down with paper and pencil to list all the songs he felt he might have heard unconsciously. They did this for three consecutive nights. "It was very eerie," said Bridgers. "We both put down some of the same titles—like, we'd both have 'Stormy Weather' and 'Blue Moon.' We discussed it, and then we decided it didn't prove anything, and we weren't sleeping very soundly. So we gave up the experiment. But it showed how interested Billy was in the mind and what happens deep below the surface. He was extremely fascinated with the world of the mind and what goes on without words." Indeed, Strayhorn clearly preferred nonverbal communication to talking, even with Bridgers. The men rarely discussed their deeper feelings, including those for each other. "Billy and I both felt that you don't have to talk about such things. You communicate them better in other ways," said Bridgers. "We never pried into each other's minds or demanded to know what the other was thinking or feeling, particularly when it comes to your feelings for people. How we felt, whatever we thought about our feelings—him, me, our friends, how he felt about Duke—these things he felt, I know and I always did, too, you should know already. You shouldn't have to ask."

Their silence was not secrecy. On the contrary, many of the people who knew Strayhorn at the time were struck by the guileless assurance with which he and Bridgers conducted their relationship. "We accepted Aaron as a new member of the family, because he was with Billy," said Ruth Ellington Boatwright. "They came around all the time and made no bones about it. They were together, and that's how it was. They didn't go through the motions of any kind of pretense." Strayhorn seemed avid to cross then-forbidding social boundaries with Bridgers: when a new member of the Ellington Orchestra, clarinetist Jimmy Hamilton, invited him home for dinner with his wife, Vivian, Strayhorn brought Bridgers; then Strayhorn returned the gesture and had the Hamiltons over for a home-cooked meal at Bridgers' and his apartment. "It was me and my wife, so Billy thought it should be him and Aaron—as natural as that. We all hung out and ate beans and drank together like it was nothing, even though it was actually something, really," Hamilton recalled. "There wasn't a lot of guys who was homosexual and acted like that, like there it was and you have to accept it—and if you don't, that's your problem."

Around Convent Avenue, Strayhorn and Bridgers were so intimately associated with each other that a neighbor, the dancer Royce Wallace, couldn't distinguish them in her mind; seeing Bridgers on the street alone once, she called out Strayhorn's name. "To me," said Wallace, "they were like one person." Strayhorn was even outward about Bridgers in the company of old hometown friends. According to George Greenlee, who visited Convent Avenue shortly after Strayhorn and Bridgers moved in, "Billy was really happy to be with Aaron and so proud that you had to be happy for him. He didn't worry that I might think differently about him all of a sudden, because he never really made any secret about who he was in Pittsburgh, even if he didn't have anybody yet." Only with his parents did Strayhorn remain cryptic about Bridgers, although his sister Georgia developed suspicions when she made her first trip to New York. Lovely and confident, Georgia was accustomed to pursuing what she wanted. "As soon as Billy was out of the house and she and I were alone, she tried to seduce me," recalled Bridgers. "She was trying to see if I was gay. I didn't respond to her, naturally. So she came out and asked me, 'What's going on with you and my brother? What's the story? Are you two lovers or what?' I tried to explain to her, first of all, that not responding to her advances does not necessarily mean that a person is gay. When it came to Billy and me, I said it was something she should properly talk about with her own brother. I don't know if she ever did that, but she didn't come back to our house for a long, long time."

As he came into his own in New York, Strayhorn began to move in a circle of like-hearted spirits, most (though not all) black and gay. Beyond Bridgers, the core members of this group included Haywood Williams; Bill Patterson, a psychology student at NYU; and Bill Coleman, a probation officer for the Queens County Supreme Court who had been best man at Patterson's wedding. Honorary initiates included the arranger and composer Ralph Burns, then working for Charlie Barnet, and the theatrical-set designer Oliver Smith. With various combinations of these friends, Strayhorn set out to bring to life the lyrics he inscribed in block letters in the Mad Hatters' band book, images of penthouses and champagne, "some cocktails, some orchids, a show or two."

"I'd pick up the phone and Billy would say, '*Allez-y!*' That would be the signal, and we'd be off," recalled Williams. Strayhorn might hire a limousine and spirit a few friends off for a spin through Central Park, a tray of martinis balanced on their laps as they rode. All points seemed in time to lead to Cafe Society. "Going there was like going home for us," said Williams, who first met Strayhorn on an outing to the downtown club. "Aaron said, 'Let's go to Cafe Society—there's somebody I want you to meet,'" recalled Williams. "So we took the subway downtown, and we met Strayhorn, who was waiting for us in a subway station in midtown. I looked over, and there was this little guy standing on the subway platform in a porkpie hat. He looked so silly—still a square-head from Pittsburgh trying to be cool. But he was already getting known in the in-the-know crowd. People were starting to talk about the fact that Ellington brought this guy in, and everybody wanted to know who this guy Billy was." Before long, the bartenders knew: at Cafe Society, any customer could get a chilled martini glass of gin with a light spray of vermouth by ordering Billy's Martini. Switching to rum one night, at Mary Lou Williams's suggestion, Strayhorn adjusted poorly. "He used to come down to the café practically every night," Williams said. "I said, 'Oh, we have some wonderful rum.' He didn't know that this rum would knock you out if you drank a glassful of it. So he was standing at the bar while I'm playing, you know, and everything's cool. And I looked around to the side, and I saw him reel a little bit, and he had the glass in his hand. All of a sudden I heard this 'Whoosh!' They were carrying him out, and he had the glass in his hand."

The night would go on, typically, well after Cafe Society closed, when Strayhorn would lead whoever still had the life to a piano joint uptown called Luckey's Rendezvous, named for its proprietor, Charles Luckeyth "Luckey" Roberts. He was a pianist's pianist of the vigorous "stride" school and composer of "Moonlight Cocktail," a sweet ballad that was a 1942 hit for Glenn Miller, and his club was located partway below street level at St. Nicholas Avenue and 149th Street; there were red walls, opera-singing waiters and wait- resses (hired from Columbia University's music program), shoulder- to-shoulder drinkers, fried-shrimp sandwiches, and a piano that Strayhorn would likely end up playing by dawn. Sam Shaw, a film- maker and photographer with ties to the music business through his brother Eddie, a song publisher, caught Strayhorn at Luckey Rob- erts's often. "Billy would be there every time I was at the place, and I went an awful lot," recalled Shaw. "That was a place you could really let go, and he would. He was never there alone. It was one place uptown where nobody looked twice or cared about a couple of gay guys coming in. Billy and his friends could have themselves a good time out in public. And he had started to get quite a following there for his piano playing."

The gay social world in 1940s Manhattan centered around friends-of-friends-only parties in private homes; held at regular hours several nights a week, these events were de facto gay bars where drinks and, often, light meals were sold. By all accounts, Strayhorn was not well known in these quarters; he preferred more intimate gatherings with Bridgers and their friends in his own home. Strayhorn would cook for a full day or two, preparing mounds and pots of home-style dishes like fried chicken and beans with rice. Bridgers acted as bartender, and the doors opened for thirty or so friends and their friends. "Billy loved to play host and make sure everybody was eating. That's the kind of party he liked to have," according to Ralph Burns. "It would be great, because a lot of us had so much in common. A lot of us were in the music business, and we were gay, of course—not that we would stand there and talk about being gay. That wasn't it. It was just really good to be in each other's company. Billy would put these parties together, and they were just a great, easy, natural good time." When there was another pianist in the house, and there usually was, Strayhorn would invariably sit the musician down for a four-handed duet; he reveled in collaboration and was small enough to play standing up while his partner sat alongside him on the piano stool. "That was one of his favorite things," said Williams. "He'd do wonderful, incredible things with another musician. People would get up after playing with Billy and say they never sounded better in their lives." On occasion, Strayhorn and his partner, or perhaps a whole group, would write a song on the spot. "It would happen like a game," said Bridgers. "Somebody would start with a line of words, and Billy would make up a melody for it. Somebody else would throw out something else, and Billy would put it all together right there. The next day, none of us would remember any of it—unfortunately, because Billy had the ability to make something pretty good out of nothing."

When he socialized beyond Convent Avenue or Cafe Society, Strayhorn gravitated toward other musicians. Among members of the Ellington Orchestra, he would pal around with most of the regular barhoppers, including Ben Webster, the celebrated tenor saxophonist, who joined the band in January 1940. According to Helen Oakley Dance, Webster, "a big guy, instinctively fathered him. Besides, they both liked a good drink." However, Strayhorn drifted naturally to the vocalist Herb Jeffries, a fellow Francophile closer to Strayhorn's age (Webster was six years older). Jeffries, a fair-skinned mixed-race baritone with chiseled good looks—he starred in several all-black movie westerns as the Bronze Buckaroo—shared Strayhorn's faith in the ennobling power of gentility. "We both spoke French, so we loved to go to the very chicest French restaurants around New York," Jeffries remembered. "There was a tremendous amount of discrimination, and you could show a certain amount of sophistication by the mere fact that you could speak a language that the next white person couldn't. Strayhorn and I both felt this showed you weren't that lowly person, that Amos 'n' Andy character that everybody thought you were. If you knew a thing or two about good food and wine, it made people wake up and think, Hey, he's not that watermelon figure I expected. So it gave you a bit of a mental kick too."

When he was on his own for an evening, Strayhorn went off in search of music. In the early 1940s, he became known and swiftly accepted at Minton's Playhouse on 118th Street in Harlem, according to both Dizzy Gillespie and Max Roach, two of the creators of the then-gestating music some were calling bebop. Though he generally just listened—Gillespie remembered him paying special attention to the great pianist Thelonious Monk, another of the music's pioneers—Strayhorn sometimes sat in on the probative Minton's jams that gave birth to bop. "Strayhorn was on the scene, and he played with the best of them," said Gillespie. "He never made a big deal out of it or looked for any attention. One night, he and Bud [Powell] decided to cut [compete, taking turns at the piano], and, man, I'm telling you, he turned that piano inside out." A teenage Max Roach witnessed something similar another night at Minton's. "Pianists loved to play for each other, you know, and for the crowd," said Roach. "One night, Strayhorn sat down after somebody, I don't remember who, and nobody would go to the piano after him. He was that good."

In a corner of his new life, Strayhorn retained a place for his family. He rarely disclosed much about his background to his friends. "He wouldn't say anything about his childhood or the members of the family unless you asked him straight out, and then you would only get a few words," said Haywood Williams. To Bridgers alone, Strayhorn was a bit more revealing. "He said he didn't care much about keeping in touch with a couple of his brothers, because they weren't the nicest people to him," recalled Bridgers. "Of course, he loved his mother very much, and he talked about her—for instance, what she would probably say if she were in a certain situation he might be in. She was like a guiding force in his life, even while he was in New York." Strayhorn and his mother stayed in touch by phone; he wasn't a letter writer, evidently out of embarrassment over his herky-jerky penmanship. "Half the family told him, 'We can't read your handwriting,'" said Lillian Strayhorn Dicks. "So he said, 'To hell with you. I won't write.'"

Every three or four months during his first years in Manhattan, Strayhorn would take the train and visit Pittsburgh for a few days.

More than once, his father wouldn't be there; he would leave for periods, at first for weeks, sometimes months, at a stretch, then for several years at a time. "I don't know how she did it," Lillian Strayhorn Dicks said, "but Mama always took him back. That was what a wife was supposed to do." With James contributing sporadically, Lillian could no longer keep up her house without financial help from her sons, who pitched in according to their means. As the best-off among them, Billy Strayhorn not only sent cash regularly but helped his mother move out of the "zenith way" and onto Tioga Street proper. While young Lillian was sent to stay with her aunt Julia in New Jersey, her mother moved into a comfortable two-story rented house across the street from the Bucket of Blood; Strayhorn and his brothers took care of the monthly rent. "Mama had always dreamed of something better," said Lillian Strayhorn Dicks. "She finally got it, thanks to her boys—and mostly Bill."

He would bring his mother a fancy gift—a pair of imported gloves, for instance—whenever he came to Pittsburgh and take her shopping downtown for stockings and some other finery she couldn't or wouldn't get herself. Lillian Strayhorn Dicks remembered every visit as a family holiday. "He seemed like an exotic visitor," she said, "because he always had beautiful clothes and different things. Naturally, everybody would come around to see him, and he'd be so charming, so New York—tell all the women they were beautiful. We'd catch him up on what the latest family scandal was, if any, and he'd laugh and give his opinion on what was going on. He'd look at all the new babies—there were always more children since he was there last—and tell you how to raise them. Mama was in her glory. She was so proud of him, and that was the most important thing to him. I think she's the only reason he came home. At one point, he almost said as much. Somebody was saying something about something that somebody in the family was upset about, and he said, 'F them! I'm not concerned about anybody but Mama.' " The men in the family, never involved in that distaff talk, would chip in a few questions about New York's spicier side, much to Strayhorn's discontent: his brother Johnny made one remark about the "joints in New York," and Strayhorn snapped, "There are no joints in New York." As Lillian Strayhorn Dicks recalled, "Nobody could say anything negative about New York. For Bill, everything in New York was very posh. They just didn't have joints in New York. Joints were reserved for Pittsburgh, and that was a place Bill was very far away from"—even when he was in his parents' living room.

Strayhorn didn't so much transform in New York as take form; in New York, his amorphous youthful ideal of urban élan could finally be made real. "He had always had a certain vision of himself," said Lillian Strayhorn Dicks. "But it never had a chance to come out until he went to New York and met the right people and went to the right places. Then he really came alive." As his intimates saw him, Strayhorn emerged during his first years in Manhattan as nearly a caricature of sophistication, at least in appearance. Strayhorn dressed like a dandy: he liked striped or dark-colored shirts, sometimes paisley prints, and colorful ties; his favorite tie designer, Countess Mara, specialized in whimsical, cartoonish figures on bright backgrounds. Alto saxophonist Marshall Royal left Birdland on Broadway, around the corner from West 52nd Street, at around four one morning and found Strayhorn window-shopping at Layton's men's store. "He was admiring a suit jacket," recalled Royal. "There was another one he liked a couple of blocks away, at Phil Kornfeld's. He took me down to look at that one, and it was real nice." Strayhorn was fond of the feel of silk and cashmere on his body, and he collected socks; he had two sock drawers. Bred to regard good manners as elevating, he purchased an etiquette guide that he read as intently as one might a novel. When he bought a new suit, he kept the front pockets sewn up, because his mother had taught him to keep his hands out of his pockets.

Strayhorn had two favorite phrases: "Ever up and onward" was one. As Aaron Bridgers recalled, "It was his constant message of encouragement and good cheer. It meant, Don't look back—yesterday was yesterday and today is today. Look ahead." The other was, simply, "That's great!" and its variants: "He's great!" or "She's great!" Bill Patterson explained, "That was the thing he said more than anything. It was part of his philosophy, his approach to being alive, which was very generous, very open, almost too much so. He could see what was unique and worthy in almost any individual he came upon. Like, a waitress would wait on us, and she'd walk away, and Strayhorn would say, 'She's great!' Why? We didn't see it, but Strayhorn would see something there. The big and the small—these weren't real distinctions for him. Strayhorn would always see something he felt was truly great." Strayhorn treated those around him—and those around them—well. "He was a gift giver," said Williams. "When he came to your house, it was never empty-handed. He'd bring a little something that he saw in a shop that he thought you might like, a decorative box or something like that. If you were in a bar and Billy came into the bar, he'd buy you a drink and whoever was with you a drink, no matter how many people were in your party." Strayhorn's generosity wasn't limited to others, however. As Bridgers affirmed, "If I said to him, 'Billy, don't buy that shirt or that pair of pants. It's too expensive,' he said, 'Mind your own business.' He said, 'Life is too short.' He'd slap me down with words if there was something he wanted." Strayhorn was a reader, and he said his favorite Shakespeare was sonnet 97 ("How like a winter hath my absence been / From thee, the pleasure of the fleeting year!"). His friend Bill Coleman dropped by Convent Avenue one afternoon and found Strayhorn reclining on the sofa, poring over the orchestral score to Stravinsky's *Rite of Spring;* it was pleasure reading, not work, Strayhorn said.

Strayhorn and Bridgers had a copy of the *Kama Sutra* that Strayhorn would study at length. He liked erotica: he had a set of translucent Japanese discs that, held up to a light, revealed arty etchings of men and women having sex, and he collected beefcake postcards. Among Strayhorn's friends, graphic (though not flirtatious) conversations about sex were common. "There was an awful lot of talk about sex—positions and how to do this or that. Straight, nonstraight, whatever," remembered Patterson. "Oils, powder, esoterica. Strayhorn loved, really loved, to talk about that stuff. But it was mostly in fun. He laughed so hard he couldn't stop." Strayhorn laughed easily and heartily, though the sound came as a breathy giggle, as if the biggest part of the laugh had stayed inside.

"Billy was much stronger than he looked," said Aaron Bridgers. "Once when we were out together, I turned to him, and I said, 'Billy, I'm getting drunk.' And he said, 'Well, that's fine. You enjoy yourself.' So I did, and I eventually got so drunk I couldn't get up to go home. Now, Billy was about half my size, but he picked me up, actually picked me up, and carried me outside, put me in a cab, and picked me up again and carried me in the house." His emotional strength was both more obvious and far more impressive, according to those close to him. "The one thing that stood out about Billy then," said Ruth Ellington Boatwright, "is that no matter what anyone said or did, he was never sensitive about his own feelings or anyone trying to hurt him, and he was always understanding and sympathetic and seeing every point of view, without any reference to himself whatsoever. If I saw somebody had said something about him that I thought wasn't right, he'd say, 'Oh, darling, don't worry about it,' and he'd go on." Bill Patterson saw Strayhorn's psychic wherewithal in vaguely spiritual terms. "Billy wasn't delicate or soft at all. He had an extraordinary presence. You got the distinct feeling that he was functioning from a place that's different from where the rest of us come from, and from that place within himself, he seemed to be able to see people in a different way than a lot of people get seen or most of us see people. He listened, he actually listened to you. He was always present." In teasing honor of his deeper side, Bridgers gave Strayhorn a nickname that stuck within their circle: Buddha.

Virtually everything about Billy Strayhorn made him a good match with Duke Ellington. Stately to the verge of ostentation, Ellington used vast resources of ingenuity and will to project an image that promoted pride in and respect for black identity. Yet the priorities of a traveling bandleader—and one who was a tireless composer, arranger, record producer, and entrepreneur as well—prevented Ellington from delving into the high culture he strove to embody. Strayhorn, by contrast, had both the time and the inclination to study the music scores of the masters, to visit museums, and the like. "Duke was a magnificent role model. He was brilliant at it," said Herb Jeffries. "But some of it was hocus-pocus—grand gestures and particular five-dollar phrases that he'd pronounce with dramatic emphasis. Meanwhile, he never really read anything except the Bible, which is great, mind you, if you're only going to read one book, and he knew far less about the fine arts, including other composers, than he liked to let on. In Billy, Duke saw that image he considered so important, in flesh and blood."

Famously egalitarian, Ellington accepted Strayhorn's homosexuality much as he had long embraced gifted musicians regardless of their backgrounds or idiosyncrasies. "Pop never cared one bit that Strayhorn was gay," said Mercer Ellington. "He was never prejudiced against anybody he thought was really worthy. More to the point, he had been exposed to homosexuality his whole life in the music business. It was nothing new to him. He knew plenty of gay men and women, so there was no question about, 'Hey, is this person a freak or something?' Pop knew the story. He backed up Strayhorn all the way." This support was priceless to Strayhorn, according to his intimates—particularly after his frustrations with prejudice during his early career in Pittsburgh. "With Duke, Billy said, he had security," remarked George Greenlee. "Duke didn't question his manliness. It wasn't like that for him back home." Another gay black musician who was a close friend of Strayhorn's evoked the virtue of Ellington's patronage empathetically. "For those of us who were both black and homosexual in that time, acceptance was of paramount importance, absolutely paramount importance," the musician said. "Duke Ellington afforded Billy Strayhorn that acceptance. That was something that cannot be undervalued or underappreciated. To Billy, that was gold."

In a sense, Strayhorn made himself a triple minority: he was black, he was gay, and he was a minority among gay people in that he was open about his homosexuality in an era when social bias forced many men and women to keep their sexual identities secret. "The most amazing thing of all about Billy Strayhorn to me was that he had the strength to make an extraordinary decision—that is, the decision not to hide the fact that he was homosexual. And he did this in the 1940s, when nobody but nobody did that," declared his gay black musician friend. "We all hid, every one of us, except Billy. He wasn't afraid. We were. And you know what the difference between us was? Duke Ellington." Ellington provided Strayhorn with a high-profile outlet for his artistry, as well as with emotional support. Free to compose for the Ellington Orchestra, albeit behind the scenes, Strayhorn was also freed from the hardships he would have faced had he sought a career as a pianist or bandleader. "Billy could have pursued a career on his own—he had the talent to become rich and famous—but he'd have had to be less than honest about his sexual orientation. Or he could work behind the scenes for Duke and be open about being gay," said his friend. "It really was truth or consequences, and Billy went with truth. It was just incredible." Forsaking public prominence, Strayhorn found personal freedom in service to the Duke Ellington Orchestra. Now there might not be a Billy Strayhorn Orchestra. But there was a Billy Strayhorn.

5

BEYOND

CATEGORY

This is the way you played this number; now, this is the way I would play it. During the first few years of their association, Duke Ellington increasingly called on Strayhorn to do what he would with what Ellington had done—or what Ellington had put aside, had done partway, or wanted to do at some point. Much of this labor fell within a staff arranger's responsibilities. As Fletcher Henderson did for Benny Goodman and Sy Oliver did for Tommy Dorsey, Strayhorn created orchestrations of pop hits and other material, including compositions by the bandleader, for the orchestra to play in its vein. Unlike Henderson or Oliver, however, Strayhorn was working with a world-class composer who had, over two decades, developed a brilliantly distinctive imprimatur. Strayhorn called it "the Ellington effect": Duke's way of designing compositions for specific musicians and their personal voices. "Ellington's concern is with the individual musician, and what happens when they put their musical characters together," explained Strayhorn in an article for *Down Beat*. As for the relationship between composer and arranger, Strayhorn added that Ellington's only piece of advice was unfettering. "His first, last and only formal instruction for me was embodied in one word: observe." The two of them would rarely discuss projects in detail. "I'd see Billy walk into Duke's dressing room, and Duke would say, 'Oh, Billy, I want you to finish this thing for me,' " recalled Ruth Ellington Boatwright. "Just like that: 'I want you to finish this thing for me.' And Billy would sit and stare into his eyes for about ten minutes, and Duke would stare back, and then Billy would say, 'Okay.' They wouldn't even exchange a word. They'd just look into each other's eyes, and Billy would go out and write what Duke wanted."

Strayhorn also added his own touches to Ellington's compositions, such as "Sepia Panorama," which briefly served as the band's theme song; though most of this episodic mood piece is Ellington's, sixteen bars of it came from a Strayhorn arrangement of Erskine Hawkins's theme song, "Tuxedo Junction," that the Ellington band didn't record. Strayhorn revamped an aborted Ellington effort, "Take It Away," and it became the exploratory bass vehicle "Jack the Bear." "Duke originally wrote the thing as an experiment," explained Strayhorn. "It didn't work out, and the piece was dropped. Then [bassist] Jimmy Blanton came into the band, and Duke wanted to feature him as a solo man. We needed some material quickly, so I reworked 'Take It Away' as a showpiece for Blanton's bass." Ellington resisted completion (and not only in music: he never divorced his first and only wife, Edna Ellington, after making a new home with Mildred Dixon; as a bandleader, he never fired a musician but would simply hire a replacement, leaving the problem musician to get the message and quit on his own). "As long as something is unfinished," Ellington said, "there's always that little feeling of insecurity, and a feeling of insecurity is absolutely necessary unless you're so rich it doesn't matter." With Strayhorn on hand, Ellington could keep that insecurity and gain the security of knowing that something he dropped could now not only be finished but possibly improved. As for Strayhorn's reputation as a composer in his own right, two of his songs had been recorded and released as 78s by the end of 1940: another of his Mad Hatters numbers, "Your Love Has Faded," as well as his lushly evocative "Day Dream."

Along with "Something to Live For," the records marked the emergence of Strayhorn's individual voice, an emotive one distinct from Ellington's; even so, as with "Something to Live For," the labels on both "Your Love Has Faded" and "Day Dream" listed Duke Ellington as co-composer.

Publishing credits and such were business, however, and didn't much concern a Stravinsky-reading aesthete like Billy Strayhorn—at least until 1941. In December 1940, he was in Chicago, where he had supervised and played piano on Johnny Hodges's small-group recording of "Day Dream," as well as three other Hodges-group numbers (Ellington's "Junior Hop" and Hodges's own "Good Queen Bess" and "That's the Blues, Old Man") and a few tunes by ensembles featuring Ellington trumpeter Rex Stewart and clarinetist Barney Bigard. Ellington and the orchestra had just moved on from Chicago to Culver City, California, to play the Casa Mañana, a new backlot-Mexicana nightspot built on the site of Sebastian's Cotton Club, once the top West Coast showplace for black entertainment, when a message came from Ellington. Strayhorn and Mercer Ellington, who had traveled with the band to Chicago, were to head west immediately. A prolonged legal scuffle between the American Society of Composers, Authors and Publishers (ASCAP) and the radio industry had just come to an unexpected head: radio stations were refusing to submit to an ASCAP-proposed increase in the fees that stations were obliged to pay for the right to broadcast music by ASCAP-member composers. Launching their own organization to compete with ASCAP, called Broadcast Music Inc. (BMI), the stations announced that as of the first of the year they would refuse to air any music by ASCAP members. This was tantamount to a ban on most popular music, including virtually all the best-known compositions by Duke Ellington, who had belonged to ASCAP since 1935. In order to perform on radio, Ellington needed practically a whole new repertoire, but he couldn't write it—or cowrite it; the music had to come solely from composers unaligned with ASCAP, such as Billy Strayhorn, who had never been urged to join, and Mercer Ellington, who hadn't composed much music.

"Strayhorn and I got this big break at the same time," remembered Mercer Ellington. "Overnight, literally, we got a chance to write a whole new book for the band. It could have taken us twenty years to get the old man to make room for that much of our music, but all of a sudden there was this freak opportunity. He needed us to write music, and it had to be in our names." Rooming at the Sutherland, a small but pleasant South Side hotel for blacks, Strayhorn and Mercer Ellington had a couple of days in Chicago before the next available train to Los Angeles. "We were sharing the same room and we had all this work to do," said Ellington. "It was one room and two people. When I was up during the day, Strayhorn would use the bed, and while he was up at night, I would sleep in it. The maid never got a chance to change the sheets—she gave us some hell. But we were writing so much music so fast we didn't care." For fuel, they brought in a gallon jug of blackberry wine; as Mercer Ellington recalled, Strayhorn needed "some loosening up" to increase productivity. "At one point, he was having some sort of trouble," said Ellington, "and I pulled a piece of his out of the garbage. I said, 'What's wrong with this?' And he said, 'That's an old thing I was trying to do something with, but it's too much like Fletcher Henderson.' I looked it over—it was ' "A" Train'—and I said, 'You're right.' It was written in sections, like Fletcher Henderson. But I flattened it out anyway and put it in the pile with the rest of the stuff." Happily frantic, the two composers boarded the train waving to their friends, a bottle of whiskey in each hand; once en route, they traded two bottles for a carton of cigarettes, which they considered a superior composing aid. "We were having a time," admitted Ellington. As Strayhorn remembered, "There was a big mad scramble to build up a new library. So I sat down and started writing. I don't know how on earth I got through it. Mercer did 'Jumpin' Punkins' and all those things of his. And out of that, of mine, came ' "A" Train' and, oh, a whole lot of other things—big stacks of things." "Loosened up" by Mercer Ellington, a bit of booze, and at least half a carton of cigarettes—and perhaps most significantly, freed for the first time since his arrival in New York to write entirely as himself—Strayhorn produced a big stack of things indeed, including "After All," "Clementine," "Chelsea Bridge," "Johnny Come Lately," "Rain Check," "A Flower Is a Lovesome Thing," and "Passion Flower" (the last two recorded by Ellingtonians in small bands), every one a creative triumph.*

Ellington picked the hard-swinging new arrangement of "Take the 'A' Train" for his orchestra's latest radio theme, replacing the ASCAP-controlled "Sepia Panorama" (itself a recent replacement for the band's longtime theme song, Ellington's atmospheric "East St. Louis Toodle-O"). Ellington was evidently undeterred (and perhaps encouraged) by the song's debt to Fletcher Henderson, the Georgia-born bandleader and arranger who played an incalculable behind-the-scenes role in Benny Goodman's rise as the King of Swing. Indeed, " 'A' Train" became not only Ellington's signature song but his greatest success. Recorded for the high-profile Victor label in Hollywood in February 1941 and issued as a 78 shortly thereafter, the song was an immediate best-seller (the record stayed on the charts for seven weeks that summer) and jukebox sensation; a few months out of the Sutherland Hotel trash, "Take the 'A' Train" became a leitmotif of the swing era. Infectiously upbeat, the number derives its propulsion from the arrangement's kicky rhythmic figures, and its peppy main theme is at once unusual and hummable.

Most of Strayhorn's other new contributions to the Ellington Orchestra band book were more characteristic of the young composer's musical personality and serious orientation. The most ambitious among them was "Chelsea Bridge," an impressionistic miniature composed, Strayhorn said, with a painting by James McNeill Whistler in mind. (Whistler rendered several scenes of rivers and bridges in London, although none of the Chelsea Bridge.) Unlike conventional tune-based pop and jazz numbers of the day, "Chelsea Bridge" is "classical" in its integration of melody and harmony as an organic whole. A bridge is not an apt metaphor for the composition, which more vividly evokes the water below; it flows naturally, inevitably, and with hidden depth. There is more

---

* Strayhorn's compositions during this period also included a significant number of pieces not known to have been performed at the time, some shelved for use by Ellington many years later and others unrecorded until the 1990s, when they were unearthed by the musicologist Walter van de Leur. These works include the original "Tonk," scored for full orchestra and later known as a piano duet; "Lament for an Orchid," which Ellington recorded as "Absinthe" in the 1960s; and the twelve-minute rhapsody "Pentonsilic."

Debussy than Ellington in "Chelsea Bridge," although Ellington had long experimented with imaginatively colored tone poems. Comparably sophisticated though much different in style, "Johnny Come Lately" brought the hipster experimentalism of Strayhorn's after-hours sessions with Dizzy Gillespie and Max Roach to the Ellington organization: the piece is proto-bop, rhythmically vigorous and angular, harmonically modernist. "Rain Check," a somewhat more traditional up-tempo number, springs with all the ebullience of "Take the 'A' Train," but its snappy melody and jitterbug beat disguise progressive structure and some sly, almost inaudible dissonance. Strayhorn also applied his advanced musical sensibility to new orchestrations of other composers' works, most notably "Flamingo," which Ellington described as "the renaissance of vocal orchestration." When Strayhorn arranged it, "it began to blossom," said Ellington. "Before then, an orchestration for a singer was usually something pretty tepid, and it was just background—that's about all. But now, this had real ornamentation, fittingly done, supporting the singer and also embellishing the entire performance of both the singer and the band." Originally a virtually unknown instrumental by pop composer Ted Grouya, the tune was discovered by Ellington's friend Edmund Anderson, a businessman, who added lyrics. Strayhorn's arrangement suggests early-twentieth-century orchestral composition in its heady chromaticism and liquid movement. Yet it's not pretentious; Strayhorn harnessed his conservatory skills in the service of feeling. "It was a good song," recalled Anderson, "but Strayhorn's arrangement gave it a deeper quality."

As this wave of tunes hit the record stores, musicians—composers and arrangers, in particular—started buzzing about Billy Strayhorn. "I grew up in New Mexico, and Duke was my idol," recalled pianist and composer John Lewis. "One of the outstanding things for me was the first Strayhorn thing I heard. It was the arrangement of 'Flamingo.' It had nothing to do with what had gone on in jazz at all before. It sounded as if Stravinsky were a jazz musician." The baritone saxophonist and composer Gerry Mulligan recounted, "I was part of a small community of very young musicians and arrangers, and we paid a lot of attention to who was doing what with all of the bands. When Strayhorn came on the scene, he just blew us away, because he was doing very complicated, sophisticated things, and they didn't sound complicated to the ear at all—they sounded completely natural and very emotional. To bring all that complexity to bear and have it be so beautiful was something incredible to everybody who knew anything." Gil Evans, who was writing for the Claude Thornhill Orchestra in the early 1940s, recalled, "From the moment I first heard 'Chelsea Bridge,' I set out to try to do that. That's all I did—that's all I ever did—try to do what Billy Strayhorn did." Also the saxophonist and arranger Benny Carter: "Strayhorn's compositions were so *complete*. They weren't just riffs or chord changes like so many others were doing. It made us all think a little differently about what we were doing." Dizzy Gillespie: "All those sevenths—man, I never heard anything like those things until him. I got ideas from hearing him that I knew I could use forever." Bill Finegan, who wrote for Glenn Miller: "It didn't take a thing away from Duke to recognize that Strayhorn, like Duke, was an original. There was so much all-around musical knowledge in those things he did, and always something original, the element of surprise." Billy May, who wrote for Charlie Barnet and Glenn Miller: "Now, I knew Billy in Pittsburgh, so I knew what he was capable of. Then he came up with 'Chelsea Bridge' and 'Mid-Riff' and 'Passion Flower' and all those songs in the 1940s. He had a tremendous amount of consistency. There wasn't a clinker in the bunch. That's what was truly amazing, I think—every single song had something great." Ralph Burns, who wrote for Woody Herman: "Billy took big-band music and moved it up a couple of steps musically. He was really writing classical music for the Duke Ellington Orchestra." Slide Hampton, then a young trombonist (and later an arranger): " 'Chelsea Bridge,' 'Passion Flower'—at that time, people weren't writing with that extensive level of theory. His compositions were very involved. But the thing that stood out was that, with all that theory that was there, you still had a very human and spiritual side to his music."

Gone was the mimicry of Gershwin and Porter that tainted Strayhorn's first major efforts, Concerto for Piano and Percussion and *Fantastic Rhythm*—experimentation as homage. Gone was the mannered fuss of his more pretentious early songs, such as the river-flivver rhyming "If You Were There"—social climbing in B-flat.

Mature and honest, his first big-band masterstrokes for the Ellington Orchestra are debtless Strayhorn, and revealingly so. Many of the pieces share a feeling, an essential component of their "Strayhorn sound," of darkness. "Chelsea Bridge," "Passion Flower," "After All," "A Flower Is a Lovesome Thing"—different statements in the same voice, they suggest a personal anguish. Just as all the floral-related titles (like "Violet Blue" and "Lotus Blossom" of the later 1940s) evoke their author's formative experiences in his grand-mother's Hillsborough garden, the inner torment of the music casts light on the private world Strayhorn explored in his walks along the Eno River. Friends like Mickey Scrima, Herb Jeffries, George Green-lee, and Haywood Williams assumed that he found music the one way to release the frustration and hurt concealed under the armor of politesse. "The guy went through a lot of shit in his life, from his father right on through school—the kids calling him a sissy, you know," said Scrima. "He kept it all in and put on a big front that everything was fine, nothing bothered him. Then he sat down and wrote all that music with all that emotion. All his feelings came out in the music. That's what made his stuff so incredible and different from Duke's. It was great music, like Duke's was, and it was so full of dark feeling."

Just when Strayhorn's classicism was becoming a vital compo-nent of Ellingtonia, the orchestration got a monumental boost with the arrival of two new band members, the bassist Jimmy Blanton and the tenor saxophonist Ben Webster. Blanton, a quiet and lanky young recruit from St. Louis, had a gift for contrapuntal melody, a ringing tone, and impeccable intonation that broadened his instru-ment's orchestral possibilities; before Blanton, bandleaders had es-sentially used the bass as a string tuba. By taking Ben Webster as the orchestra's first full-time tenor saxophone soloist, Ellington not only caught up with Count Basie and his influential tenorist Lester Young but gained a strong and versatile solo voice to match his own instrumental muscularity and eclecticism. (On his music for Juan Tizol's driving "Perdido," Webster wrote a note in the margin: "Swing like Pres.") With the Blanton-Webster band under him and Strayhorn submitting ambitious work, a freshly challenged Ellington reached a watershed of his own. The compositions he was recording in the early 1940s (even during the ASCAP ban, which affected radio broadcasts only)—the dizzying "Cottontail," the forceful "Main Stem," the quirkily expressive "Harlem Air Shaft," and the commanding "Ko-Ko"—mark an invigorated master working at his resolute best. "Duke was really reborn with that combination of talents in his organization," said the composer, critic, and historian Leonard Feather, who was in the studio during several of Ellington's recording sessions with Blanton in early 1941. "Duke said, 'Listen, you're going to hear something you never heard before—a bass player who plays melody, and in tune.' Blanton was wearing the wildest zoot suit you'd ever see—big, wide stripes—but he played like an angel. Strayhorn had a proprietary interest in Blanton—he had heard him play before Duke did and was one of the people who brought him to Duke's attention—so he was watching very closely and helping out a bit, making little changes in the chords and the voicings. Duke was in his glory at the center of it all."

Outside the studio, Blanton, Strayhorn, and Webster carried on as close friends. Webster, under six feet but beefy, was physically daunting—musicians called him The Brute—but unashamed of his sensitive side; he lived with his mother and grandmother for much of his adult life and, in a moment of sorrow, was known to cry as easily and shamelessly as, in a moment of anger, he would pummel an antagonist. It was Webster, Feather recalled, who gave Strayhorn the affectionate (though subtly belittling) nickname that fellow musicians quickly embraced: Swee' Pea, taken from the troublesome, one-toothed baby in the *Popeye* newspaper comics and cartoons. (Feather and others speculated that the nickname might also have alluded to Strayhorn's fondness for sweet-smelling cologne. Some sources, most notably Ellington, credit the name to drummer Sonny Greer; others, including Ellington's first biographer, Barry Ulanov, attribute it to saxophonist Otto "Toby" Hardwicke.) Strayhorn called Webster Uncle Benny. "Ben, Billy, and Blanton became very attached to each other, probably partly because they were the new guys, which made them outsiders in the eyes of the longtime members of the band," said Helen Oakley Dance. "Ben—the big, darling tough guy, and he was older—loved them dearly. He adopted them. If one of them didn't get on the bus on time or couldn't get a seat or something, Ben would take care of it. He established himself as their protector." The threesome carried on musically as well, playing together after hours. Pianist Jimmy Rowles, then a student at Gonzaga University in Spokane, remembered hearing Blanton, Webster, and Strayhorn play together at a no-name joint in Seattle late one night in the spring of 1941 when the Ellington Orchestra was in town. "I came into town to hear Ellington and went out that night, and in walked the three of them," said Rowles. "It was amazing—the most beautiful trio I'd ever heard in my life. They had perfect taste. Every note was just right. And they could swing. I mean, they really swung."

Midway into the seven-week Casa Mañana run, Ellington invited Strayhorn to accompany him to a private party being held late one night at the home of an MGM gag writer, Sid Kuller, who had introduced himself to Ellington at the club earlier that week. The two of them found Kuller's extravagantly stylish Art Deco house in Culver City (designed by Columbia Pictures art director Steve Gooson, a former architect) jammed with Hollywood types—Kuller's celebrity friends such as John Garfield and Mickey Rooney; the screenwriter W. R. Burnett, who wrote *Scarface*; and starlets and would-bes and their various predators. The black character actor Frank Fay and some of his friends were regulars, earning Kuller's parties praise (and, more important to Kuller, publicity) from gossip columnist Louella Parsons for breaking the social color line. "Duke and Billy weren't used to this, see," recalled Kuller. "But it was all right, and they liked that, and they came back the following Saturday, and this time they brought half the band," including Harry Carney and drummer Sonny Greer, who danced that night with Lana Turner. "He was cute," Turner recalled, "but not as cute as Billy, but he wouldn't dance with me. That was okay. We talked and became great friends. He was so charming, but not in a come-on way. He was very real, even at a Hollywood party." Around 2:00 a.m., as Kuller remembered, "the place was wall-to-wall people, and Duke was at the piano. I said, 'Boy, the joint sure is jumping,' and Duke said, 'Jumping for joy.' He started to turn the line into a song, right there. After a few more drinks, we decided to write a show together—*Jump for Joy*." Kuller was serious: with Garfield and Burnett as backers, he quickly put the funding together for Ellington, a few collaborators, and him to stage a musical revue. Ellington was equally serious about the potential of this, his first major theatrical project; he approached it as a musical vehicle for black pride, a showcase for black talent, and a gutsy swipe at Uncle Tomism.

Jump for Joy opened on July 10 at the 1,600-seat Mayan Theatre, the premier venue for black acts in Los Angeles. Though Duke Ellington was given top billing, he played piano and led his orchestra from the pit, largely out of sight; on stage, the show featured singers Dorothy Dandridge and Ivie Anderson, plus comedian Wonderful Smith, dancers Henry "Phace" Roberts and Andrew Jackson (The Rockets), a dance chorus of twelve, and a choir of ten. The score was a bit of a hodgepodge and far from pure Ellingtonia: Mickey Rooney wrote the music for one number ("Cymbal Sockin' Sam") and Kuller's pal Hal Borne, a white MGM journeyman, contributed five songs, including such black-themed numbers as "Sun-Tanned Tenth of the Nation" and "I've Got a Passport from Georgia." The standouts among the originals, however, were credited to Ellington: the rousing, gospel-inspired title song, the gorgeously mournful ballad "I Got It Bad and That Ain't Good," the liltingly romantic "Brown-Skinned Girl in the Calico Gown," and the tuneful swinger "Subtle Slough" (an instrumental that later became the popular "Just Squeeze Me" after Lee Gaines added lyrics). The show was poorly received by most critics, with a few exceptions, such as Ed Schallert of the *Los Angeles Times* and Almena Davis of the *Los Angeles Tribune,* a black weekly. "The audience loved us, but they were almost completely black," recalled Wonderful Smith. "The critics were white, and they had never seen anything like this. They didn't know what to make of it. The music was magnificent and the performers were all tops, but it was all in a completely different style than what you'd see in a white theater. The big difference was style, not quality. But that wasn't understood." Operating at a cost of about seven thousand dollars per week, the show was pulling considerably less by its fifth week and closed after twelve weeks and 101 performances. "It was a pity," said Henry Blankfort, the show's producer and director. "We were hoping to move to New York and open on Broadway, but we ran out of money. Broadway might have been more receptive to a black show. We'll never know."

No one ever knew how much Billy Strayhorn had to do with *Jump for Joy.* Somewhat akin to Strayhorn's musical *Fantastic*

Rhythm, it might have been a natural project for Ellington and Strayhorn to collaborate on. Ellington and Hal Borne, however, were the only composers credited in the show's program and promotional materials. Only on the last page of the program is William Strayhorn acknowledged, along with Duke Ellington and Hal Borne, for "musical arrangements." According to Blankfort and Kuller, however, Strayhorn cowrote much of *Jump for Joy* with Ellington as a composing collaborator rather than as an arranger. "We should have listed Billy, too: 'By Duke Ellington and Billy Strayhorn.' But Ellington had the name. He was the big draw," said Blankfort. Kuller said he dealt with Ellington and Strayhorn as artistic equals: "Billy really did write a whole lot of the show. They were writing together all the time. They were collaborators in fact, in spirit, in mind, and in talent. When we were writing the thing, sometimes I'd work with Duke, sometimes I'd work with Billy. It didn't matter—we were all writing it, as far as we were concerned." Sometimes, according to Phace Roberts, Strayhorn composed alone. Roberts visited Strayhorn's dressing room often and watched him work; there was an upright piano in the basement room and a small bar, at which Strayhorn would mix a concoction he called a Heater Booster Cooler (brandy, rum, and ginger ale in secret proportions). "Billy was always writing new songs for the show, and he'd play them for me to try them out," said Roberts. "One time, I was there waiting for Billy to mix up this drink, and Duke walked in. Duke said, 'What's the latest?' Billy sat down and played a new number he was working on. Duke was listening—'Uh-huh, uh-huh.' And that was that. It was in the show."

As the manuscript score for *Jump for Joy* illustrates, Strayhorn had a big hand in no fewer than five compositions, including "Rocks in My Bed," "Cindy with the Two Left Feet," "Uncle Tom's Cabin Is a Drive-In Now," and "Bugle Breaks" (the only number whose copyright includes Billy Strayhorn, cited as coauthor with Duke and Mercer Ellington). "The thing is, see, Duke was the front man," explained Kuller. "It was a big enough shock to the world to have Duke Ellington's name up there. Listen, the world wasn't ready to accept a show by Duke Ellington. It certainly wasn't ready to accept Duke Ellington *and* some other guy nobody ever heard of." At the heart of this arrangement, Ellington and Strayhorn themselves seemed to share an attitude of resigned complicity. "Duke knew this was the way it had to be for this thing," said Kuller. "So did Billy. They both knew the ropes. Hey, they were beside themselves to be doing this at all. Once we started this thing, it was tremendously important to Duke. His name was out there in front. And anybody could see that Billy loved working on the music and being involved in the theater. He was content just to be doing it. If Duke Ellington's name was out there, so be it. That was okay with them."

The chance to live for most of the year in California, where he was invited to Hollywood parties and Lana Turner was there, appeared to be a compensatory thrill to a lifelong easterner like Strayhorn. "He got into the whole exotic trip of the West Coast," remarked Jeffries. "It was a kind of mecca to us—all the glamour. Everything was new and sunny. Strayhorn bought into all that." One of Kuller's houseguests, Harry Salzman, a young Canadian who had just come to Hollywood looking for work, invited Strayhorn to come along on a visit to a winery near Santa Ana. "The whole zeitgeist of touring a winery and sipping the vintages really appealed to Strayhorn," said Kuller. "It wasn't something a lot of Negro kids from Pittsburgh did."

By night, Strayhorn explored the black music scene around Los Angeles, where he was an uncommon sight again: there, he was the celebrity. When Strayhorn and Blanton, roommates in a private home on Pico Boulevard below Hollywood (they weren't allowed in most hotels), found the hippest jam session in town—at Billy Berg's packed little club on Sunset and Vine—they were received like New York royalty. The house rhythm section vacated at their arrival, according to Lee Young, a drummer who was then leading a seven-piece group with his brother Lester, who had left the Basie band the previous year. "Strayhorn and Blanton were recognized as heavyweights," said Lee Young. "They played, and the place stopped cold." Through Blanton, whom Young had already known well, Strayhorn became friendly with both Lee and Lester Young and wrote some music for their band: new arrangements of three tunes, "Flamingo," "Take the 'A' Train," and one of the numbers from *Fantastic Rhythm*, "My Little Brown Book." Lee Young paid Strayhorn seven dollars for each one. "They were hip charts," said Young.

"It wasn't easy to write for seven pieces with two tenor saxophones. Billy got a great, full sound out of those seven pieces. He made us sound like fourteen." While he was at it, Strayhorn passed on some tips to one of the Youngs' regular arrangers, trumpeter Gerald Wilson. "He really taught me how to arrange," remembered Wilson. "Chord structure, how to get from one point to another—I couldn't figure out how he did all those things. He sat me down and showed me: 'Here, Gerald, you can just do this.' It was so natural, so easy to him, like writing a letter. I don't think he had any realization that what he could do was incredible. It just doesn't come like that to other people."

Wineries and parties and Billy Berg's jams aside, Strayhorn's West Coast excursion peaked shortly before the show closed, when Ellington called on his polished young colleague's grace with an extramusical assignment: Lena Horne duty. About a year earlier, in New York, when Horne was twenty-three and starting out in cabaret, she and Ellington had had a secret fling. Horne had since come West to do some nightclub work and poke around the movie business, and Ellington arranged for her to see *Jump for Joy*. At intermission, Strayhorn approached her. "This small, wonderfully brown little man with great big glasses walked down the aisle. He was like an owl," Horne recalled. "He said to me, 'Miss Horne, I've been commissioned by Mr. Ellington to keep you company. My name is Strayhorn.' You see, Duke could be very possessive with women. He wanted to make sure that no other man came after me, so he arranged for Billy to be my chaperon. He assumed that Billy was safe, which I guess he was in the way that Duke saw me, which was as a sex object."

Strayhorn and Horne connected nonetheless. "He sat with me in the theater, and he was soft-spoken," said Horne. "I liked him immediately, and that's very unusual for me, because I'm very inward. We watched the rest of the show, and we talked as if we had just left each other the day before and had things to catch up with. We talked a little about Pittsburgh, because we both came from there. There was an immediate recognition by both of us that we would be friends. For me, it was as if my other self came up and spoke to me—we were that much in sync." After the show, Strayhorn accompanied Horne home to the apartment (on Horn Avenue) in whites-only Hollywood that she had rented under another woman's name. "I took him to my house, which is another unusual thing, because I was never there myself. I didn't want to be seen there. But I wanted so much to be alone with Billy, to talk to him, and with him I felt totally safe. I didn't care who saw me and where they saw me. I felt strong. So we went to the house. He played 'Lush Life' for me on the piano, and we talked all night."

For the several weeks remaining in Strayhorn's California stay, he and Horne kept constant company, discovering restaurants and dropping into nightclubs, usually the Capri, a top jazz spot, and Brothers, the black club where white actors loved to be seen. "I was lonely in California when I first went. I had always been a lonely person, until I met Billy," said Horne. "We went to museums, we went out at night to hear the blues. He was the one I wanted to be with all the time. He was my guru." Mostly, Strayhorn and Horne stayed in at her house or went for walks and talked. "I never met another man like him. He liked to stop and look at a tree," she said. "We stopped on the street once, because there was a carving on a door that interested him. He could tell I was a person who had missed a lot in life and wanted to know everything, and he was so bright. I hadn't gone to school very much, and he was very scholarly. I'd always been a snob against education. But I learned from him; things I would never have thought to ask a teacher about, I could ask him. We talked about everything. We talked about what it was like to be a woman and what it was like to be a man, and we talked about how mixed up each of the sexes were and how better off we'd all be if we were even more mixed up together. He wasn't like a professor—he was like you imagine a professor to be. He was brilliant but gentle and loving. He never made you feel dumb. He was very sure of himself and decisive in his thinking. You wanted him around you, and he made it bearable to have other people around.

"I wanted to marry him so badly. He was just everything that I wanted in a man, except he wasn't interested in me sexually. If I could have had him, I would have taken him. We were in love, anyway. He was the only man I really loved." These are things Lena Horne loved about Billy Strayhorn: "He had a face like an elf. You'd want to put your hands up and hold it. He loved food like he loved trees and nature. He thought food was beautiful—the texture of an apple. He was very unhappy when people didn't handle food respectfully. When he got angry, he never showed it. I knew he was seething inside sometimes, but he rarely showed his anger. If he heard somebody say something that he disagreed with, he'd deal with it in a very relaxed and easy way. He'd say, 'Well, I don't like what you said.' That's all, yet it would seem very forceful. Nobody was offended, but he made his position clear. He was very, very strong and at the same time very sensitive and gentle: he was the perfect mixture of man and woman."

Applying his gift for musical empathy to the artist he loved so, Strayhorn worked closely with Horne to refine her singing style and repertoire. "I wasn't born a singer," said Horne. "I had to learn a lot. Billy rehearsed me. He stretched me vocally. Very subtly, he made me stretch—he raised keys on me without telling me. He taught me the basics of music, because I didn't know anything. He played good music for me to hear, because I hadn't heard anything. He went around with me to auditions and played piano for me. I was terrified, but he kept me calm and made me good." Horne finally landed an engagement at Los Angeles impresario Felix Young's Little Troc cocktail lounge, a smaller version of Young's failed nightclub extravaganza The Trocadero. Something close to a Cafe Society West, the intimate Little Troc was located in a Sunset Strip space about the size of a grade school classroom. The floor-level stage was so tiny that the Katharine Dunham dancers, who opened for Horne, kept knocking over patrons' drinks and quit after three performances; the dressing rooms were small as well, recalled the dancer and choreographer Talley Beatty, then with the Dunham troupe: "Billy and Lena were working together in her dressing room, which was really a little closet. They were right up against each other, but it didn't matter to them. They only needed the space of one person, they were so close." To Horne's old New York club material, Strayhorn added arrangements of four new numbers for her pianist, Phil Moore: "Blues in the Night," "Honeysuckle Rose," "There'll Be Some Changes Made," and "When the Sun Comes Out." "He knew what songs were right for me. He knew my personality better than I did," said Horne, "and he wrote arrangements that had my feeling in the music." Hollywood talk made the show a must-see—"People who never went to nightclubs pushed their way into the place four or five nights a week," the *New York Times* reported—and Lena Horne seemed on her way to a screen career.

Strayhorn worked well with singers. Ever since the imaginary lush life of his teens, he had had a fondness for theatrical songs in the Gershwin and Porter vein; he knew the Tin Pan Alley and Broadway repertoires thoroughly and favored the vocal song form in his most personal work. (Although he might zip through an arranging assignment in the midst of a house party, while guests noodled on the piano or records played, he would craft his own songs alone, refining the work for weeks or longer, according to Aaron Bridgers.) A facile pianist and adaptive collaborator, Strayhorn served as a sensitive accompanist and vocal arranger, roles of growing value to the Ellington Orchestra as singers emerged as a popular focal point of the major bands in the 1940s. When Strayhorn first took over the Ellington Orchestra vocal wing in 1939, Ivie Anderson was the only singer; by the mid-1940s, he was supervising a roster of full-time singers, including Joya Sherrill, Maria Ellington (no relation), Kay Davis, and Al Hibbler.

Herb Jeffries, who left the band in November 1941 to pursue a full-time film career, acknowledged his debt to his friend for nurturing his singing style as well as the orchestra's larger vocal identity. "When I was hired for the band, I used to sing in a high, high voice," said Jeffries. "I used to clown around and do some imitations. So one night we were down in Nashville, and I was imitating Crosby backstage, and when Strayhorn heard that he said, 'Oh, I like that. That's great.' So he told Duke, 'That's the voice, that's the voice he should sing in.' So he brought me all the way down from a very high voice into the mellow voice that I've used ever since. That's the kind of thing he did with the singers in the band. He'd work very, very closely with you, and he sensed what your strengths were. Then he picked songs and did the arrangements to bring out the best in you." Joya Sherrill, a fair-skinned, impishly cute teenager from Detroit when she joined the Ellington Orchestra in 1942, said she grew up under Strayhorn's tutelage as well. "I had never sung professionally before," said Sherrill, who auditioned for Ellington by performing her own lyrics to "Take the 'A' Train." "Billy would teach me my songs and get in lots of lessons about music at the time.

But he would never act like he was teaching me. As things came up, he would explain something or help me with something. By the time he was done with me, I had learned a lot about my craft. That's the way he did things." Maria Ellington, elegantly winsome, sang relatively little; when Ellington signed her in 1944, he referred to her as "the beauty department." Strayhorn did teach her the sexy novelty "Rocks in My Bed." "I hated it, because it was basically a silly song," recalled Maria Ellington Cole (who later married Nat "King" Cole). "I think they used me more for show than anything, because of my looks. Billy worked with me on my songs and played piano for me. But when I asked him how I was doing, he'd say, 'Oh, you look divine.' "

Among the orchestra's female singers, Strayhorn seemed closest to Kay Davis, a mousy concert vocalist with a master's degree in music from Northwestern when Ellington hired her in 1944; her specialty was performing the abstract, wordless vocal parts that Ellington pioneered early in his career with such compositions as "Creole Love Call." "I mostly did Duke's obbligato vocalizing rather than standards or Billy's tunes," she explained. "But Billy and I rehearsed all the music together, and we became fast friends. We both loved classical music, and that was a very strong bond. He taught me 'Lush Life,' which was very flattering, considering how special that song was to him. He had very particular ideas about the way that song should be sung and very high standards. Eventually, he and I did it together in public." (Strayhorn and Davis finally gave "Lush Life" its first major performance at Carnegie Hall on November 13, 1948; it was essentially a duet, with the full Ellington Orchestra contributing only the climactic final chord. Although his notebooks show that Strayhorn was working on an arrangement of "Lush Life" for the Ellington Orchestra at this time, he abandoned the project.) Strayhorn taught her "down to every little inflection," according to Kay Davis Wimp. "He was very particular like that. For instance, he taught me how to drink a martini. He told me that the proper drink for me was a martini, and he told me how to drink it. He said, 'It tastes bad. But drink it anyway—you'll adjust.' And he was right."

Strayhorn worked less closely with the orchestra's principal male vocalist of the 1940s, Al Hibbler, perhaps because the Arkansas-born singer's style was so untouchably idiosyncratic, a mercurial amalgam of earthy tones, part-growls, and abstractions, all imbued with a jarring hint of a Cockney accent. "I didn't need Strayhorn very much," said Hibbler, who was born sightless and learned singing with the choir of the Arkansas School for the Blind. "Strayhorn was all right. He was something else. I may be blind, but I know who's in the room with me. Ray Nance was in the room, I knew Ray Nance was in the room. Cootie Williams was in the room, I knew Cootie was in the room. Strayhorn was in the room, I didn't know he was there. He was like a ghost—there's no way you knew if he was even there."

The Second World War affected Billy Strayhorn's life less than he had expected. When the news of Pearl Harbor broke, Strayhorn and Lena Horne were alone, drinking cocktails in her apartment; they sat on the floor holding their drinks with two hands, staring at the knobs of the radio. "Billy turned to me," recalled Horne, "and he said, 'It's all over.' We thought that was the end of the world." It was, certainly for now, the end of their private happy hour: Strayhorn left immediately for New York and, with Aaron Bridgers, undertook what would be a less than traumatic adjustment to wartime. Both Bridgers and he were declared 4F, Bridgers for a hernia, Strayhorn for his severe myopia. Ellington, who was forty-two when the United States entered the war, wasn't drafted; he maintained a homefront version of his usual relentless touring and recording schedule, adding armory dances all over the country (these tended, though, to be largely civilian events to which servicemen and their dates were admitted free of charge) and making sure to pitch in with benefit appearances. Sharing a bill with Bette Davis, Abbott and Costello, and Rudy Vallee and his Coast Guard Band at the Hollywood Canteen in October 1942, Ellington performed a duet with harmonica player Larry Adler, a private in the army infantry. Strayhorn accompanied the band to this event and, while he was in California, met Francis Goldberg, a sinewy, strong-featured black sailor stationed at the San Pedro naval base; Strayhorn and Goldberg clubbed together around Los Angeles over the course of several days and agreed to reunite in New York after the war.

Both with Ellington and outside his organization, Strayhorn

composed and arranged material, including the only complete studio recording of an extended collaboration with Ellington called "The Deep South Suite," for morale-boosting "V-discs" distributed without charge within the armed services. A political buff and Roosevelt booster, Strayhorn hoped the 1944 presidential election would bring a prompt end to the war. On election night, he arranged to listen to the returns with a few friends at Ruth Ellington's apartment. "He was very anxious about the election," recalled Claire Gordon, a friend of the Ellingtons' who was part of the group that evening. "He felt it was imperative that Roosevelt win. We went out to buy something to drink to have as the returns came in, but since it was election night and the liquor stores were closed, we couldn't get any alcohol. We went from store to store, wandering all over the place. Finally, we found a place that would sell us some slivovitz, a ceremonial plum brandy. We went back, and we listened to the returns, and we drank. Roosevelt won, but we weren't very happy because we were sick as dogs from the stuff we were drinking." None of Strayhorn's friends or members of his immediate family died in the war, although George Greenlee encountered trouble stateside. Commissioned as a first lieutenant in the U.S. Army Air Force and assigned to the 477th Bombardment Group of black pilots (the Tuskegee Airmen), Greenlee was rejected for intelligence training while seemingly less qualified whites were accepted; he protested in terms accurately deemed disrespectful and was court-martialed near the end of 1944. Strayhorn traveled overnight by train to McCoy field in Orlando, Florida, to visit his friend in the brig, only to find that Greenlee's uncle Gus had pulled strings with the army brass and gotten his nephew relatively lenient confinement to base. Strayhorn and George spent the weekend in the officers' club, as Greenlee recalled, drinking "to victory and the numbers games." Meanwhile, Strayhorn had already played a more tangibly constructive part in the war effort, though he didn't know it: his old Westinghouse High School friend Boggy Fowler was serving in the special services and spent three years producing *Fantastic Rhythm* at navy bases throughout the Pacific.

In the expansive postwar spirit, a rich opportunity came Ellington's way. Perry Watkins, a young black set designer and stage manager esteemed for his work with Harlem's WPA Negro Theatre (as well as with Orson Welles on his all-black production of *Macbeth* for the Federal Theatre), set out to produce his first Broadway show, a daring contemporary fable based on John Gay's *The Beggar's Opera*, first produced in London in 1729. Though the antihero tale of a thief and a jailer's daughter had been updated relatively recently by Kurt Weill and Bertolt Brecht as *Die Dreigroschenoper* (*The Three-penny Opera*), Watkins's twist was to use a multiracial creative team and cast for what he called *Beggar's Holiday*. Spotting Ellington and a small entourage finishing dinner in a midtown Manhattan restaurant, Watkins walked up to him cold and offered him a commission to compose the score in collaboration with the librettist John Latouche, who had a track record with black-themed material as the author, with the composer Vernon Duke, of *Cabin in the Sky*. Watkins was surprised at first to find Ellington unfamiliar with *The Beggar's Opera*. "I realized all of a sudden that Duke never went to the theater very much," remarked Watkins, who was equally surprised when Ellington accepted the offer anyway, on the spot.

Watkins's proposition was another step in forming Ellington's reputation as a composer who transcended big-band jazz. Nobody was asking Tommy Dorsey to write for the Broadway stage; moreover, this was a full "book" show in a "legit" theater—not a revue in a "Negro-circuit" house—and one based on a work by an old, dead white Englishman. "Ellington wanted the recognition of writing a Broadway show," recalled Luther Henderson, a lifelong friend of the Ellingtons (and a Juilliard classmate of Mercer's), who helped prepare the show's music for the stage. "In fact, he wanted the recognition of writing a Broadway show more than he wanted to write a Broadway show."

Ellington's endless loop of band engagements prohibited him from working on Broadway for a prolonged period. Latouche found it nearly impossible to collaborate with Ellington and threatened to quit, complaining that he needed to talk to him—Ellington was the composer. "I can't work like this," said Watkins. Henderson explained: "Duke Ellington would give up his band and his traveling from one city to another only under the penalty of death. Ellington would never leave his band—never, ever, not for anything. Now, you cannot do a Broadway show without the composer present, because a Broadway show is a collaborative effort between composer, lyricist, choreographer, and the performers." However, Henderson added, "*Beggar's Holiday* was not produced without the composer present—one of the composers, at any rate. Ellington said, 'I will leave you Strayhorn.' " It was no secret: An item in the September 9, 1946, edition of the *New York Herald Tribune* reported, "Billy Strayhorn, composer-arranger, arrives from the West Coast tomorrow to begin work on a new jazz version of 'The Beggar's Opera' in collaboration with Duke Ellington."

Working alone at home on Convent Avenue, as well as with Ellington as often as possible, including by phone—the band was away from New York for several months prior to the show's first rehearsal on October 21, 1946—Strayhorn applied himself to *Beggar's Holiday* with striking seriousness of purpose. "Strayhorn had the theater bug," said Aaron Bridgers. "That show meant a lot to him. He gave it everything he had in him." The result was a collection of sophisticated yet swinging, harmonically uncommon theater songs, including the pretty "Brown Penny," "Women, Women, Women," "Girls Want a Hero," "Maybe I Should Change My Ways," "The Wrong Side of the Railroad Tracks," and "I'm Afraid," all composed either by Ellington in collaboration with Strayhorn or solely by Strayhorn. During the rehearsals in New York and tryouts in New Haven, Newark, Hartford, and Boston, Strayhorn handled the music through whirligig revisions and additions to the show. "It was in a lot of trouble out of town," recalled George Abbott, who replaced Nicholas Ray as director. "I don't know what Nick was doing, but it wasn't working. I was brought on board, and it was evident to me that a great many changes had to be made, including some new songs and other changes to the music. I never saw Duke Ellington, never worked with him. Billy took care of whatever I asked for. He sat down and wrote it right there, whatever was needed."

In New Haven, it was decided that what the show needed was a ballet number. "We were out of town and they needed this ballet," said Luther Henderson. "And I remember in the hotel at about two o'clock—I was there—I watched Billy talking to Ellington [by telephone] for a few minutes. And Strayhorn stayed up the rest of the night, and the next day the orchestra read the music, and they put the ballet [titled the "Boll Weevil Ballet"] in the show the following day." In Hartford, the first act was being performed on stage while the second act was being revised backstage. "That's what Billy Stray-horn was going through," said Perry Bruskin, a comic actor in the show. "He was writing music during the actual production." As the set designer Oliver Smith recalled, "It was hectic because they were cutting and adding songs all the time, and Billy had to write them on the spot. I used to sit in his dressing room and watch him. I'll never forget it, because of the way he worked. He sat down with the music paper and very methodically wrote the song. He heard it in his head. And only when it was complete would he sit down and read it through on the piano. He'd ask me, 'Well, what do you think?' Once I told him, 'That doesn't really sound like an Ellington song,' and he said, 'It's not supposed to.'" Luther Henderson un-derstood. "The misconception was that Ellington put Strayhorn there because Billy knew what Duke would do," said Henderson. "The truth was the opposite: Ellington put Billy there to do what he wanted, because Duke knew that whatever Billy did would be great."

Strayhorn made a hit with the cast. "Despite how important he was to the show, when he came into a group, he would stand on the side," Bruskin recalled. "He projected that kind of very pleasing, gentle intelligence. But he had an authority that we accepted im-mediately—that this was the man with responsibility for the music. That's all. And everything he said was the last word as far as the music was concerned." Bill Dillard, a singer and actor, was also struck by Strayhorn's warm authority. "He had an air of 'I know what I'm going to do,'" said Dillard. "When he came up with a song or when he changed anything—some of the music or whatever it was—you had a feeling that he really knew what he wanted to do. His directions and his corrections to us were all done in a very friendly way. We all enjoyed whatever he wanted us to do." Among the dancers, above all, the men, Strayhorn made a special impres-sion. "He always came around us and delighted in being around us," remembered the dancer Albert Popwell. "This was unusual, because we were more or less a clan—they called us the gypsies, because we were really in a world of our own. And Billy always seemed to merge toward us, one, because so many of us were gay, and that was a very important connection, especially if you were black *and* gay. Also, dancers are always like kids, and he was short and looked very boyish. I don't mean that Billy was childish, because he was very sophisticated and incredibly strong in that way of still water runs deep. It was like you knew that if he wanted to and you crossed him, he could lash at you. He reminded me of a cat like that."

Beggar's Holiday was staged at a record cost of approximately $300,000; the show promptly settled in at a draw of some $5,000 per week less than the $27,000 it required to break even. "Perhaps it was too daring for its time," speculated George Abbott. "Audiences then were shocked by the very sight of blacks and whites together on stage." The show had only a sixteen-week run at the Broadway Theater on West 53rd Street before closing in the last week of March 1947, despite reviews that found much to praise, principally in the music. The *New York World-Telegram*'s reviewer wrote, "Mr. Ellington's score is a generous outpouring of his individual talent, filled with the spirit and the warmth of his music, the pulsing beat of his rhythms, the strength and the refreshing colors of his modern harmonies," and the critic for the *New York Times* observed, "Mr. Ellington has been dashing off songs with remarkable virtuosity. No conventional composer, he has not written a pattern of song hits to be lifted out of their context, but rather an integral musical composition that carries the old Gay picaresque yarn through its dark modern setting." Strayhorn's program credit read: "Orchestrations under the personal supervision of Billy Strayhorn." "What credit could be given?" asked Luther Henderson. " 'Duke Ellington and Billy Strayhorn'? Uh-uh. This was supposed to be a Duke Ellington show. 'Billy Strayhorn'—who was he? 'Duke Ellington and Billy Strayhorn'—what was that? You couldn't sell it."

This time, however, Strayhorn wasn't buying so easily. "Billy didn't say 'boo' about Duke or how the credits would read the whole time," recalled Oliver Smith. "But on opening night on Broadway, there was a grand, gala party. Duke was there in all his splendor, receiving his public." Ellington moved among the first-nighters in a disembodied glide that impressed the dancers; he acknowledged others with only a slow beginning of a nod of the head and never appeared to move the rest of his body, apparently powered by something outside himself. "Billy said to me, 'Let's get out of here,'" said Smith. "I said, 'But the party's just starting.' And he said, 'Not for me it isn't.' I told him no, I really should stay, and he walked away and out of the theater alone."

6

I'M

CHECKIN'

OUT,

GOOM BYE

Da-dee day! Da-dee day!" Billy Strayhorn scat-sang the opening theme of Gershwin's *An American in Paris* into the microphone of his parlor record-cutting machine. Two days earlier, New Year's Eve 1947, Strayhorn had thrown a bon voyage party for Aaron Bridgers, who sailed for France the following morning. Through Moune de Rivel, a leonine and faintly talented French West Indian chanteuse-turned-restaurateur once featured at Cafe Society Uptown, Bridgers had gotten his first job in music, as a cocktail pianist at Chez Moune de Rivel, a simple spot on the busy Latin Quarter corner of rue St. Jacques and rue du Sommerard. Strayhorn's bash was still in full swing the evening of January 2. Bridgers was some six hundred nautical miles across the Atlantic aboard the *Queen Mary*, his bags stuffed with the powdered milk and chocolates he expected to find in short supply in postwar France, while his old gang topped three days of loosely Gallic celebration by shellacking regards for their friend in Paris. Strayhorn played host on the recording, announcing each speaker with bilingual savoir faire. *"Bonsoir messieurs, mesdames!"* proclaimed Strayhorn. His little voice, sweet and sibilant, formed the French words limberly. "Aaah! *La vie parisienne—et le théâtre! Aaah! Pour Monsieur Aaron Bridgers, écoutez!* This record we're making for Aaron apropos his coming visit to the City of Lights. We are gathered here, quite a quiet little gathering, to make this little farewell disk to our good friend, Aa-ron. *Vous avez l'esprit de Paris, n'est-ce pas?* Aaron, you must take this to the Sorbonne and play it for all the *professeurs.*" Haywood Williams said a few gentle, nervous words into the mike; Ruth Ellington phoned and delivered her wishes, entirely unintelligible, through the receiver; and two relatively new members of the Convent Avenue group chimed in—Francis Goldberg, the sailor Strayhorn had met in California during the war, now discharged and working as a cook in New York, and his imponderably named fraternal twin Frank, a postal worker with movie-star looks and a boxer's frame. "When you gonna come bouncin' around there, Strayhorn?" cracked Frank Goldberg. "Oh," responded Strayhorn coyly, "I'll probably spend April in Paris." Precious continentalism underlined the self-enhancement in Bridgers's and Strayhorn's Francophilia: if their lives ever seemed less than lush, a dose of Paris would ease the bite of it. "Ever since I was growing up in North Carolina, I had always fantasized about sipping champagne on the Champs-Elysées," said Bridgers. "Going to Paris was an experience I had to have, and Strayhorn knew that, because he felt the same way. He was very happy for me. It was a bit sad for both of us when I went, but we thought this was a wonderful thing for me. This was a transition time for us, and we both believed it would work out well, because I was going to Paris. We thought of Paris as a wonderful place. There was no problem, because I was in Paris. This was also a good time for me to go away. Strayhorn needed some time alone. He was going through some things of his own."

Paris was becoming a locus of change for Strayhorn and those dearest to him. A few months before Bridgers sailed for France, Strayhorn returned on the SS *America* from an intercontinental trip that had been a virtual secret mission. He had accompanied Lena Horne to her unpublicized Paris wedding to Lennie Hayton, her longtime beau, an MGM arranger and conductor; California law prohibited mixed-race marriages, and Hayton was white, of Russian Jewish heritage. Horne found a compatible Strayhorn surrogate in Hayton: bourgeois and vigilantly so, Hayton relished introducing Horne to wines and classical music, mostly that of Bartók, Ravel, and Stravinsky. With his aquiline features and longish graying hair, Hayton, thirty-eight, looked like the old Georgian nobleman he behaved as if he were. He frequently wore a yachtsman's cap, and he never sailed. "Since I couldn't have Billy, I let myself fall in love with Lennie," allowed Horne. "I submitted him to Billy for his approval, and he gave it to me, or else I wouldn't have married him." She did so in a civil ceremony on April 16, 1947, Hayton standing on her right, Strayhorn on her left. "Billy and Lennie were as compatible as Lennie and I, and that just had to be," added Horne. "They got along well. They'd stay up together and talk and play music after I went to bed." Strayhorn and Hayton decided to learn chess together; they bought an instruction book and played for days straight, keeping a record of their moves on a notepad both for future study and to document their improvement, neither of which occurred, as far as Lena Horne could tell.

Hayton, a jazz-oriented arranger and onetime pianist for the Paul Whiteman Orchestra (during this stint, he recorded a perky duet version of "Sweet Sue" with one of Whiteman's vocalists, Bing Crosby), developed a growing interest in Strayhorn's music and career. He was exploring the prospect of developing his own music production and publishing company and asked Strayhorn about his agreement with Ellington. Alarmed to find that Strayhorn had none—and had no idea how much his arrangements and compositions might be worth on the open market—Hayton urged him to be more attentive to the business side of his career with Ellington. "That was the beginning of problems with Strayhorn," said Mercer Ellington. "Lena and Lennie really took him under their wing, and because Aaron was away in Paris, they got a lot more of his attention than Pop. We didn't see very much of Strayhorn for a while."

At every party Horne had in Los Angeles, she recalled, Strayhorn played "Lush Life." When Marie Bryant, the star of *Beggar's Holiday*, had a bash at her Los Angeles home, Strayhorn played

"Lush Life." "I never intended for it to be published," Strayhorn explained. "No, I really didn't. You know, you have your little private projects? Well, that was 'Lush Life.' It was something that I did and I had written and that I liked for myself, and I just did it at parties." Were another musician or admirer to remark on the song's complexity, Strayhorn would protest in self-deprecation, slide to the left of the piano bench to make room for one more, and demonstrate how to play a rendition of "Lush Life" using three fingers. At Marie Bryant's house in the fall of 1948, however, Strayhorn's little private project fell on the ears of Norman Granz, the thirty-year-old entrepreneur who brought a refined sensibility to the Clef and Norgran record labels he had founded. Hearing Strayhorn's performance, he asked him to record the composition for an inventive jazz anthology album he was putting together, *The Jazz Scene,* a bound album of six 78s showcasing performers such as saxophonists Charlie Parker and Lester Young, pianist Bud Powell, and bandleader Machito, as well as arrangers such as Ralph Burns and Neal Hefti. "At that party was one Norman Granz, and he loved it—'You must record it!' I didn't particularly like the idea of doing an isolated [song] in a collection of things," Strayhorn said. "It didn't seem to me to have any kind of form. I mean, just to have works of this person, that person, and the other person, at least the way he explained it to me. I didn't like the idea. He said, 'You can have anything you want. You can have any size orchestra.' I said, 'There's only one way to do "Lush Life," and that's with piano.' And since I was the only one who knew it, I was the only one who could do it, because I had never written it down. So I recorded it, and as we finished the date, Nat [Cole] came in, because he had to do some retakes on a piano album he was doing—he came in a little early. He said, 'What's that?' I said, 'Well, a song of mine.' So he said, 'I'd like to do that.' Well, you know, I paid that no mind whatsoever." *The Jazz Scene* was released in late 1949, but without "Lush Life"; Strayhorn was represented, nonetheless, in two selections featuring Harry Carney, "Sono" and "Frustration," for which Strayhorn played piano and wrote string quintet arrangements. Both compositions were by Ellington, who also supervised the two recordings. "We didn't include Billy's 'Lush Life,' because we could only accommodate a limited number of selections," said Norman Granz, "and Billy also contributed two beautiful string pieces." (The arrangements were credited to Ellington on the release.)*

"Lush Life" remained a party treat until the fall of 1949, when Strayhorn discovered that Nat Cole had indeed recorded the song, in an exuberantly un-Strayhorn vocal rendition set to an exotically theatrical orchestral arrangement by Pete Rugolo, released as the B side of a commercial tune, "Lillian." Strayhorn preferred the A side, in part for the way it rhymed his mother's and his first names, Lillian and William. "When he first heard Nat's 'Lush Life,' that was the only time I ever, ever heard Billy really upset," said Aaron Bridgers. Strayhorn had called immediately after hearing Cole's recording. "I never heard him talk like that. He was screaming, 'Why the fuck didn't they leave it alone?'" Rugolo took liberties with the composition, streamlining the modulations and adding a few bars at points. ("Nat said he didn't know what to do with it," said Rugolo. "So I took it and I worked on it for a while, and I got this idea—I kind of expanded the verse, I made like a tone poem out of it. I added bars, and I tried to catch a weekend in Paris—I put a little Paris thing in, and I tried to make it that kind of a thing.") Moreover, Cole muffed some of the lyrics: he replaced the ethereal allure of "your siren song" with the strange alarm of "your siren of song"; he sang "strifling" for "stifling" and "those who lives are lonely, too" instead of "those whose lives. . . ." Strayhorn "was snorting, he was so angry," said Bridgers. "Of course, any other time, it might not have bothered him quite as badly. I think it was just the icing on the cake. He was getting frustrated at that time." And his next trip to Paris only sharpened the bite of it.

In the spring of 1950 Ellington took on a third theatrical project, his most intellectually enterprising yet. He was to compose the score for a dramatic musical version of *Faust*, with book, lyrics, and direction by Orson Welles, whom Ellington had met in California. In July 1941, almost immediately after the opening of *Jump for Joy*, Welles and Ellington had announced plans to collaborate on a doc-

* Two unidentified solo piano performances recorded at the time of the *Jazz Scene* sessions were attributed to Strayhorn for Verve's expanded edition of the album on CD. At the request of the Strayhorn estate, this author suggested titles for the pieces: "Tailspin" and "Halfway to Dawn." However, the compositions' authorship has not been verified to the author's satisfaction.

umentary to be called *Saga of Jazz*, but it had never come to be. As he was during the gestation of *Beggar's Holiday*, Ellington was busy touring, this time through Belgium, Italy, Switzerland, and other points in Europe; and once again, Ellington dispatched Strayhorn to the theater, this time the little Théâtre Edouard VII in Paris. Alerted that Welles wanted to work independently on the script, the sets, and other aspects of the effort, Strayhorn met with the production manager, Herbert Machiz, a young American studying in Paris on the first Fulbright fellowship in drama, and he set out to compose. Strayhorn began notes for four pieces to be sung by the three characters Welles had decided to use at that point, Dr. John Faustus, Mephistopheles, and Helen of Troy: "Me Is the Trouble," "Zing, Zing," "In the Dungeons of Guilt," and "Song of the Fool."

Imminently, however, Strayhorn's experience appeared inadvertently Faustian: the assignment looked doomed. Titled *The Blessed and the Damned*, the hybrid Faust tale—parts Milton, Dante, Marlowe, and Welles, plus whatever music Strayhorn would contribute—evolved into a one-act third of the evening, augmented by a short Welles spoof of Hollywood called *La langouste qui ne pense à rien (The Unthinking Lobster)* and, as the finale, Welles's magic act. "It was a salad," recalled Samuel Matlovsky, the music director for the whole production, which was in the end billed as *Le temps court (Time Runs)*. "Worst of all," said Matlovsky, "Welles kept changing it completely in rehearsals. One day he'd decide to do something from *Richard III*. The next day there was something by Oscar Wilde. It was crazy." As Helen of Troy, Welles cast Eartha Kitt, a twenty-two-year-old unknown whom Welles had caught in a thrown-together performance at Kyle's nightclub on the rue de Pontier after she was fired from the Katherine Dunham troupe. To audition her, Welles turned his back and only listened to her voice; during rehearsals, he insisted that the untrained first-timer needed no direction. "Whenever he directed anyone in the show, he wouldn't speak directly to the actor," recalled Kitt. "He would speak only to Machiz. He'd say, 'Tell such-and-such a person to do such a thing.' And he never directed me at all. I asked him, 'What should I do here?' And he said, 'Don't worry about it. I'm not directing you. A director only directs stupid people.' "

As opening night, June 17, drew near, Welles had written no

lyrics for Strayhorn's music and, accordingly, decided to use no songs in *The Blessed and the Damned* except "Me Is the Trouble," which he finished with Strayhorn one night in early June over wine at the Café de la Paix. As Helen, Eartha Kitt sang Welles's lyrics to Strayhorn's simple twelve-bar lament: "Hungry little trouble, bound in a bubble, yearning to be, be or be free / All that you see, is all about me, / Hungry me." Responding as a chorus, two actresses, Rosalind Murray and Tommie Moore, chanted, "Now Satan got lonely way down in the pit / So he grabbed Dr. Faustus and put him on the spit." "It was terrible," admitted Kitt. "The music might have been good. But nobody could tell. The whole show was a disaster. Incoherent." Though Strayhorn had originally begun writing arrangements for a six-piece ensemble made up of piano, flute, clarinet, French horn, bass, and drums, Matlovsky's piano ended up as the only instrument. "We didn't get to use most of Strayhorn's music," explained Matlovsky. "So there was no entrance music for Orson. I didn't know what to do at that point, so I played the *Third Man* theme, which had been a big international hit. Orson shot me a glare like he was going to kill me—then the audience burst into applause. That night he said to me, 'The *Third Man* bit was great. Keep it in.' " With Ellington billed as composer of the music for *The Blessed and the Damned*, *Time Runs* tottered for several weeks in Paris, then moved to Hamburg and promptly closed. Strayhorn was clearly disappointed, according to Welles's personal assistant on the French production, Janet Wolfe. "The guy was awfully frustrated," said Wolfe. "Orson was driving us all crazy, but that was Orson, and you had to love him. It was the music that really suffered. It got lost in the shuffle, and he—Billy Strayhorn—he looked like a little lost lamb. He looked to me like any minute he was about to cry."

Not all the sadness in Strayhorn's Paris venture was professionally rooted, however. When Strayhorn saw Aaron Bridgers, his old housemate was living at the Villa Pax, an old brick boardinghouse popular among students and young performing artists, including, at that time, the American jazz pianist Jimmy Davis and the mime Marcel Marceau. Bridgers was settling in for an extended stay, having begun to build a local reputation as a bar pianist and having been offered a regular slot at the hottest new *boîte de nuit*, the Mars Club, owned by an American, Ben Benjamin. Returning to New

York this time, Strayhorn wasn't quite going home: much of his life, both as an artist and as a man, had changed.

Strayhorn moved out of the Convent Avenue basement den he had shared with Bridgers and into his first place of his own, a contemporary one-bedroom apartment on the second floor of 15 West 106th Street, a clean-lined building a hundred feet or so from the rocky northwest corner of Central Park. For continuity, Strayhorn kept most of the furniture he had bought with Bridgers, including their moderne, low-to-the-floor turquoise couch; for freshness, he decorated with lots of color: long pink curtains hung on the windows, framed by wide woodwork painted light purple; the insides of the closets were in bright red—when he selected his clothing, the mood was festive. With no built-in bar and stools and no garden, the apartment was less a party pad than a single man's home; it wasn't as well equipped for entertaining. But it was an exciting place in which to get dressed. In fact, although Strayhorn continued to entertain his old friends about once a month while he was in town, his post-Paris retrenchment brought him into a much more "downtown" social circle, if only geographically.

In late 1940s' Manhattan, an informal group of creative people emerged outside the public eye, its members virtually all black men, artists—painters, dancers, writers, musicians—and gay. There were exceptions, of course: John Cage, white and gay, participated occasionally; Harry Belafonte and the painter Felrath Hines, black and straight, were active members; Eartha Kitt dropped in sometimes. The very point of the group, however, was to defy the reductiveness of category. The Neal Salon, as it came to be called, was founded by Frank Neal, a dancer (formerly with Katherine Dunham) and painter (trained at the Art Institute of Chicago), and his wife, Dorcas, known as a stimulating hostess and chef. Every weekend night and, often, once or twice during the week, insiders knew to convene at the Neals' parlor, no earlier than midnight. It was a moderate-sized second-floor space with wide windows that overlooked a row of storefronts on 28th Street between Broadway and Fifth Avenue; a view without charm, it turned the eye inward. A few paintings by Frank Neal, depictions of working people and still lifes in both watercolor and oils, spotted the walls, though they were not lit—the room tended to darkness. There was always food: a pot of chicken and rice or ham and beans, plus a plate of sandwiches on the table, and Dorcas Neal kept everything coming as long as anyone was eating. She drank coffee compulsively, always a whole pot a night herself. Everyone else drank beer or whatever people brought. These were not parties, however. "It wasn't like a raucous atmosphere, with a lot of drinking. It was a way for a particular group of people to get together and talk and support each other," explained Dorcas Neal, an exquisite woman with an easy charm and a smile that started tentatively and grew very slowly until, as if in triumph, it took over her face. "I guess you could say this was a safe place to be. It was a place for a group of people who were just *different* to be in the company of those who were *the same*. It was all like a family situation. This was a breeding ground for a certain group of artists at a certain time when they had nowhere else to go. It was like Bloomsbury. In this group, these people could be the artists they were and be dealt with like artists. They all faced a lot of the same problems and a lot of the same questions regarding their careers and their place in the world, which was white at the time. I think they were able to answer many of those questions for each other and solve those problems and become successful in the world." The regular members were Dorcas and Frank Neal, of course; Felrath Hines; the dancer and choreographer Talley Beatty; Art Smith, a jeweler who was a friend of Beatty's; the painter and playwright Charles Sebree; the actor and singer Brock Peters; the composer Lou Harrison; the writer James Baldwin, when he was in the city; the historian Bill Coleman; Belafonte; and, starting shortly after his return from Paris in 1950, Billy Strayhorn.

"Ours was a group that never saw the light of day. People stayed until at least five or six in the morning, a lot of times straight through until breakfast," said Dorcas Neal. "Strayhorn was a night owl, like the rest of us, so he became very active. At first, people would step back a little when he came in, because he had such a reputation as a genius—among people in the know, you know. But he was a very charming and very generous person, and he got very close to everybody and even started working on things with people." Strayhorn had been acquainted with Talley Beatty since the dancer had appeared in a short film set to the Ellington Orchestra recording of "Flamingo" in 1942; together, they now laid the groundwork for a ballet (to be produced years later as *Road of the Phoebe Snow*). In much the same way, Strayhorn and Sebree started outlining a musical drama showcase for Belafonte, to be called *Fisher Boy*. Although *Variety* published a brief mention of the project, it was never produced and is not known to exist in any form. It was Strayhorn who purchased the first painting that Felrath Hines ever sold, an abstract of circles in bold reds and yellows. "He was very cosmopolitan and knew much more about art than you might expect," remembered Hines, who had studied at New York University and the Art Institute of Chicago, where he met Frank Neal. "He was very supportive of my pursuing art when we were at the Neals' and talking about our problems. It was nearly impossible to be black and try to be accepted as a fine artist at that time. Billy was having the same experience in music, and he encouraged me to keep on. Then, when I had my first gallery show, he came and bought the first painting. That was the kind of support I really appreciated."

As a rule, intangibles were the currency of the Neal Salon. "For those in the group who were black and gay, and that wasn't everybody, it meant the world just to see that there were others like them in the arts," noted Dorcas Neal. "They didn't have to talk about homosexuality, and, in fact, they practically never did. It was an understood thing. The only one who was perfectly willing to talk about it, as far as I knew, was Strayhorn. One night he said, 'I'm not going to change for anybody, and if they don't like it, that's their problem.' Of course, it wasn't just their problem. If it wasn't anybody else's problem, we wouldn't have had the salon. Nevertheless, it was always more understood than talked out." The "main thrust," as Talley Beatty recalled, was "art, every kind of art. It was highly animated—wonderful. Everything was criticized. No one came away unscathed. It was very sociopolitical. A black gathering, very sociopolitical. We had all worked with prominent white people—myself, with Jerome Robbins—and we had done well with them, up to a point. At the salon, we could discuss our observations and frustrations together and argue about them, which is what inevitably happened. I had been reviewed in the *New York Times*, and I said, 'This should be worth about fifty thousand dollars. But look at me—I can't get a job!' " Adversity fortified the salon's insularity, according to Brock Peters. "I guess we felt we were kind of special," he said. "We were all daring to try to have careers in an arena where everything was structured against the possibility of having a career. And we got fuel from seeing each other and encouragement in talking with each other and comparing notes and laughing about things and gossiping about things in the business as they looked from our perspective. I wanted a career in concert music and was having trouble coming to terms with the necessity of doing popular work, and Strayhorn and I talked about that a great deal. He encouraged me not to compromise. He said he knew all about compromise, and things hadn't always worked out the way he expected." For his part, Strayhorn appeared to come away from the Neal Salon sessions with a renewed sense of worth, according to Dorcas Neal. "It was a big shot in the arm for him at that time," said Neal. "He said to me, 'You know what? There are some things I want to do for myself for a change. I think I'm going to do them.' "

Early in 1950, Strayhorn accepted an invitation to become a member of a more formal organization that he might have seemed unqualified to join. It was a society of black tap dancers called the Copasetics, founded in honor of tap icon Bill "Bojangles" Robinson, who was credited with coining the term to express soft-shoe felicity, as in, "How's everything, Bojangles?" "Everything's copasetic!" It was a state the often indigent dancer likely felt less than his language suggested. Waiting in pitiless cold on a snaking mourners' line outside the 69th Regiment Armory on Lenox Avenue in Harlem, where Robinson's wake was held on December 5, 1949, a few younger dancers agreed to start a social organization in their idol's memory. One of them was Charles "Cookie" Cook, partner with Ernest "Brownie" Brown in the comic dance team of Cook and Brown. Small and quick-witted—he moved with spring-action surprise and talked the same way—Cook knew Strayhorn through mutual friends in gay circles and asked his fellow dancers to accept the musician in the Copasetics. "We were looking for gentlemen—*who* you were, not *what* you were," explained Honi Coles, half of the "class act" of Coles and Atkins and first president of the Copasetics. Along with Cook, Brown, Coles, Cholly Atkins, and Strayhorn, early membership included the dancers James "Catfish" Walker and Luther "Slim" Preston, Phace Roberts and his partner, Johnny Thomas, Eddie West (of the Chocolatiers dance troupe), the comedian LeRoy

Myers, and Louis Brown (a veteran member of the Cotton Club Boys and close friend of Robinson's who became a liquor salesman).

Five of the members (Cook, Brown, Coles, Atkins, and Myers) had already formed an unofficial club by steering one another into the same apartment building, 2040 Seventh Avenue, at 122nd Street, known around Harlem as "the dancers' house." Gathering at the Showman's Cafe ("uptown's smartest rendezvous," a hangout for Apollo regulars on 125th Street) a few weeks after Robinson's wake, the members drafted a charter: "The Copasetics is a social, friendly benevolent club. Its members pledge themselves to do all in their power to promote fellowship and to strengthen the character within their ranks. With these thoughts ever foremost in our minds, it should be our every desire to create only impressions that will establish us in all walks of life as a group of decent, respectable men. Bearing in mind that these achievements can only become a reality by first seeking the aid of God." The Copasetics met every Sunday afternoon in the early years, rotating the location among the members' homes. For the first meeting held at his place, Strayhorn tacked little signs all over the apartment pointing directions to the refrigerator, the telephone, the bathroom, and other points of possible interest, and he prepared one of his specialties, red beans slowly cooked in beer. "Strayhorn's house became our favorite place to meet because he was such a great host and fantastic cook," recalled Phace Roberts. "After a while, we met there most of the time. His apartment was like our clubhouse." Ritualized with the keeping of minutes and the recitation of the preamble, the Copasetics' meetings, much like Strayhorn's beans, boiled down to alcohol-steeped indulgence. "Well, we talked about all sorts of things," said Cholly Atkins. "We talked about what was happening in the business, different trends and the like. Who was up and who was down. Nothing in particular, just talk. Lots of laughs and lots to drink, that sort of thing." Busmen on holiday, the Copasetics always seemed to end up dancing at some point in their meetings, if only on the pretense of settling an argument about a step; Strayhorn would hop to the piano stool, and a Sunday gathering of gentlemen upended into a cutting session. "We communicated with our bodies—that's what we did," explained Honi Coles. "If we were celebrating, if we were debating, if we were fighting, we did it in dance." At the close of every gathering, the elected treasurer would pass a hat for donations in lieu of prescribed dues, to cover whatever food and however much drink attending members had enjoyed; if there was a surplus in the hat, the members would remember who was up and who was down. As Atkins explained, "It was the type of thing like if, let's say, somebody didn't have any engagements at that particular point and we knew his rent was due or there were doctor bills and he could use a little help. It might be a member or it might be somebody else we knew. The money would go there."

Though ostensibly an outsider, Strayhorn was accepted as a peer—or something more—by the Copasetics, and he clearly treasured their affection and respect. "He was just a lovable person," said Atkins. "He had such a level-headed attitude toward everything. He was a great inspiration to most of us guys." To Phace Roberts, "He was the brains of the group. He knew about everything and explained it to us." LeRoy Myers said, "He was well respected among the guys in the group because his demeanor, his personality, was such that he commanded attention." So dedicated a Copasetic was Strayhorn that he was elected president of the group. "A club like this needed a decisive personality," said Atkins. "I mean, guys would get into heated things. Everybody had an idea about what we should do, what should be happening. There were fist fights sometimes. And Strayhorn was the guy who would keep all of this down. It wasn't that he was pushy. He was just so sharp and even-keeled that everybody listened to him. Everybody felt that if Strayhorn wanted to do this, this is what we should do." He returned their faith with loyalty—and work. "I think the reason Strayhorn was so dedicated to the Copasetics was that he recognized how much love was in the Copasetics for him," added Atkins. "Most people shunned people like him for being how he was, and here was a bunch of guys who were crazy about him—not because of his lifestyle or anything but for him, as a person. We made him our leader." As president, Strayhorn focused his enthusiasm on a new initiative, a Copasetics show, which he would write for the group to perform. The organization had already sponsored an affair in September 1950, a dance at Big George's Barbecue in Queens, the highlight of which was an impromptu performance on bass fiddle by the prizefighter Ezzard Charles; Strayhorn composed a song for the event, "Let's Have a

Ball," an up-tempo trifle. Next time, Strayhorn promised, he'd produce a whole Copasetics musical revue.

Emboldened through the Neal Salon, invigorated by the Copasetics, Strayhorn eventually heeded Lennie Hayton's counsel and applied himself to the business of his musical life. For guidance, he turned to Leonard Feather, the expatriate Briton who, through a range of journalistic, public relations, composing, and record-producing projects, had built a reputation as an all-purpose jazz whiz. (Shortly before this, Feather and Strayhorn had collaborated on a forty-four-page booklet on Ellington's instrumental approach, entitled *Duke Ellington Piano Method for Blues*, which credited Ellington as its author.) "He asked me for a crash course in the music business. He wanted to know how everything worked," said Feather, who met with Strayhorn in his apartment office above Cafe Society Downtown at 1 Sheridan Square in Greenwich Village. "I'm not sure how much of the music business I really ever understood myself, but we went over all the various aspects of the business fairly thoroughly. He went away in typical Strayhorn fashion; he was very nonchalant. The next time I saw him, a week or so later, I asked him if our conversation had been of any use to him. He said, 'Oh yes, thank you very much. I've found the skeletons. They give their regards.' He had looked into his publishing and found a variety of problems."

Strayhorn's work since his arrival in New York, virtually all of it performed or recorded by Duke Ellington or members of his orchestra, had been published by several companies in a manner fairly typical for the time—that is, through a knotty mesh of conflicting strategies difficult to untangle from the outside. It was axiomatic that the composer would not necessarily be the immediate or the primary beneficiary of his own work. In fact, Duke Ellington had been a historic victim of this system years earlier, when he was under contract to Irving Mills; the publishing mogul took credit for co-composing or writing lyrics—and took the related royalties—for more than fifty Ellington works, including such masterpieces as "In a Sentimental Mood," "Mood Indigo," "Prelude to a Kiss," "Solitude," and "Sophisticated Lady." Fortunately for Ellington, no one really thought Mills wrote anything. Strayhorn's case was more complex, since his responsibilities in the Ellington organization included aiding Ellington in both refining and completing works clearly conceived as Ellington music; on stage, Ellington referred to Strayhorn with cryptic aesthetic intimacy as "our writing and arranging companion." Moreover, in jazz a fine musical line often divides composition and arrangement. As a result, Strayhorn could hardly be shocked to find his name missing from the credits of Ellington pieces in which he had a hand, notably, "The 'C' Jam Blues," "The Mood to Be Wooed," "Tonight I Shall Sleep (with a Smile on My Face)," and the "Sugar Hill Penthouse" section of Ellington's long-form masterwork, *Black, Brown and Beige*. Since it was not the convention to publish arrangements, neither did Strayhorn have reason to expect his orchestrations for "Flamingo," "Frankie and Johnny," and "Blue Belles of Harlem" to be copyrighted in his name. Three other kinds of publishing conflicts, however, involved Strayhorn uniquely. The strangest of these "skeletons" were compositions correctly credited to Strayhorn on record labels but not copyrighted in his name: "Flippant Flurry," a 1947 Strayhorn composition, and "Overture to a Jam Session," another Strayhorn original from the same year. Both were filed with the Register of Copyrights in the name of Duke Ellington, who in turn received all royalties for them. Some other Strayhorn works—for instance, his "Tapioca" and "Feather Roll Blues"—were recorded and issued with the proper composer credit but not copyrighted at the time. The least unusual of these cases were compositions Strayhorn created alone for which he shared credit with Ellington, including the Mad Hatters' "Something to Live For" and "Your Love Has Faded," as well as "Day Dream," "Grievin'," "Brown Betty," and "I'm Checkin' Out, Goom Bye," not to mention Strayhorn's contributions to the scores of *Jump for Joy* and *Beggar's Holiday*.

Since the most recent (though not all) of these compositions were published by Ellington's own company, Tempo Music, Inc.—set up for Ellington's new repertoire during the period of the ASCAP radio ban and managed by Ruth Ellington—some of Strayhorn's publishing problems were problems with Ellington. "That was the first time I saw any conflict between the old man and Strayhorn," remembered Mercer Ellington. "Strayhorn had looked into his royalties and such, and he was upset. They had a talk about it, but Strayhorn wasn't satisfied, and he pulled away. There was some distance between them there." (In the handful of interviews published or broadcast during his career, Strayhorn refrained from noting this rift with Ellington; with few exceptions, he responded to inquiries about Ellington with generous praise for his artistry and leadership.) Ellington had, however, given Strayhorn some stock in Tempo Music (ten shares) when the company was formed in 1941, and through it Strayhorn had been profiting from all compositions published by Tempo, including the many Ellington pieces that Strayhorn had nothing to do with. Moreover, Ellington's financial generosity toward Strayhorn had long been seemingly boundless: Strayhorn's rent and living expenses, his vast and lavish wardrobe, the finest food and drink, travel—anything Strayhorn seemed to need or want was his. "Money wasn't quite the problem. How could it be, when Billy had everything?" asked Leonard Feather. "The problem was the lack of independence that his business problems represented. Billy couldn't very well do very much [work] of his own if he was entirely tangled up with Ellington's and he was totally dependent upon Ellington for all his needs. The actual source of his frustration was artistic. He hadn't had very much of a chance to do much of his own thing since the whole period of 'Chelsea Bridge,' during the ASCAP strike. Surely he knew he wasn't being acknowledged for many of the things he was doing. He was obviously frustrated as an artist. He decided it was time to do something about it." Leonard Feather, along with both Duke and Mercer Ellington, ended up helping.

Unique in jazz history for sustaining a musical organization for decades, Duke Ellington engendered loyalty through liberation: one of the ways he kept his cats at home was by letting them loose to do their own projects—under his general supervision, whenever possible. As the big-band era receded in the early 1950s and a new musical era took form, Strayhorn wasn't the only Ellingtonian with an itch for independence. Ellington's star saxophone soloist, Johnny Hodges, was grumbling about leaving. "For a couple of years before he finally left [in January 1951], Johnny told Duke he was going to go," recalled his wife, Cue Hodges. "Duke said, 'What do you want to do? Make your own records? You can do that with me.' " With instrumental combos on the rise again, Ellington set out to revive the dormant small-band phase of his operation and launched a new label, Mercer Records, jointly owned by him, Leonard Feather, and the company's namesake. Strayhorn had a minority position in the business, but his creative role was not insignificant. He was to serve as musical director and arranger as well as pianist on many of the label's dates, and he would be given full credit for every aspect of his participation. The operation's biggest problem was technical: Mercer Records produced 78 rpm singles—and not particularly good ones, acoustically—while record buyers were shifting to 33⅓ rpm LPs. A few Mercer Records sessions, including some of Strayhorn's most imaginative ones for the company, were released as albums before it folded less than ten months after it was launched. "We were releasing the right music the wrong way," said Mercer Ellington.

Strayhorn was featured on several sides credited to Billy Strayhorn and His All-Stars (most notably a boppish version of Lester Young's "Jumpin' with Symphony Sid" and a hard-swinging "Hoppin' John," composed by Jimmy Hamilton), as well as in a small group called the Coronets, which included Ellingtonians Juan Tizol on valve trombone and Willie Smith on alto saxophone (the group's high points were both moody Tizol compositions, "Moonlight Fiesta" and "She"). The Billy Strayhorn–Johnny Hodges Sextet backed blues singer Chubby Kemp on a handful of minor releases. Most notably, Strayhorn was responsible for several sessions featuring Al Hibbler and an extremely hip midsized band including alto saxophonist Benny Carter, bop trumpeter Red Rodney, and Max Roach—plus Mercer Records' most original project, a ten-inch LP of piano duets by Strayhorn and Ellington, released, in a switch, under the name of the Billy Strayhorn Trio. (Alternating bassists Wendell Marshall and Joe Shulman completed the trios.) Issued in an altogether artless, text-only sleeve with (all lowercase) printing on one side, the album sold dismally—just a thousand or so copies, according to Feather. The record was no Strayhorn showcase, however; once more, it essentially proved how deftly Strayhorn could weave his voice around Ellington's. Side by side at two grand pianos, Ellington and Strayhorn ran through some of their standbys—Ellington's "Cotton Tail," Strayhorn's "Johnny Come Lately," their collaboration "The 'C' Jam Blues," a real blues jam in the key of D-flat they called "Bang-Up Blues"—shifting solo voices and appropriating each other's voice with intuitive ease. The unmistakable masterpiece among this batch of tossed-off gems is "Tonk," a precision two-piano adaptation of an intricate composition that Strayhorn had originally written for full orchestra but that was never recorded in that form (here, credited jointly to Ellington and Stray-horn).

After fourteen years of dueting with Ellington figuratively, lit-erally, publicly, or secretly, Billy Strayhorn made his first steps out of Ellington's sphere of influence in mid-1953. The first move was a small one, but in a propitious direction. Herbert Machiz, Stray-horn's old colleague from *The Blessed and the Damned*, home from Paris and trying to build a New York theater career, put together a summer-stock production of Vernon Duke and John Latouche's *Cabin in the Sky* and asked Strayhorn to supply the musical accom-paniment. Having endured that hellish Paris experience together, both working in the wings for American geniuses of their art forms, Strayhorn and Machiz had kept in contact since returning from France. There were evident similarities in their family histories: no money, an abusive father, a nurturing female (in Machiz's case, a maternal aunt) who encouraged the young boy to pursue the arts. "He was also theatrical, that kind of boy," said his sister Miriam Machiz Dworkin. "He could entrance anyone and everyone." Machiz, however, was as manically egocentric as Strayhorn was de-mure; before his Paris stint, he had been drafted into the army but was pulled out of basic training for "eccentric" behavior and as-signed to duty producing entertainment in military hospitals. Stray-horn took on the summer-stock job with Machiz and brought in another friend from his theater experience, Luther Henderson, one of the arrangers who had worked on *Beggar's Holiday*. Much like the Billy Strayhorn Trio, the two musicians performed the *Cabin in the Sky* score at two pianos offstage, accompanied by percussionist Dean Sheldon on drum kit and bongos. "Strayhorn loved the idea of four hands at pianos," explained Henderson. "It's very East Side. It's Cole Porterish, it's European, it's English. Two pianos are very special, when they work. But one of the musicians has to be flexible and listen and feel and bend with the other one. One of the people has to be a Billy Strayhorn."

Working in the theater without Ellington for the first time since *Fantastic Rhythm*, Henderson's collaborator revived his old billing and went by the name of Billy Strayhorne. A few more of his old theater connections were in the all-black cast, including Juanita

Hall and Bill Dillard, both of them *Beggar's Holiday* veterans. "I was so happy to see Billy there," recalled Dillard. "I knew the music would be taken care of and he would take care of me. We didn't do very much rehearsing, so I made a few mistakes here and there. Billy covered them up before I even knew what I did." One of the show's dancers, Joyce Mordecai, was equally grateful for Strayhorn's responsiveness. "A lot of things had to undergo quite a few changes as we went along, in terms of the rhythms and stuff," explained Mordecai. "Billy was incredibly sensitive to what we needed as dancers and always made whatever changes were necessary in the music instead of telling us to change—that's what you find nine times out of ten." Just a stock revival, after all, the show got only one review, a bit of praise in *Variety* that singled out the music: "Song and dance are sparked by a three-piece pit combo that's as good as any full-strength orch. Luther Henderson and Billy Strayhorne man the two pianos . . . [and] the drive they develop is almost incredible."

Brainstorming backstage, much like everyone else in summer stock, Machiz and Strayhorn once drifted into a discussion of a dream project for Strayhorn, Bill Dillard recalled. "They were talking ideas. And Strayhorn started talking. He had this idea about doing this all-black show, and it had something to do with homosexuality. It was wild talk as far as I was concerned." Strayhorn's notion—a theatrical vehicle for both black and gay pride—was certainly extraordinary in 1953. Herbert Machiz happened to be working, however, on an extraordinary forum for extraordinary propositions. Shortly after Machiz returned to the States from Paris, he met, and soon moved in with, John Bernard Myers, an influential early dealer of abstract art renowned for his droll charm; Myers's favorite word was *marvelous*, which he could infuse with a seemingly infinite range of meanings. "John exposed Herbert to the art world, and that gave Herbert the idea to start a new kind of theater, bringing together theater people and fine artists, and John was able and willing to pay for it," said Myers's business partner, Tibor de Nagy, a gallery owner. In February 1953, with Myers's backing and administrative support, Machiz founded the Artists Theatre, a groundbreaking forum for interdisciplinary experimentation that was vital in establishing the experimental identity of Off Broadway. "At the time, there was no Off Broadway as we would come to know it," recalled the playwright Lionel Abel (who wrote his now-classic *Death of Odysseus* for the Artists Theatre). "Off Broadway was a stepping stone to Broadway, where the daring work was supposed to be done. With the Artists Theatre and a few efforts like it, that turned around."

In its first year, the Artists Theatre presented, among other productions, new plays by Tennessee Williams, Frank O'Hara, John Ashbery, and James Merrill, with sets designed by Larry Rivers, Elaine de Kooning, Grace Hartigan, and Albert Kresch. "A lot of smart, very talented people trying to show that we were smarter and more talented than everybody else" is how Rivers depicted the group. Bringing to fruition his "wild talk" of a black-gay statement, Billy Strayhorn joined this heady roster and contributed the theater's only play with music, a dramatic musical adaptation of Federico García Lorca's tragic lament to doomed romance, *The Love of Don Perlimplín for Belisa in Their Garden,* to be performed by a black cast. "It was a terribly brave thing, very, very unusual for any time and absolutely unthinkable in 1953," recalled Bernard Oshei, a young fashion designer who took on the task of costuming the show. "Of course, everybody thought of Lorca as the great gay martyr. Herbert and his boyfriend were the producers, and Strayhorn and I did the music and the costumes. I think the only key participants who were straight were Alfred Leslie [the set designer] and the leads, who were both black." (Gladys Bruce, a newcomer, and Elwood Smith, a Juilliard-trained actor-singer, were the principals in the six-character cast.) Subtitled *An Erotic Lace-Paper Valentine in Four Scenes,* Lorca's lyric allegory tells of a bittersweet romance rendered impossible by social convention.

Like all the Artists Theatre productions that year, *Don Perlimplín* was produced at the cozy Amato Opera Theatre on Bleecker Street. "We didn't charge Herbert or anybody else very much money," recalled Sally Amato, co-owner of the theater with her husband, Anthony. To stimulate attendance for all the Artists Theatre productions, only season tickets were offered; for $7.50, one could see the entire season's program of six plays. Though *Don Perlimplín* opened on election night—the New York mayoral race went to Robert F. Wagner, Jr., "young scion of the New Deal"—the four hundred or so seats of the Amato were filled that evening and for the two following weeknight performances. "That one was one of the best of the Artists Theatre productions, as I recall," said Oshei. "I thought it was delightful, and it had a finished and polished look to it." Oshei's costumes, standard nineteenth-century period outfits rented from a theatrical supply shop, added a bit less flair than did the sets by Alfred Leslie, the fiery young abstract expressionist who once boasted, "Art begins with me." In place of realistic sets, Leslie positioned five oversized canvases (ten feet wide and eighteen feet high) at points on the stage; on each, he had painted a stylized version of a work by another painter, by Velázquez, for instance, and by the American landscape artist Albert Pinkham Ryder. "I envisioned each space sort of with an historical motif going back into some segment of some artist or some element of the Western world, whatever. I was thinking of all the Western artists of the past and using elements of their work in order to create the ambience of a particular space," said Leslie.

Strayhorn composed four main pieces for the fifty-minute production, some parts set to passages of Lorca's text. (Only two of the Strayhorn compositions, "Wounded Love" and "Sprite Music," were titled on the manuscript.) Musically, Strayhorn's *Don Perlimplín* ranks with the richest of his jazz work, an original achievement of dizzying beauty and sophistication. As performed by Strayhorn himself on piano, the instrumental music woven through the play served the dual purposes of inspiration and expression, according to Alfred Leslie: "It was like he knew exactly what the actors needed to bring out the character and the scene."

Theater became the fulcrum of Strayhorn's disengagement from Ellington and emergence on his own. Just as the frustrations of Strayhorn's stage experiences with Ellington contributed to his urge for independence, the small triumphs of his first solo dramatic efforts stimulated him to pursue the theater. He immersed himself in Broadway productions of the 1953–54 season, catching *The Trip to Bountiful, Kismet,* and two plays rich in gay subtext that Strayhorn took friends to see repeatedly: Robert Anderson's melodramatic *Tea and Sympathy* and *In the Summerhouse* by Jane Auer Bowles (wife of composer-writer Paul Bowles, an intimate of Strayhorn's friend Oliver Smith). *In the Summerhouse* gave Strayhorn a new favorite phrase of ironic repartee: "Describe it to me, darling." A few months after *Don Perlimplín,* in early summer 1954, Strayhorn set his creative sights on Broadway. For a theme, he applied his adventurism to one of his own passions again, and set out to write a musical incorporating elements of jazz. For a collaborator, he engaged his Juilliard-trained friend Luther Henderson. "We both had the theater bug and a bit of experience, so we decided to sit down and write a Broadway show," recalled Henderson. "At that time, Broadway was pretty square, and we thought we were pretty cool. This was the time of Dizzy Gillespie——'Oo-Bop-She-Bam' and all that stuff— so we thought we would write, I guess you'd say, a bebop musical. Not bebop music necessarily, but with that feeling, that coolness, that hipness. One of the things we talked about was looking at the world through rose-colored glasses. We fancied ourselves as pretty savvy about things. So we decided that that would be our theme. What's reality? What's perception? What's the difference? And what does love mean with this going on? And we called the thing *Rose-Colored Glasses.*"

Working a few nights a week for about a month at Strayhorn's apartment, Henderson and Strayhorn developed ideas for the show's principal scenes, along with sample sections of dialogue; Henderson's wife, Steffi, would type (and edit) the partners' creations, drawing from her husband's notes. To celebrate a good day's work one night, Strayhorn and Henderson went out to hear Ram Ramirez, the pianist and co-composer of the Billie Holiday signature song, "Lover Man," who was playing a club date in Greenwich Village. Feeling particularly cool, they each ordered the faddish drink at the time, a zombie (two ounces dark rum, two ounces light rum, one ounce 151-proof rum, one ounce Triple Sec, one teaspoon Pernod, one ounce lime juice, one ounce orange juice, one ounce papaya juice, one teaspoon grenadine, mixed over cracked ice and sprinkled with sugar). "That was *the* ultra-cool thing of the day," said Henderson; indeed, urban folklore had it that New York City law prohibited the sale of more than one zombie per customer. Strayhorn and Henderson broke the law five times. "We were feeling pretty fantastic," said Henderson. "One of us said to Ram, 'Hey, Ram, man, how about letting us do a number?' And he said, 'Sure.' You know, we were Billy Strayhorn and Luther Henderson—this should be interesting. So we sat down at the piano bench, and we went at it. We were *inspired.*

We were way out—avant-garde—countermelodies, relative keys, two different tempos at the same time. It was genius, or so we thought. We finished the number with great flourish, and we stood up, and everybody in the place was just staring at us. We walked out of the place, and the next morning, Ram called me, and he said, 'Man, don't you ever do that to me again! You guys almost got my ass fired. What the fuck did you think you were playing?' So Strayhorn and I gave up zombies and went back to gin."

Rose-Colored Glasses was a surreal romp around the Land of Ool-Ya-Coo, peopled by whimsical eccentrics such as Brother Big Eyes, a grinder of lenses for eyeglasses, and the object of his blind affection, Honey Ooh La La. "It wasn't *Finian's Rainbow*, but it was that kind of thing," explained Henderson. "Brother Big Eyes traveled around the Land of Ool-Ya-Coo grinding lenses for people, and he came on these crazy characters like Papa Doo Dah and Johnny No Love. It wasn't realistic at all. It was supposed to be like a dream. Very cryptic, very weird." The main set, as imagined by Strayhorn, was a colossal pair of horn-rimmed glasses dominating the stage, a perhaps unintended evocation of his own face. Innovatively, some of the dialogue was to be recitative; bringing a bit of jazz into the musical theater, Henderson and Strayhorn wanted some instrumental accompaniment to be improvised each night. Such was the intent of the following first-act passage written by Strayhorn, in which Brother Big Eyes describes himself:

> *Once upon a time there was a man named Brother Big Eyes,*
> *At least that's what everybody called him.*
> *He was a queer-looking duck:*
> > *Kinda funny*
> > *Kinda sad*
> > *Kinda quiet*
> > *Kinda . . . well, kinda* MA-A-AD!
>
> *Well, Brother Big Eyes had a little trailer*
> *Hitched to the back of his bicycle*
> *And from this trailer he conducted his business,*
> *Quite a business it was, for, you see,*
> *Brother Big Eyes made magic glasses.*

> He ground them, tinted them
> And polished them himself.
> You could get them ready-made,
> Right off the rack,
> Or tailor-fitted
> To suit your own individual psyche.

A few of the show's songs came from the collaborators' respective trunks: they finagled ways to wriggle in Henderson's pert "Hey, Cherie" (later recorded by the Ellington Orchestra), as well as Strayhorn's "Let Nature Take Its Course" from *Fantastic Rhythm* and "Lush Life," which they chose, in a break from Broadway convention, as a quiet and bittersweet finale to the show. Among the new numbers, Henderson wrote five on his own: "It All Depends on Your Point of View," "Hip Hoe Down," "Hey, Cherie," "Well, Well," and "You, You, You." One song was a Henderson-Strayhorn collaboration—"Got No Time" (music by Henderson, lyrics by Henderson and Strayhorn)—and Strayhorn wrote both words and music for nine: "Brother Big Eyes," "Ool-Ya-Coo," "Cottage on the Hill," "If I Can't Have You," "Beauty and Talent," "Looking for a Male," "Still in Love with You," "Love Has Passed Me By, Again," and "Oo, You Make Me Tingle." The most intricate and mature of these was surely "Love Has Passed Me By, Again," a grim lament over unrequited love in the mode of "Something to Live For." Several, such as the bouncy romantic duet "Still in Love with You" and the sexy "Oo, You Make Me Tingle," were solid, hummable show tunes. (The remaining songs are incomplete or lost.) Sung by Brother Big Eyes, "Ool-Ya-Coo" distills the central notion of *Rose-Colored Glasses* in one verse:

> Nearly everyone has a rosy view
> But every now and then
> It seems that something happens
> Which even I can't understand
> And the perspective of such nice people as these
> Seems to go askew.

Turning to his closest contact in the New York theater world, Strayhorn asked Herbert Machiz for an informal critique of the outline, the sample scenes, and the songs he and Henderson had written for *Rose-Colored Glasses*, then turned to the matter of whether he could make some money without Ellington. Strayhorn's basic expenses were still being covered by the Ellington organization, since reissues of his old compositions in the new LP format were pulling in royalties; in addition, Strayhorn was still accommodating Ellington with new arrangements. "He wasn't on the scene a lot like he was before," recalled Jimmy Hamilton, the Ellington Orchestra clarinetist. "It was a situation where Duke still called him if he needed him, and Billy, he was there if he was needed. But their heads was somewhere else." Indeed, Ellington was increasingly employing other arrangers (drummer Louie Bellson and the West Coast bandleader Gerald Wilson contributed arrangements), and he discussed a full-time slot with at least one musician, a little-known black orchestral composer named Frank Fields. "Duke offered him Strayhorn's job," said Fields's friend Sam Shaw, who saw Ellington and Fields at Luckey Roberts's place the night Fields declined the bid. "Ellington really laid on the charm," said Shaw. "He told Fields how brilliant he was and what an honor it would be to work with him. He said he could really use someone with Fields's abilities because Billy was doing other things now. Now, Fields respected both Ellington and Strayhorn, but he turned Ellington down. He just didn't know enough about jazz." With his involvement with Ellington scaled back, Strayhorn found the Ellington money diminishing. "That was a time when he really didn't have very much," recalled his friend Bill Patterson. "He was taking the subway again when he had to go downtown, which says something about him," as one who used to call a limo for the kick of the ride.

Strayhorn earned a bit for some recording-session work over the course of 1955, though he certainly didn't do the work for the money: he accompanied Lena Horne on piano for fourteen recordings made under Lennie Hayton's supervision for RCA. As was the convention for popular vocal LPs at the time, none of the musicians was credited on the records, but recording-session ledgers identify Strayhorn as the pianist on Horne's renditions of "You Go to My Head" (one of Strayhorn's favorite songs, according to both Horne and Aaron Bridgers; it celebrates drunken delirium as a metaphor for love), "Love Me or Leave Me," "It's All Right with Me," "Fun to Be Fooled" and ten other recordings made from March through July 1955. "She was real comfortable with Strayhorn at the piano. She was nervous and shy, and she wouldn't do a take without Strayhorn, even though her own husband was the leader and a hell of a pianist," remembered Jimmy Maxwell, who played trumpet on seven of these dates. Elegantly restrained, Strayhorn cushioned Horne's eggshell voice with gentle support. "He was a great accompanist for me because he understood me and loved me," said Horne. "But he was also musically great for me; he had a trick of hearing the breath. When you sing, you need air, and he made a soft little bed right there to support the structure, so while you're taking your breath, nobody knows. It takes an awful lot of sensitivity." That summer, Strayhorn took to the road with Horne and served as her pianist for several months of engagements, including three weeks at Chicago's Chez Paree. (In its review, the *Chicago Defender* noted Horne's performance of Strayhorn's "Oo, You Make Me Tingle," composed for *Rose-Colored Glasses*.) The two old friends romped like reunited schoolmates. During the days, they'd phone up acquaintances for lunch, usually shop some, or lie about Horne's hotel room reading magazines. Once, in the spirit of café-society scholarship, they decided to learn mixology and bought a *Mr. Boston Official Bartender's Guide* and every variety of liquor, cordial, and mixer required for each major drink in the book, which they made in alphabetical order: the Abbey cocktail, the absinthe cocktail, the Acapulco, and on through several dozen concoctions mixed—and tested—over three days. Horne and Strayhorn got very sick.

"A lot of time that year, when Billy was the pianist in the trio, it was like he had a direct psychic link to Lena," said Chico Hamilton, the drummer, who rounded out the group with bassist George Duvivier. "When she was singing, he translated what she was feeling on the piano and sent back to her in his music at the same time. It went both ways." Taking that bilateral musicality deeper still, Strayhorn composed a pair of new tunes intimately tailored to Horne's personality and vocal approach: a graceful love song titled "You're the One" and a bitingly cynical swipe at the caprice of romance called "Maybe":

Love is a shoestring.
Any way you tie it, it may come undone.
Life is a new thing.
Every day something lost, something won.

Maybe I'll see him again,
Maybe the moon will be there big and bright again,
Maybe . . .
Then again, maybe not.

Strayhorn had both songs, as well as "Oo, You Make Me Tingle," published by Hayton-Horne Music, Inc., rather than by Ellington's Tempo Music. (The other new music from *Rose-Colored Glasses* was not published.) "I was lying on the couch reading while Billy was writing 'Maybe,' " said Bill Patterson. "He said, 'I'm working on a new song for Lena—what do you think?' And he played me some of it and sang it for me. And to be perfectly honest, I thought it was awful. There just wasn't very much there. It wasn't much of anything. I said something like, 'Oh, what do I know?' or something and kept reading until Lena came in a little while later. She sat down with him on the piano stool and they went over it, and then she stood up and she sang the song, and I couldn't believe it. It sounded like a completely different song. He had written this thing perfectly for her and her attitude—her voice, the way she sang a line. There wasn't a trace of Billy Strayhorn in that song. There was nothing in it except pure Lena Horne. I was amazed."

With his new work apart from Ellington, especially *Rose-Colored Glasses* and his custom songs for Lena Horne, Strayhorn indulged his love for writing lyrics as well as music, a passion that had lain more or less dormant since his early career in Pittsburgh. His duties as a composer and orchestrator for Ellington's projects allowed little time for coming up with words too. Despite the enthusiasm for Strayhorn's lyrics that Ellington had expressed when they first met, Strayhorn proceeded to generate relatively few for the Ellington Orchestra and its offshoots: "A Flower Is a Lovesome Thing," "Grievin'," "I Don't Mind," "I'm Checkin' Out, Goom Bye," "Love Like This Can't Last," and "Take the 'A' Train." Lyricists were called on to set a few other Strayhorn compositions to words: "Blossom" (lyrics by Johnny Mercer), "Day Dream" (John Latouche), and "Just A-Sittin' and A-Rockin' " (Lee Gaines). (Mercer Ellington, delving into artist management briefly in the early 1950s, asked a young singer-pianist protégé from Washington, Dini Clarke; to set words to two Strayhorn compositions, "After All" and "Johnny Come Lately," but they were never published, evidently having been rejected by Strayhorn. As Clarke recalled, "They introduced me to Billy, and he wasn't very happy about my writing words for his songs. He wasn't very nice to me.") "Billy couldn't do everything and didn't choose to, so various lyric writers were brought in sometimes," said Ruth Ellington Boatwright, who, as the president of Tempo Music, contracted most of the lyricists involved in Strayhorn's songs. "Billy assisted Edward where his wonderful talents were most helpful to Edward."

When Strayhorn applied himself to both words and music, as he was doing on his own now, the work had an eager charm and intelligence. Like Ira Gershwin, principal lyricist for Strayhorn's boyhood idol George Gershwin, Strayhorn valued cleverness, especially in lighter up-tempo numbers such as "Still in Love with You":

> *I bought some new fur*
> *Went on a spree*
> *Looked into the future*
> *Yes, and what did I see?*

At times, however, he could slip into self-consciousness or artificiality, as in the bridge of the same song:

> *I thought the bright city lights*
> *Would blot out your eyes*
> *Or at least dim them a bit . . .*

In more serious-minded ballads such as "Love Has Passed Me By, Again," Strayhorn tended to temper his wordplay:

> *Love has passed me by again*
> *Don't ask me why*
> *I simply cannot tell you*

> *How love could pass me by again*
> *And cast me in the role of Romeo at large.*

Nevertheless, he succumbs to pretense:

> *I have traveled far and wide*
> *Cupid's cavalry to ride*
> *But there's only gravel deep inside*
> *Down inside my heart.*

Among professional lyricists, Strayhorn was widely seen as a gifted original whose skills were neglected. "Strayhorn had a beautiful way with words," said Mitchell Parrish, who wrote the lyrics to Ellington's "Sophisticated Lady." "Strayhorn loved language. He didn't write very much, though, did he? If he did more, I think he could have been a major lyricist." Humility—or full-blown insecurity as a lyricist—might have kept Strayhorn from writing more words, according to the jazz singer and lyricist Jon Hendricks. "I was working at Basin Street East [in New York] with Duke and Art Blakey, and while Blakey was on, I was back in the dressing room with Duke, and Strays was there," recalled Hendricks. "And he said to me, he said, 'You know, Jonny, I would like for you to come up and listen to some of my tunes and write some words to them.' And I said, 'Didn't you write the lyrics to "Lush Life"? You don't need a lyricist!' He didn't realize how good he was—that was how humble he was. I'll tell you how good he was. When he applied himself, he was as close to perfect as you'll find. And I'll tell you why. Several reasons. He wrote everything—the theme of the words, the melody, and the actual language—as a complete whole. He was a perfectionist. And he was honest. His words were real. Oh, yeah—and he was a genius. That comes in handy." Sammy Cahn, though unfamiliar with much of Strayhorn's work, always held the words to "Lush Life" in esteem. "Frank [Sinatra] and I love that song," he said. "Those words, the maturity. Sophistication. You really had to have *lived* a life to write that. Frank adored that." On learning that Strayhorn wrote "Lush Life" as a young man in Pittsburgh in the 1930s, Cahn added, "Then I amend my words, which I rarely do, by the way. He wasn't only talented. He had some balls."

Working as a musician outside of Ellington's projects, Strayhorn participated in a couple of recording sessions for artists other than Lena Horne during this period, but for friends, resisting the temptation to beef up his income with studio work. "Billy could have done a million sessions," said Jimmy Maxwell. "He was fast. He was good. Half the studio piano players I worked with weren't that good. Why didn't he? Billy wasn't what you'd say a professional. He was an artistic man." In two sessions a year apart, Strayhorn recorded with Ellington's former tenor saxophonist Ben Webster and the singer Carmen McRae, an Ellingtonian once removed, having sung with one of Mercer Ellington's bands. The Webster date, for Norman's Granz's Verve label, on May 28, 1954, was another of Granz's efforts to expand jazz's popularity by backing illustrious soloists with string orchestras. Earlier, Granz had featured Charlie Parker in a string setting to mixed critical reaction but great success in the marketplace. Granz commissioned one of his favorite arrangers, Ralph Burns, to handle the orchestrations for Webster; it was a comfortable match, since Webster used to drink with Burns on 52nd Street. Of course, Webster drank with everyone on 52nd Street, including Strayhorn, whom Granz brought in, to the delight of both Webster and Burns, as the arranger for four songs: the Gershwins' "Love Is Here to Stay"; "It Happens to Be Me," a dulcet ballad by the pop songwriters Arthur Kent and Sammy Gallop; the Ellington ballad "All Too Soon"; and Strayhorn's own "Chelsea Bridge." "I knew Billy wanted to write for strings, and he could do it, unlike most straight jazz guys," said Granz. "Since he never got the chance to write for strings with Duke, he jumped at it." Marking Strayhorn's debut as an arranger for full string orchestra, the three songs for Webster sounded much like his best mood pieces for the Ellington Orchestra, naturally flowing, with currents of melodic and harmonic movement. The arrangements seem to wash all around Webster rather than float underneath or fill up the background. Strayhorn also played piano for all three selections, complementing Webster's hefty tone with Tatum-influenced delicacy. "I don't know why he didn't arrange the whole album," said Ralph Burns. "I got the feeling he did all he wanted to do."

For Carmen McRae on June 14, 1955, Strayhorn sat in on one number, his "Something to Live For," replacing the session's pianist,

Dick Katz. Recorded at the Pythian Temple, a big catering hall on Manhattan's Upper West Side that became a hot recording location because of its enviable acoustics, the "Something to Live For" session had been arranged by McRae and Strayhorn at a party the previous weekend. "I wanted him to play for me, and I asked him," said McRae. "I didn't think he would show up. I thought he was drunk. He *was* drunk. I thought he was just being nice, nice and drunk. I never really expected him to come. The day came, and I looked out from the stage they had there where you recorded, and Swee' Pea walked through the door and sat down in the auditorium area they had. We finished one song, and I said, 'You want to play, Swee' Pea?' He said, 'Sure!' And we cut it. No sheet music. We just cut it." The bassist on the date, Wendell Marshall, relished playing with Strayhorn, whom he knew well from his stint as Ellington's bassist. (Marshall had left the orchestra after seven years in January of that year, preferring New York studio work to the road.) "It was the easiest thing in the world playing with Strayhorn," said Marshall. "He carried you along."

Strayhorn turned forty on November 29, 1955, and he seemed to be at a halfway point. Behind him, there had been Homewood, Ellington, and Aaron Bridgers. In the present, there was Lena Horne, the Copasetics, the theater, and the subway, and not only the A train. Before him . . . it seemed that Luther Henderson had an idea. Since both he and Strayhorn had so much in common, why not go into business together? "He was extricating himself from Ellington, and I was working independently at the time," explained Henderson. "Between the two of us, we had the know-how and the connections to make it. We could develop new artists, put together nightclub acts, write material, make records. How could we lose?" After a day of reflection, Strayhorn said he agreed, and with a handshake the two new partners mapped out some plans. The first order of business: tell Ellington.

7

ALL

ROADS

LEAD BACK

TO YOU

It no longer meant everything to have that swing. As former jitterbuggers settled into Levittowns, demand for the dance-floor instrumental music of the big bands gave way to a new market for the lounging sounds of crooners like Doris Day and Vic Damone. One swing-era showplace with wall-to-wall dancers, the Oceanliner nightclub on New Jersey's Route 22, a few miles outside of Manhattan, became a carpet showroom. Jazz bandleaders scrambled through the early 1950s: Basie broke up his big band and started touring with a septet; Woody Herman, suffering constant personnel changes in his orchestra, put together a series of small groups; Artie Shaw formed a quintet, the Gramercy Five, then just gave up and retired to Spain; Harry James went into semiretirement; Andy Kirk went into real estate. Ellington fared comparatively well, though not without his own problems. In January 1951, Norman Granz lured away the restless Johnny Hodges, who took along trombonist Lawrence Brown and drummer Sonny Greer (the latter had been with Ellington since his first band in Washington in the 1920s), to record and tour for Granz's Clef label. "I didn't have to persuade Johnny. All he wanted was the financial and organizational support to permit him to pull the plug with Duke," said Granz. "Although Duke didn't call me directly, he let it be known that he thought I was making a terrible mistake—Johnny wasn't good enough to make it under his own name. This came from Duke, who had been producing Johnny as a small-band solo act for many years." As Hodges's wife recalled, "Johnny knew Duke was hurt. That wasn't what he wanted. He wanted something good for himself. He didn't want something bad for Duke." (As turnabout that March, Ellington gained drummer Louie Bellson, alto saxophonist Willie Smith, and his own former valve trombonist Juan Tizol when the three of them left the Harry James organization.) The singer Al Hibbler quit at the end of that year in a squabble over whether he could freelance; he had accepted a booking on his own at the High Hat Club in Boston. "Man, [Ellington] was mad at me," said Hibbler. " 'How dare you sing without me? Who do you think you are, Billy Eckstine? Frank Sinatra?' I said, 'I don't think I'm none of those guys. But I don't belong to you. You don't own me, you baggy-eyed cocksucker. I quit.' "

Ellington fell prey to criticism: "THINGS AIN'T WHAT THEY OUGHT TO BE WITH ELLINGTON'S BAND" read the headline of *Down Beat*'s contorted review of a one-night stand at the Civic Auditorium in Portland, Oregon. Yet Ellington was still producing work of a high musical order, some of it with participation by Strayhorn. In December 1951, Ellington recorded one of his most sharply drawn long-form compositions, "A Tone Parallel to Harlem," a programmatic fourteen-minute tour of black Manhattan; Strayhorn, uncredited, contributed about thirty seconds of music to end the piece. More notably, Strayhorn helped fashion extended new arrangements (again unacknowledged) of Ellington compositions ("Mood Indigo," "Sophisticated Lady," "The Tattooed Bride," and "Solitude") to be recorded for an LP titled *Masterpieces by Ellington;* the pieces range from eight to fifteen minutes in length, and each is a distanced reconsideration of an Ellington piece, expanded with mercurial shifts in tempo and timbre. Most constructively, Strayhorn fleshed out an Ellington riff sketch with harmony and lyrics—an ode to Strayhorn's mother, spun around Strayhorn's pet name for her—and ended up with "Satin Doll." Though Johnny Mercer was brought in to replace Strayhorn's oedipal lyrics with ones evoking more commercial male-female love, "Satin Doll" was recorded as an instrumental and became a modest hit (and the last single-record success of Ellington's career), peaking at number 27 in three weeks on the *Billboard* chart. (Strayhorn's original lyrics to "Satin Doll" are not known to have survived.)

The timing was good: unlike most other swing bandleaders, Ellington was able to support his orchestra with his earnings as a composer. "That was the old man's secret," said Mercer Ellington. "That orchestra was his instrument; more than that, it was his whole life. Nobody else was able to keep their band together year after year, through all the changes in the music scene. But nobody had that catalog of compositions that he had. With all those royalties coming in, he was able to meet his payroll, which was substantial, because a lot of those cats had been in the band for a long time. Harry Carney—that was the only job he ever had in his life. And they all made good bread. They were top men. Without those royalties, the old man would have been operating at a loss. He would have gone under, just like the rest of them." Surviving a sea change in musical tastes, Ellington accepted a kooky mix of bookings in the early 1950s: corny battle-of-the-bands dates with Stan Kenton at the acoustically disastrous Rollerdome in Revere Beach, Massachusetts; an extended engagement at the Aquacade on the World's Fair site in Flushing Meadows, New York, where the Ellington Orchestra shared the bill with ice skaters, a ballroom-dancing competition, and water-fountain tricks. Had it not been for his publishing holdings—all those songs by Ellington, Ellington-Strayhorn, Strayhorn, Mercer Ellington, and others in the Ellington roost—the bandleader might not have held on through the decade.

Much as he rejected closure, Ellington avoided confrontation: he didn't resist when Strayhorn broke the news of his decision to enter into a partnership with Luther Henderson. "Strayhorn and I had it all figured out," recalled Henderson. "We figured we could bring in $300,000, $400,000, maybe $500,000 or so a year. That was nice money. But I think a great deal of it was, for Strayhorn, he wanted to do something for himself. Strayhorn went and told

Ellington, and he called me. He said, 'I talked to Edward. Everything's fine.' The next day, Ellington called me. He said, 'Luther, Strays was telling me all about your plan. It sounds great. It's brilliant. Marvelous. But you know, there's one thing I think I should tell you. You know, I've worked with Strayhorn for a long time. I know what he can do. And I have to tell you, you don't need Strayhorn, not with your talent. He can't do what you can do. He just puts notes down on the music paper. When the music paper sees *you* coming, it comes alive! It leaps up in joy! When you write a piece of music, the music paper feels privileged. It's the happiest day of the music paper's life.'

"What a snow job!" said Henderson. "It sounds ridiculous when I hear myself repeat it. The funny thing is, when Ellington says it, you believe it. Don't ask me why. You fall for it." At once puffed up and insecure about his own judgment of Strayhorn's abilities, Henderson was relieved to find his prospective partner equally hesitant to proceed with their agreement. "I don't know what Ellington said to him," added Henderson, who didn't tell Strayhorn about Ellington's call. "I have to assume it was the same kind of thing— Strayhorn didn't need *me. I* wasn't as good as him. In any case, we just let the whole thing slide. We didn't go through with it." Their momentum lost, Henderson and Strayhorn never picked up *Rose-Colored Glasses* again either, despite an encouraging critique in a memo from Herbert Machiz, who said the work could succeed with its characters humanized. "We left all that undone," said Henderson. "It was the biggest mistake of my life. I should have never let him go."

Strayhorn didn't go right back to Ellington, however. To realign his life his favorite way, lushly, Strayhorn gravitated to Europe and Aaron Bridgers. In Paris he found an environment that seemed uniquely hospitable to blacks, gays, and artists; indeed, a whole colony of black musicians, painters, and writers had emerged on the postwar Left Bank—the place of his Pittsburgh dreams transformed into a European branch of the Neal Salon. The writers James Baldwin and Chester Himes, the painter Herb Gentry, the jazz musicians Kenny Clarke and Art Simmons were part of a growing group of blacks who, seeking acceptance and opportunity outside the homogeneity of Eisenhower-era America, looked to notoriously liberal

France. "A number of us stayed there after the war because we felt like we found a place where there was less racism, and we were treated like professionals and artists," said Simmons, a veteran, along with Clarke and John Lewis, of the seventeenth Special Services band. Roundish and funny, a nice guy from the States, Simmons became de facto den father of America's jazz expatriates, French division. He liked his whiskey and, nonetheless, played disciplined piano in the style of Hank Jones. "Some of what we thought when we first came to Paris was probably naive," said Simmons. "Pretty soon, I noticed some of the French people talking in a terrible way about 'the Arabs' and 'the Jews,' and I started wondering what they said about me when I wasn't around. And there was something kind of superior in the way they embraced American blacks, a 'noble savage' attitude or something. But it was better than the situation in the States in a lot of ways. And I think it was better for other guys who were black like me but gay on top of it." Bridgers certainly found comfort in the French brand of detached tolerance. "Nobody cared who you were or what you were," he said. "There was no judgment. That's one of the reasons Billy and I loved it here [in Paris].

"From the moment he came to Paris, it was like nothing had changed and we had just been together the day before," said Bridgers. "We did everything together. Everything was the same again. It was good for us; things were better when we were together." As members of a community of their own within Parisian culture—the French called them *Am-Am*—black Americans had established social centers, cafés like Chez Honey, a small box on rue Jules Chaplain in Montparnasse operated by Herb Gentry (and named for his wife), where expatriates met one another as well as visitors from the States. Strayhorn stopped by in passing—a courtesy call—but relished the more glamorous elements of the city: he had come for old Paris in all its extravagant glory, not for the tempered familiarity of an American colony. Bridgers in tow, Strayhorn spent the days shopping. He liked to walk around Claridge's, a luxurious hotel with pricey French specialty shops in the lobby (Bridgers said, "He thought it was a palace"), and he ordered monogrammed leather luggage—there would be no confusing his bags on the Ellington band bus. At one shoe store, he picked out several pairs of loafers.

" 'A pair of these, a pair of those. Have you got them in black?' " as Bridgers recalled. A favorite stop was Fauchon, the famous boutique for delicacies and spirits; Strayhorn bought a case of exotic liquors in colorful elongated bottles and had the order shipped home. For dinner, the two of them—some nights with a Parisian friend of Bridgers's like the industrialist Jean Berdin or the pianist Raymond Fol—favored Le Doyen; Strayhorn experimented but had to have his smoked salmon and foie gras.

On Bridgers's nights off, he and Strayhorn roved the jazz clubs: Bricktop's, beloved by the Parisian elite; the Club Saint-Germain, favored by the university set; the Olympia, a musicians' hangout; and two popular nightspots, the Ringside and the Living Room. "Americans like Billy and Aaron believed the Parisian nightclubs were freer than the American nightclubs," said the French jazz writer Maurice Cullaz, who accompanied Strayhorn and Bridgers in some of their club hopping. "They believed there was reason to be comfortable here. They had a good time. They didn't have to worry about what people thought. Naturally, no one really knows what Parisians are thinking, including we Parisians." Most evenings, Strayhorn and Bridgers relived their treasured Cafe Society days at the Mars Club, where Bridgers was the house pianist. It was a little room in the eighth arrondissement, off the Champs-Elysées: Annie Ross, a naturalistic jazz vocalist and no belter, didn't need a microphone, and instrumental trios were booked rarely, since there was no place for a drum kit. The walls were painted with loose-line sketches of planets and stars asserting the rocket-age Mars theme. Ben Benjamin, a balloon-shaped gay American, ran the place for the Parisian woman whom he had married and with whom, accordingly, French law permitted him to share ownership of the business. In the estimate of one of the Mars Club's managers, the American singer Nancy Holloway, the clientele was nearly half gay. Featured performers during this period were virtually all Americans, including Annie Ross, the singer-pianists Blossom Dearie and Bobby Short, and the pianists Peter Matz and Richard Allen. A gathering place for song aficionados, the Mars Club was what the singers would call a verse club: instead of starting with the chorus, you could do the whole composition, including the opening verse. "A majority of the audience was like dear Aaron and Billy, brilliant listeners," said

Dearie. Between sets, Aaron Bridgers played solo cocktail piano. "Poor Aaron," said Cullaz. "When he sat down, the people started talking, like a record was playing." Before closing, whenever he was there, Strayhorn yielded to inexorable demand and took a turn at the piano for a murmuring, self-referential rendition of that song about a week somewhere romantic. "It was an internationally known gay hangout," said Peter Matz, a young music student at the Ecole Normale when he played the Mars Club. "They'd all come there to check in and hear the latest news. Strayhorn was a star there because everybody knew all about him through Aaron. At the Mars Club, man, Strayhorn was *it*. He was the main man." Bobby Short, too, was impressed: "When he came into the room, he had an aura. He looked very, very, very much like he should have been in white robes or something."

Strayhorn returned to New York and the world of Duke Ellington in the second week of 1956. Throwing his own homecoming party after more than a month overseas, he took Francis Goldberg and a few other friends to Cafe Society Uptown, bought a few rounds in salute to Bridgers, and charmed the group with droll descriptions of the Mars Club and its Continental clientele. "He was like Noel Coward, a miniature, black Noel Coward," recalled one of the group that night, a gay black musician familiar with the Paris scene. "Now, I knew all about Paris—I *played* at the Mars Club. And *I* was hanging on his every word. Billy loved that place so much. The way he described Paris, it was all new to me." Meanwhile, Cafe Society had also changed: as declining demand for big-band music had lowered the surviving orchestras' asking prices, Barney Josephson, the owner, was able to afford the Duke Ellington Orchestra. Strayhorn's musician friend recalled, "Billy saw a bill on the wall: 'Coming Soon: Duke Ellington and His Orchestra!' And he said, 'Well, I'll *have* to come to see Duke Ellington—and hear all those Billy Strayhorn songs.' He looked around the tiny little club, and he puffed on a cigarette, and he said, 'If there's room for them.' "

As it turned out, Ellington was inclined to make room for Billy Strayhorn, more so, in fact, than he had been at any time since the ASCAP ban. When the Duke Ellington Orchestra opened at Cafe Society on January 12, 1956, Strayhorn was there, sharing a table with his musician friend. He greeted seemingly every one of the more than three hundred customers shoehorned into the cabaret and drank several Billy's Martinis. "Halfway into the show," said his friend, a pianist well known at Cafe Society, "he said to me, quietly, 'I talked to Edward. He would like me to be more *engaged* again. He asked *me* what sort of project *I* would like to do.' So I said to Billy, 'Well? What are you going to do?' He lifted up his martini, and he looked straight ahead. He didn't look at me. And he said, 'Take one sip at a time. One sip at a time.' " Before the evening's end, Strayhorn had the first metaphoric taste of his new relationship with Ellington. The bandleader, who was considering signing with Columbia Records, introduced him and his guest to Irving Townsend, a Columbia producer who was a clarinetist and a longtime Ellington buff. "We exchanged the usual pleasantries," recalled Strayhorn's friend, "and Duke said, 'Mr. Townsend, you're so fortunate to have come tonight because you have the pleasure of meeting the wonderful man I told you so much about, Mr. Strayhorn. Mr. Strayhorn has many wonderful, wonderful ideas for recordings, and if Mr. Strayhorn has an idea, it must be truly wonderful. Why don't you two get acquainted so we can get started right away with all of Mr. Strayhorn's ideas?' " Strayhorn shot his friend a get-this-guy look and proceeded to follow Ellington's lead.

Townsend and Strayhorn, chatting while Ellington shook hands and nodded to his fans, got as far as one of Townsend's own ideas: a vocal album pairing the Ellington Orchestra with the pop singer Rosemary Clooney, a hot commodity for the wave of hits she had given Columbia under easy-listening mastermind Mitch Miller, including "Mambo Italiano," "Botch-a-Me," and "Come On-a My House." The task had a taint of the old novelty "Jumpin' Jive" and Strayhorn's earliest work in Ellington's vocal wing. Nonetheless, Strayhorn apparently saw promise in the project—he said he thought Clooney was underrated, his friend recalled—and before the two of them left Cafe Society, Strayhorn, Townsend, and Ellington had agreed on a basic approach to the album: whatever Clooney and Strayhorn wanted to do.

Strayhorn flew to Los Angeles and took a taxi to Clooney's home in Beverly Hills, a Spanish-style split-level she shared with her husband, the actor José Ferrer, and their three children; she was very pregnant with a fourth child and under doctor's orders not to fly.

Working under deadline to begin recording in less than ten days and unfamiliar with Clooney's style (her range, best keys, and preferred tempos), Strayhorn set priorities: "He made me breakfast in bed," said Clooney. The twenty-seven-year-old singer was suffering nearly constant nausea, and Ferrer was in England directing and acting in a film, *The Cockleshell Heroes.* Sleeping in one of the children's rooms, Strayhorn stayed with Clooney for more than a week to act as nurse and play Ellington Orchestra records, occasionally at the same time. "We didn't know each other at all before that, and we became incredibly close immediately," said Clooney. "I was having a very difficult pregnancy. I was really suffering, and he got me through it. I'd say, 'Oh, God, I'm going to throw up again,' and he would say, 'Okay, now. It's okay,' and he would take care of me. He said, 'Don't get up, honey,' and he'd make me crackers and milk. I felt a bit better one day, and he baked me an apple pie. He cared about that baby. He cared about the fact that I couldn't afford to get tired, and he watched out for me. I would just stay in my bedroom, and he would come upstairs, and we'd sit on the bed and talk about things. Most of the time, we didn't even talk much about music. When we did work on the music, it was like I was working with my best friend. I wanted to do my best for him, and I would do anything he wanted."

Strayhorn and Clooney chose their numbers (a mix of Ellington favorites, including "Sophisticated Lady" and "It Don't Mean a Thing," and lesser-known Strayhorn songs such as "Grievin'" and "I'm Checkin' Out, Goom Bye") and ironed out the arrangements (to accommodate Clooney's range, he slipped a key change into the bridge of "Sophisticated Lady"). Songs and singer were ready for the first recording session, scheduled for January 23. It wasn't practical, however, for the Ellington Orchestra to perform on the end of Clooney's bed. Irving Townsend came up with a resourceful solution: the Ellington Orchestra would record the instrumental music in New York, and Clooney would overdub her vocals in a studio near her home, under Strayhorn's supervision. The trumpeter Clark Terry recalled the East Coast dates, which Strayhorn flew back for, as tense: "Nobody had ever worked that way before. When we played for a singer, we were used to hearing the singer sing and playing around it. I said to Strayhorn, 'Hey, Strays, why don't you sing the songs, and they can erase your voice? Wouldn't that be better, if we could hear your voice?' He looked at me deadpan, and he said, 'No, I believe silence would be preferable.' "

As at many other Ellington Orchestra sessions, the work was hurried: John Sanders, a valve trombone player enlisted as a second copyist, shared space with Tom Whaley at a card table set up in the recording studio; as soon as they inked the parts, the band members would pick them up and play them for the first time, tape running. "I didn't know what to expect picking up a part for one more version of 'Sophisticated Lady,' " said Terry. "Then I played it, and I told Strayhorn, I said, 'That chart we just played, man, that arrangement of "Sophisticated Lady," that is really the most fantastic chart I have heard in a long time.' And he said to me, 'Did you enjoy your part?' I'll never forget that. 'Did you enjoy your part?' That man was always thinking about *you*." (Strayhorn told a magazine interviewer, "I have a general rule. Rimsky-Korsakov is the one who said it: All parts should lie easily under the fingers. That's my first rule, to write something a guy can play. Otherwise, it will never be as natural, or as wonderful, as something that does lie easily under the fingers.") Once the instrumental sections had been recorded, Strayhorn got a flight back to Los Angeles and supervised Clooney's overdubbing at the Radio Recorders studios. Accustomed to working with a live orchestra surrounding her rather than with frozen accompaniment squeaking through a set of headphones, Clooney was jittery. "We tried a few takes, and it was a disaster," said Clooney. "I couldn't get used to being separated from the music like that. Billy was studying me very intently. Finally, he said, 'Okay, Rosie. It's okay. The band isn't here. It's just a tape. Okay? You don't have to pretend that the band is here. Listen to me, honey. You're in your house, and you're sitting in your room. You turn the radio on—and it's Duke Ellington! That's great! You love Duke Ellington. So you start singing along. You're brushing your hair. You're looking in the mirror, and you're singing along to the radio. Okay?' And that did it for me. I was all right from then on." Although overdubbing was new, this kind of collaboration was familiar to Strayhorn. "The only other really strong advice he gave me was on 'I'm Checkin' Out, Goom Bye,' " said Clooney. "He told me not to do it angry. He said, 'Just because you're leaving the other person, it doesn't mean you're

: Billy Strayhorn on the porch of his paternal aunt Julia's house in Montclair, his legs bowed from rickets. ABOVE LEFT: The Strayhorn family's house in Homewood. HT: Georgia, Billy, and Johnny Strayhorn in Hillsborough in 1923

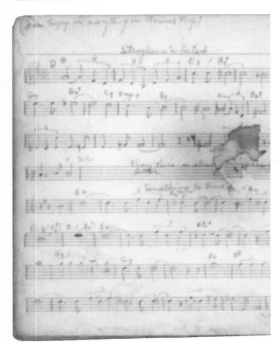

Posters for <u>Fantastic Rhythm</u>, and, top
right, Strayhorn's pencil manuscript for the
revue's theme song. LEFT: The "band book"
for Strayhorn's jazz combo included
"Something to Live For"

Strayhorn in Pittsburgh, around 1937

During the ASCAP strike in 1941, Strayhorn came into his own within the Ellington organization

ke Ellington with his orchestra in the late 1940s

rcer Ellington and his first wife, Evelyn, with Strayhorn, a member of Duke Ellington's
ended family since 1939

ABOVE: **Aaron Bridgers, Strayhorn, and Billie Holiday at Manhattan's Cafe Society Uptown.** BELOW: **Strayhorn and Bridgers with unknown revelers in a Harlem bar**

ᴏᴠᴇ: **Strayhorn aids Ellington and Louis Armstrong in a 1946 recording session of
e Esquire All-Stars.** ʙᴇʟᴏᴡ: **In the studio for Mercer Records, Strayhorn poses with,
m left, Oscar Pettiford, Ellington, Lloyd Trotman, and Leonard Feather**

"Lush Life" in its first edition, published in 1949, and in a piano
score Strayhorn wrote in 1960 for Aaron Bridgers to perform

angry. You're in charge. You're leaving, because you're the strong one. You might even come back. Who knows?'"

As thanks for his musical guidance and prenatal care, Rosemary Clooney gave Strayhorn a Cartier watch inscribed "To Svengali." "He was anything but," said Clooney. "I was never associated with a man who was so completely unthreatening and uncontrolling *and* so completely in charge." The album, completed on January 27 and entitled *Blue Rose,* included ten vocal tracks and one instrumental, a full-band arrangement of Strayhorn's "Passion Flower." "Having 'Passion Flower' on there was sort of a wink," explained Clooney, "an inside thing to those in the know that this was basically Billy's record." Along with the overdubbing, a first for a major artist, the album heralded a smaller breakthrough: even though two of Strayhorn's compositions were described as Ellington's alone in the liner notes written by Townsend ("Grievin'" is called "one of Duke's most effective songs," and "I'm Checkin' Out, Goom Bye" is referred to as "an older Ellington composition with a new sound"), Strayhorn was acknowledged, with Ellington, as one of the album's arrangers. Pleasant as it is, *Blue Rose* came as a surprise to both Ellington's jazz following and Clooney's pop audience and failed to become the hit of Townsend's design, never making it onto the charts.

Privately as well as professionally, Strayhorn was at an exploratory stage. Unattached, he was seen more often at gay parties, including one of the city's more popular weekly events at a musician's home on Sutton Place. "I never saw Billy Strayhorn on the scene except for that period, which was very brief," said the gay music critic Roy Hemming, then twenty-nine. "Everyone knew him—he was a star in that society. He enjoyed it but stayed at arm's length. It seemed as if he was simply interested in good company. He was extremely charming. He had a rapier wit, and certainly he adored his cocktails. Before very long he would leave, usually alone, but not always." That spring, talk spread within gay circles that Strayhorn had been a victim of a pickup gone bad, but the facts, as Strayhorn later recounted them to Lena Horne, Aaron Bridgers, and Bill Coleman, suggested something different. On a morning around April 30, 1954, Strayhorn was returning home to his apartment on 106th Street after a night out. "He said he was pretty drunk," Bridgers recalled. For reasons unexplained, he exited his cab several blocks west of his building, near the park at Riverside Drive and 106th Street. There was a construction site on that corner, and a man was standing near a hill of sand stored for mixing cement. As Strayhorn approached him, a second man appeared, and the two strangers jumped him. They stole his wallet and beat him, and he fell into the sand pile. Fearful that his accosters would steal his black star-sapphire ring, a treasured gift from Lena Horne, Strayhorn wormed his left hand into the sand and worked the ring off, burying it there. Once he was alone, he got up on his own and walked home; his face was bruised and his ribs ached. The next morning, he returned to the scene and, digging under the imprint of his body left in the sand, he found his ring. On May 2, the *New York Journal American* reported in a one-line item, "Billy Strayhorn, composer and longtime Duke Ellington arranger, was mugged by a group of hoodlums a few nights ago." "I don't know the whole story," said Lena Horne. "We didn't need to discuss it. He just said, 'I was lucky. I found my ring.' And we talked about the cruelty of people." In a visit to Strayhorn the day after the event, Bill Coleman was taken, above all, by his friend's resilience. "There was no great outpouring of emotion about it, even though it was a rather vicious kind of thing that had happened," said Coleman. "He didn't display histrionics or anything like that. He was visibly shaken by the whole experience, of course. But he was very strong and had an extraordinary capacity to absorb things that would be devastating to someone else and carry on. He accepted it as something that happened and moved on, although I know he didn't go out as much for a while after that. He kept his focus on his work."

Jazz continued its recession from the pop mainstream, the swing generation steering its new station wagons ever further from jukebox culture, the emerging generation turning to the electrified sound of rock and roll. Jazz was evolving into an elite music for mature ears; old hipsters found a different kind of nightlife in the easy pleasures of their TVs and their hi-fis. For live music, meanwhile, since jazz is a largely improvisational form, an accommodating institution took form: the jazz festival. In Newport, Rhode Island, in the summer of 1954, twenty-nine-year-old George Wein, the owner of and house pianist at Boston's Storyville nightclub, produced the American Jazz Festival, the first of its kind. "I watched the nightclubs dry up around me," recalled Wein. A Boston University pre-med graduate who had studied jazz privately with Teddy Wilson, Wein had an aggressive, percussive style of piano playing and a felicitous touch as a businessman. He was built like a cinder block, actual size. "The idea behind the Newport festival was to make live jazz appealing again to a generation that didn't go to nightclubs anymore," said Wein. "You could bring the kids and sit outside all afternoon and hear music, all various acts in every genre of jazz. You could have a picnic. The kids could play." Wein had reservations about booking Ellington for Newport, concerned that Ellington was perceived as past his prime, but he offered the bandleader a slot at the third annual festival, in July 1956. "The festival—and the whole idea of a jazz festival—was still very young, and the kind of press we got was important to us," said Wein. "Duke was booked and all set to go on in a few days, and I called him. I said, 'Duke, what are you going to do? Do you have anything new?' He said, 'Well . . .' And I said, 'You can't come up here and do a medley of your hits. You can't. The critics will kill you. You have to come up with something new.' "

Ellington was getting the same message from Columbia Records. The label had assigned a new A & R executive to work on the Ellington account, George Avakian—a jazz enthusiast since child-hood, with a pronounced interest in Ellingtonia, as well as long experience at Columbia as head of both the popular-album and in-ternational departments—and he wanted to try something new at Newport: the first live recording at a festival. "I called Duke. He was on the road somewhere, so I got him in a hotel," explained Avakian, a continental, multilingual charmer skillful at talking any setting's talk. "I told him we wanted to record his performance at Newport for a record. I said, 'Look, the festival is making [news], and we've given them twenty-five thousand dollars for the right to record. Can you put something together that we can call "The New-port Jazz Festival Suite" or some such thing? It would be a good tie-in. I know there's not much time. Can you do it?' And Duke said, 'Okay. Strays and I always have something going. I'll put him to work on it right away.' "

To come across at the festival as more than a nostalgia act—Miles Davis, Charles Mingus, Dave Brubeck, Sarah Vaughan, and the Modern Jazz Quartet (among others) were all scheduled to perform—Ellington needed to reassert the vitality of his work and his orchestra. The *Newport Jazz Festival Suite*, composed of three parts ("Festival Junction," "Blues to Be There," and "Newport Up") and credited to Ellington and Strayhorn, wouldn't do it, however: though somewhat more involving than picnic soundtrack music need be, the piece is a loping parade of cool-jazz riffs stretched out with some clever repetition and plenty of solo space. Nonetheless, the orchestra's Newport set turned out to be the event's most celebrated performance—indeed, one that elevated the standing of both the jazz festival and the Ellington Orchestra. Ellington called for his "Diminuendo and Crescendo in Blue" in a showy version the orchestra had been performing for the past several years; in the middle of the two-part piece, Ellington added what would come to be called "the wailing interval," a mammoth twenty-seven choruses of uninterrupted solo blues improvisation by the tenor saxophonist Paul Gonsalves, a bebop-oriented veteran of Dizzy Gillespie's big band who had joined Ellington in 1951. Seemingly possessed, Gonsalves drew the festival crowd into something like a religious frenzy; Ellington egged him on, revving his arms like a drivetrain, roaring cheers from the piano. At the conclusion of the nearly fifteen-minute performance, Newport erupted into a screaming, stomping affirmation of Ellington's undiminished showmanship. "That moment was a turnaround point for Duke and us," said Wein. "If anybody needed proof that this was a band that could hold its own against anybody else out there and provide a level of music pleasure that nobody could match, there it was." For his part, Wein felt vindicated that "people got a taste of how much music the festival could provide."

Columbia released the live LP *Ellington at Newport* in the fall of 1956 to critical raves; only Ellington insiders knew that portions of the *Newport Jazz Festival Suite* had been rerecorded in Columbia's Studio D on July 8, the day after the orchestra's performance, and patched in to amend a few minor flubs in the original. After the career diminuendo of Ellington's last half decade, the crescendo of Newport rang far: *Time* magazine, in a six-page cover story about Ellington in its August 20 issue, made Newport a referendum on Ellington and his role in the evolution of jazz. "The event last month marked not only the turning point in one concert; it confirmed a turning point in a career," the story (unbylined) said. "The big news was something that the whole jazz world had long hoped to hear: the Ellington band was once again the most exciting thing in the business. Ellington himself had emerged from a long period of quiescence and was once again bursting with ideas and inspiration. . . . His style contains the succinctness of concert music and the excitement of jazz." Strayhorn was noted briefly as Ellington's arranger and shown in a "family" photo of the Ellingtons: Duke, Ruth, Mercer, and his wife, Evelyn.

Reunited, at least tentatively—yet they had never quite been apart—Ellington and Strayhorn had dinner together at the Hickory House on Manhattan's West 52nd Street in mid-August 1956. They met at Ellington's initiative, and the dinner marked the first time they had ever discussed their relationship in terms close to negotiation, as Strayhorn recounted immediately afterward to his two dearest Copasetics friends, Cookie Cook and Honi Coles. "Billy called me. He said, 'Edward wants to talk to me. We're having dinner,' " recalled Coles. "I said, 'You want me to come along? If you need some moral support . . . ' Billy said, 'No, Father'—Billy always called me Father. He even sent me Father's Day cards. 'Ever up and onward,' he said. So we agreed to meet at the Showman's after he had dinner with Duke. Cookie and I were there waiting for him. About midnight or twelve-thirty he comes in, and he's wearing the biggest Cheshire cat grin you could imagine. Cookie said to me, 'Look at that motherfucker, Honi. That is one happy motherfucker.' One of us said, 'Well, tell us all about it,' and Billy said, 'He's seeing stars again. He's been seeing stars now since Newport.' Newport could be the beginning of something big, if he took care of business, and he needed Billy for that. Billy said to us, 'He wanted to know what *I* want to do. I told him a few ideas, this and that, you know. *This* would be nice, *that* thing would be wonderful.' Billy said Duke was all over him. He's nodding up and down. He says, 'Yes, yes, that's a wonderful idea! Let's do that! Yes!' All that's all over, and Duke offers a toast. I don't know if he had a drink or coffee. Duke used to drink a cup of plain hot water; maybe he had that. Billy said he offered a toast, and he said, 'May I propose a toast? To Duke Ellington and Billy Strayhorn—to their new incorporation.' Duke basically broke down and said, 'I need you. From now, your name is up there, right next to mine. It's Duke Ellington and Billy Strayhorn.' " And what sort of project would this new incorporation produce? Strayhorn told Coles, "A Shakespeare thing."

Fifteen years after *Jump for Joy*, Ellington and Strayhorn entered a new level of collaboration, Strayhorn told his confidants: for large-scale projects of all sorts, as well as for individual pieces, Ellington offered to share the composing credit; moreover, he encouraged Strayhorn to contribute original concepts, not merely to execute ideas that came to Ellington or came Ellington's way. (Any changes in their financial arrangement are untraceable and impossible to quantify since many of Strayhorn's bills and expenditures were paid directly by Ellington and his organization, in part with Ellington's personal funds.) The partners' first project under the arrangement was to be a suite of pieces for the following year's Stratford Music Festival, an offshoot of the Shakespearean Festival in Stratford, Ontario, founded in 1953 by the acclaimed English theatrical director Sir Tyrone Guthrie. Among the most ambitious of the new arts festivals popping up to fill the vacation weeks of the newly affluent and mobile postwar generation, the Stratford event presented a Shakespeare play (Alec Guinness in *Richard III*, for example), an opera or a symphonic work (Benjamin Britten's *The Rape of Lucretia*), and a program of jazz artists, all for an admission price of five dollars. A few weeks after his celebrated 1956 appearance at Newport, Ellington had made his Stratford debut on a bill with the Dave Brubeck Quartet, the Modern Jazz Quartet, the Art Tatum Trio, and others. But his choice of program, a dance-oriented show of his hits, had disappointed the festival's founder, Thomas Patterson, and its musical director, Louis Applebaum, both of whom had solicited Ellington to present a major new work. A year in advance of the 1956 festival, Patterson had gone to Chicago to meet with him. "It was kind of fascinating," said Patterson. "The band was located in Chicago and playing gigs around, and I went to meet Duke for the first time. It was in his hotel room, and Duke was lying in bed surrounded by a whole bunch of people. It was a madhouse. Ellington was on the phone to New York and various places, and there was a guy in Chicago who had done a bust of Ellington and was there to present it to him, and the newspapers were there and everything, to get a picture of it. Ellington got out of bed in his pajamas and put a shirt and a jacket on with his pajama bottoms still on and stood beside the bust to get his picture taken. He took off the shirt and jacket and went back to bed, and we talked. I told him all about the festival, and he said, 'Oh, it sounds marvelous, marvelous. We'll certainly create something very special and worthy of such a wonderful festival.' Of course, it wasn't until he came here and played the first time and saw what we were about that he got Strayhorn to start something for the next year."

Louis Applebaum, a professional music administrator who had come from Canada's National Film Board, attributed Ellington's change of heart to two factors. "I had tried to impress upon him that we weren't interested in just another one-night-stand show— 'and then I wrote . . . ' " said Applebaum. "After he played the first year, he realized that he had missed an opportunity and offered to come back next time with something special. Also, while he was here he became very, very close to [director of music promotion] Barbara Reed, and there was no question whatsoever that their closeness had a great, great deal to do with Ellington's sudden enthusiasm for Stratford." The Reed-Ellington relationship shouldn't be interpreted reductively, however, according to Reed's boss, publicity director Mary Joliffe: "Everybody takes credit for getting Duke to write for the festival. It was Barb who did it, but not just Barb as a woman. Duke had a million women, and he didn't write music for all of them, even if he told them he did. Barb was a genius as a publicist, and she showed Duke what it could do for him to have this association with Stratford. She gave the motivation." Applebaum, in turn, specifically suggested that Ellington write a work inspired by Shakespeare. Ellington responded that the suite form, his favorite anyway, was fitting for the project. And Strayhorn took it on excitedly, glowing to his friends about having an Ellington Orchestra project geared especially to him.

Strayhorn's affection for Shakespeare was well established on the band bus. "We used to *call* him Shakespeare—that was one of his nicknames," said Jimmy Hamilton. "Not when he was around, I'm talking about." With the most literate instrumentalists in the orchestra, Strayhorn was known to indulge in an occasional debate on the Bard: the trumpeter Willie Cook, a Gillespie big-band veteran from Chicago, tangled with him on the issue of stylistic brevity at a hotel bar somewhere in the Midwest. "I told him I thought Shakespeare was verbose," said Cook. "That got Strayhorn *mad*. He was steaming. I said Shakespeare used too many couplets to make his points. I told him Kahlil Gibran could say the same thing in four or five words. Strayhorn was spouting off all this Shakespeare, all these lines from all the plays and whatnot. 'How would Kahlil Gibran say *that*?' It was funny, man—he was so mad. When Duke said he was writing a Shakespeare suite for the band, I said to myself, 'Oh, man, now Strayhorn's going to get back at me. My whole horn part's going to be four or five notes!' " Ellington's own approach to Shakespeare was imaginative, if defensively colored by his autodidact's pride. As Strayhorn explained at the time, "Ellington has always been intrigued by Shakespeare, 'cause he said Shakespeare certainly knew more about people than anyone he's ever known. Duke also said that the only way Shakespeare could have known as much about people as he did was by hanging out on the corner or in the pool room. He says that if William Shakespeare were alive today, you would surely find him down at Birdland listening to jazz." For his own preparation, Strayhorn stuck with books: he spent evenings perusing his old complete works of Shakespeare, jotting musical notes in the margins. Late one night, he came into the Showman's with one volume under his arm; he held the book on his lap for hours, chatting with Honi Coles and a few casual friends from the neighborhood until suddenly he stood up, slipped the Shakespeare onto the stool, and sat on it. "He looked me straight in the eye with a grin," said Coles, "and he said, 'Look, I'm as big as you. How do you like that? Shakespeare is so excellent for a person's growth.' " For several days, Strayhorn obsessed on the suite's title; resisting Ellington's preference, "The Shakespearean Suite," he called his friends at all hours with ideas. One was "Nova," Avon spelled backwards; another, "Madness in Great Ones," became a title for one movement. He settled on *Such Sweet Thunder*, a phrase from *A Midsummer Night's Dream* (Hippolyta: "I was with Hercules and Cadmus once / When in a wood of Crete they bay'd the bear / With hounds of Sparta. . . . I never heard / So musical a discourd, such sweet thunder").

Clearly relishing his first equal-credit collaboration with Ellington under their new understanding, Strayhorn was well into it when Ellington announced that another project would have to take priority: music for a television special. The CBS network had undertaken a competition with NBC to win FCC approval for a color-TV broadcast standard. Each network was testing and promoting its own system in the freewheeling market: CBS's was a mechanical one involving a dinner-plate-size translucent disc tinted with three colors that spun inside the TV camera, and NBC's was based on cathode-ray tubes. Although it may have seemed archaic in conception, the "color wheel" technology was said to produce more accurate colors than NBC's tube-based method, except when the color wheel spun at less than constant and precise speed, which did occasionally happen. To stimulate public enthusiasm for its system, CBS created a demonstration parlor in midtown Manhattan: viewers lined up on Fifth Avenue to buy tickets and see, via closed-circuit TV, full-color still pictures of pieces of Swiss cheese and bologna. Hoping to promote the system nationally, CBS executives commissioned an original musical production from the Theater Guild. Administered by a former patent attorney, Lawrence Langner, and his wife, Armina Marshall Langner, an actress, the Guild had come to acclaim as the producers of *Oklahoma!* and a series of George Bernard Shaw plays. Langner approached Ellington, who pitched a variant on the history-of-jazz idea he had knocked around with Orson Welles in 1941: an allegorical trip from Africa and the Caribbean through New Orleans to the rocket age. Native costumes, jungle greenery, outer space—CBS relished it for its opportunities to use color, recalled the production's set designer, Willard Levitas, who had recently jumped from *Studio One* to the higher-profile *U.S. Steel Hour*, on which CBS proposed to produce Ellington's conception.

"The main thing for them was 'Will it show off our color wheel?'" said Levitas. "They didn't know very much about Duke Ellington except that he wasn't white, so there was more color for them." This was the idea for the program as Ellington explained it: "It will be the most ambitious thing we ever attempted artistically. A *Drum Is a Woman* is a tone parallel to the history of jazz, and the heroine is called Madam Zajj, which is a funny way of spelling jazz backward. And she is the spirit of jazz, which comes about as a result of this tremendous romance that goes on between a musician and his instrument and his music—and this is a big thing, and this is how we arrive at the statement that a drum is a woman. We've seen a lot of guys who would leave a real pretty chick so that he can go off into a corner and blow his horn. And you see guys like [Ellington Orchestra member] Sam Woodyard, who is a drummer, and when he takes a solo, he'll be grunting and closing his eyes and caressing that drum and feeling the skin of its head—it couldn't be hotter. That's what they call their drums, skins. A drummer is a skin whipper. And a woman is definitely the most important accessory a man has."

The show would be an Ellington-Strayhorn collaboration, the partners' closest one ever, according to Strayhorn. "I suppose the largest hunk of collaboration was *Drum Is a Woman,* in which we just kind of did everything," Strayhorn explained. "He wrote lyrics, I wrote lyrics. He wrote music, and I wrote music. He arranged, and I arranged."

Working quickly together in New York, usually at Ellington's apartment, as well as separately while the bandleader kept up his perpetual schedule of performances, they finished the music and threads of narration that would serve as the soundtrack, and it was recorded by the Ellington Orchestra and a few guest artists in a whirl of New York sessions in late September 1956. The singers were Joya Sherrill, returning temporarily at Ellington's request; Margaret Tynes, a twenty-seven-year-old operatic singer and teacher with little professional exposure; and Ozzie Bailey, a black cabaret singer who had gotten vocal coaching from and done a bit of recording with Luther Henderson. Bailey, thirty-one and gay, hovered near Strayhorn during the production; they became friends, though likely no closer than Strayhorn and any of the other musicians. "Ozzie, what a dear boy, but he wasn't for Billy," recalled Talley Beatty, Strayhorn's old Neal Salon compatriot, who danced the role (Caribe Joe) that Bailey sang in the production. Sweetly effeminate, Bailey loved to pass the studio downtime singing American songs in French, emoting in cute gestures. Strayhorn giggled at the sight but encouraged him—"Aaah! *Magnifique!*"—and Bailey took a deep bow, perhaps (and perhaps not) acknowledging Strayhorn's irony.

Composed of fifteen musical numbers arranged for expanded orchestra (the usual sixteen pieces plus three percussionists and harp),

A *Drum Is a Woman* plays off touchstone modes of jazz from the music's African and Caribbean origins through early New Orleans music ("Hey, Buddy Bolden") to bebop ("Rhumbop"), with a stop in outer space ("Ballet of the Flying Saucers"). The disparate elements of homage are neatly filtered through the consistently distinctive sound of the Ellington Orchestra. The high points are the least referential instrumental selections ("Rhumbop" and "Ballet of the Flying Saucers") and the bop-influenced improvisations by Clark Terry (on "Madam Zajj") and Paul Gonsalves ("Congo Square"). Lyrically, however, *A Drum* is unsettling. Alternately coy and childlike, the words rarely convey accessible or mature feeling; the title song, moreover, expresses outright sadistic misogyny in the guise of an attempted joke (presumably):

> *It isn't civilized to beat women*
> *No matter what they do or they say*
> *But will somebody tell me*
> *What else can you do with a drum?*

By contrast, Strayhorn's old "Don't Mess Around with the Women" was feminist.

Working from LP pressings of the music and narration, spoken by Ellington himself, producers from CBS and the Theater Guild set out independent of Ellington and Strayhorn to stage the work as a presentation of music and dance—there would be no dialogue beyond the narration, to be handled on camera by Ellington—with the live broadcast scheduled for the following spring. In the meanwhile, the Shakespeare suite still had to be written, and more quickly than Strayhorn had originally been told. George Avakian asked Ellington to premiere the work prior to the Stratford Festival at a benefit Avakian was producing in conjunction with his wife, the classical violinist Anahid Ajemian. Dubbed *Music for Moderns*, the concert would feature Ellington and his orchestra on a double bill with the conductor Dimitri Mitropoulos and a chamber ensemble performing Kurt Weill's Concerto for Violin and Wind Orchestra, op. 12; Ajemian was to be the soloist in the Weill. "We were recording *Drum Is a Woman* and getting it together and also writing the Shakespearean suite," recalled Strayhorn. "We had a deadline for *Thunder,* as we had promised to premiere it at . . . the Town Hall. We were rushed." Indeed, Ellington and Strayhorn divvied up the composing responsibilities, each writing a group of the suite's movements, and neither was on schedule as the deadline drew close. Ellington, booked with his orchestra at Birdland, composed backstage: during an intermission, he scrawled four bars of a theme on a piece of scratch paper and asked Britt Woodman, an energetic young trombonist who had joined the orchestra in 1951, to play the fragment. The following night, Ellington had turned the melodic idea into a short piece, handed the music to Woodman, and called on him to play it for the people cold. (Entitled "Sonnet to Hank Cinq," it became the third movement of the suite.) Strayhorn was working on a theme for a segment dedicated to Romeo and Juliet, writing at home while a friend mixed cocktails, when Ellington called and told him to save time and simply steal the music—albeit from himself. Jimmy Hamilton thought there was something familiar in his part when he played the ninth movement, "The Star-Crossed Lovers." "I said, 'Hey, Strays, you think nobody's going to remember this? Nobody going to forget this, man. This is the most beautiful thing you ever wrote.' " Hamilton had recorded the same piece on Johnny Hodges's *Creamy* album just two years earlier, when it was still titled "Pretty Girl" and credited to Strayhorn alone. "I just shook my head when I saw that," said Hamilton. "Strayhorn said, 'Ellington has insisted, and when Ellington has insisted, you know what we must do. We must do what we must do.' We was together—I don't know, packing up or something— and he says to me, real quiet, 'Jimmy.' Actually, he called me James. He says, 'James, what could I do? He got me.' Like, the way Duke worked, if you're not going to give me [Ellington] what I want, I'll get it out of you one way or another. He got what he wanted, even if you wasn't giving it to him."

On April 28, *Such Sweet Thunder* was given its premiere at Town Hall in Manhattan's theater district to a sellout audience of fifteen hundred. "That night at the Town Hall concert was the very first time Duke and I had heard the whole suite without a break," said Strayhorn. "This was the first time it had been played from beginning to end. That particular night we put the whole thing together—it was very nice and went along very well." In truth, the composition wasn't performed to its end: only eleven of its twelve movements were ready that night. As a finale, Ellington told the band to vamp on the blues, and he announced to the audience that the orchestra would now perform the conclusion of the suite, a movement entitled "Cop-Out." No one laughed, Avakian recalled. "It was such a straight crowd that they didn't even know they were being put on."

Like virtually every other Ellington or Ellington-Strayhorn suite, *Such Sweet Thunder* is ostensibly programmatic in structure: each of its movements has an intended relationship to Shakespeare, and it is that commonality, rather than any purely musical thread (or threads), that links the pieces. Unlike individual sections of the other suites, however, most of those in *Such Sweet Thunder* are not traditional descriptive music. (Originally a painter, Ellington had always liked to sketch musical portraits, evoking the emotions, the ambient sounds, or the sensations he associated with a subject.) The Shakespeare connections vary from abstract to obscure: tempo changes in "Sonnet for Hank Cinq" refer to "changes of pace and the map as a result of wars," according to Ellington. A bright, prankish segment, "Lady Mac," evokes turn-of-the-century America because, Ellington said, "We suspect there was a little ragtime in soul." In purely musical terms, however, *Such Sweet Thunder* holds up without elliptical defense. The musical diversity and the emotional range of the suite are impressive, from the propulsive swing of "Madness in Great Ones" and the moody exotica of "Sonnet in Search of a Moor" and "Half the Fun" to the winking tease of "The Telecasters." Even without the romance of "The Star-Crossed Lovers"/ "Pretty Girl," *Such Sweet Thunder* would surely have been regarded as a complex and hefty work.

About a dozen blocks uptown from Town Hall, the *U.S. Steel Hour* staff was busily concocting as colorful a show as they could for the broadcast of *A Drum Is a Woman*, due in less than two weeks. The producer, Marshall Jamison, a Broadway director, had passed copies of the album on to Willard Levitas, as well as to the choreographer, Paul Godkin, and the director, Paul Felton, with these instructions: "Do whatever the hell you want, because the thing doesn't make any sense." Levitas, who didn't own a record player and didn't want anyone to know, proceeded more or less blindly until Jamison had the narration transcribed and distributed in script form. "I didn't really know much about the music, but we were all told that it didn't matter as long as everything was colorful," said Levitas, who used lots of fresh greenery and flowers in the jungle sequences. He was most proud of the New Orleans set, which, along with more flowers, included a balcony with wrought-iron filigree. Unfortunately, the bulky color-wheel cameras were so limited in mobility that much of the New Orleans set couldn't be seen on the air. Godkin devised resourceful dances for Talley Beatty and Carmen DeLavallade, a principal dancer with the Metropolitan Opera. Owing again to the cameras' immobility and relatively narrow field of vision, the dancers were restricted. "We did a lot of moving in toward the camera and back away from the camera," said Beatty, who danced in his bare feet; he bled through the rehearsals, conducted in a studio with cracking plank floors and exposed nail heads. "We had to work in very small areas in front of the cameras. But Paul did wonderful work. The dances were wonderful. They captured the music quite vividly—Paul was very respectful of the music. He loved Duke and Billy." Carmen DeLavallade thought Godkin and Strayhorn seemed temperamentally alike. "Paul was a lot like Billy. He was always calm and took everything in his stride, at least the way he presented himself to others," she said. "He never seemed unhappy about anything, and he did beautiful work. The music and Paul's dances made that show work, even though they were done completely independently." Godkin contributed an idea for the sets: a jeweled tree. "He just liked the idea. It didn't mean anything and it had nothing to do with the record," said Levitas. "We used it anyway. What did it matter?" Little was required of Ellington and Strayhorn beyond the narration and the music, both of which would be performed live before the camera by Ellington and his orchestra. While Ellington focused on the narration, Strayhorn held up the musical end, playing piano behind some of the narration; recorded tracks from the LP were used for a few dance sequences.

Broadcast on May 8, 1957, and credited equally to Duke Ellington and Billy Strayhorn, A Drum Is a Woman came off as a polished and eminently colorful execution of a largely enigmatic idea. "In those days, if somebody didn't fall on his face and you went on on time and you got off on time, the show was a success," said Levitas.

The ratings suggested otherwise: relative to most *U.S Steel Hour* productions, *A Drum Is a Woman* fizzled, reaching an estimated 5,279,000 homes (a "25 share" on the Nielsen ratings, representing slightly more than 14.2 percent of U.S. households); fewer than 100,000 viewers had the TV sets necessary to view the program in color. The program remained another kind of triumph, however. "It was unheard of to give that kind of forum to a black show done by black artists in that day. Unheard of," said Jamison. "A lot of white people would change the channel as soon as they saw black faces and never give the thing a shot. CBS took a big gamble doing it. You gotta give them a lot of credit. But they lost." In a decision unrelated to CBS's presentations of Swiss cheese or *A Drum Is a Woman,* the FCC rejected the color wheel and named NBC's tube system the color broadcast standard.

Bringing together both the new Ellington-Strayhorn collaborations in one sprawling program, Ellington and his orchestra performed the entirety of *A Drum Is a Woman,* complete with narration, as an opener to the long-promised debut of *Such Sweet Thunder* at the Stratford Shakespearean Festival on the afternoon of September 5, 1957. A capacity crowd of five hundred filled the festival concert hall, a poorly ventilated nineteenth-century barn converted into a badminton court and then reconverted into a theater. The stage protruded out into the audience, which surrounded the performers on three sides, Elizabethan style. By the day of the performance, Ellington and the orchestra, accompanied by Strayhorn, had already spent nearly a week at the festival, taking in other performances and socializing, for which Ellington allowed liberal time at this venue. Strayhorn surprised the Shakespeareans with his casual erudition. "I'm not saying I expected him to be unintelligent, but I frankly wasn't prepared for the depth of his knowledge," admitted Tom Patterson. "We were with literally the top Shakespeare scholars in the world, and Strayhorn didn't have a thing to apologize for. His knowledge was very deep." Under Mary Joliffe's wing, Strayhorn took in Benjamin Britten's opera *The Turn of the Screw;* over drinks at the reception afterward, Strayhorn initiated a discussion contrasting the Britten work with the Henry James story on which it is based. "He was very bookish. He fit right in with that crowd," said Joliffe. "At the same time, he was extremely cool. He was an incredible dresser." That evening, Strayhorn wore a pink silk shirt he had had custom-made in Paris, which Joliffe told him she found "lovely." The next day, he brought one in a gift box to her office. "He told me, 'Don't worry. If I really like a shirt, I always buy two,'" said Joliffe.

Strayhorn was so comfortable at Stratford that he wanted to perform there. "He was very eager to play piano at the festival," said Patterson. "We talked about it, but it just couldn't be arranged for that particular year. The program was completely arranged and very tightly scheduled." Instead, Strayhorn watched from backstage as the Ellington Orchestra performed *Such Sweet Thunder*, the climax of the festival. Paul Gonsalves was wrapping up the furious tenor-saxophone improvisation designed as the piece's finale—titled "Circle of Fourths," the last movement seems to climb ever higher by using intervals of fourths (supposedly representing the four dimensions of Shakespeare's work: tragedy, comedy, history, and the sonnets) in one major key after another—when Ellington waved for Strayhorn to come out front. Gliding up from the piano bench and over to center stage, Ellington kept his eyes on Gonsalves and pumped his fist, the "Keep rolling" signal. Strayhorn sat at the piano. Back to the audience, Ellington raised both hands up to his shoulders—"Finale"—and the orchestra burst into the piece's final chord. His hands slashed downward, the chord clipped short, and Ellington pointed to Strayhorn, who moved the index finger of his right hand above the fifth-octave C and lowered it onto the key to a roar of laughs and applause. "Billy Strayhorn, ladies and gentlemen!" boomed Ellington. "Billy Strayhorn!"

8

THERE
WAS
NOBODY
LOOKIN'

Billy Strayhorn and Duke Ellington inhabited the same world, but each for his own reasons and on his own terms, and you could see the difference at the Hickory House. Between 10:00 and 11:00 p.m. once or twice a week, Strayhorn slipped in alone or, less frequently, with a friend or two. He had a spot: the bar, varnished black walnut and about fifty feet long, was U-shaped—in front of it, there were twenty-five or thirty tables for six or more laid with red linens; behind it, there was a bandstand where solo pianists like Marian McPartland or small groups like the Dwike Mitchell–Willie Ruff Duo performed—and Strayhorn always sat at the very last stool on the right side of the U, where he was tucked away and turned at right angles to both the performers and the customers. He had eye contact only with the bartender, usually Jimmy Ratigan, who knew how Strayhorn liked his gin and tonics: with Beefeater's and Schweppes and in steady sequence. Strayhorn would take his seat, light a cigarette, and slide a twenty-dollar bill on the bar, rarely taking change home; one gin and tonic cost $1.75. "From where he sat, it was hard to see if he was there or not," said McPartland, whose set regularly included a disciplined rendition of "Lush Life"; when he heard it, Strayhorn would turn to face McPartland—always at the conclusion, never during the performance—eyebrows and cocktail raised high in a toast, and he'd let out an affirming "Aaaaah!" When he was in Manhattan, Ellington came in around midnight three or four times a week. Surrounded by an entourage— perhaps his sister, Ruth, the businessman and lyricist Edmund Anderson, and two or three others somehow related to his project of the moment—Ellington also had a spot: the table for eight at the center of the room. "The focus of attention immediately shifted from [the performer] to Ellington," said McPartland. Ellington ate his usual (a steak, a half a grapefruit, and a cup of hot water with lemon peel), greeted his public with smiles and nods—fearful of exposure to germs while eating, he'd slip his arms under the table to avoid shaking hands—and caught up on the news on the street from other Hickory House regulars. Strayhorn would give a little wave to the Ellington party and stop by the table for a few minutes shortly before leaving, unless Ellington was talking to Joe Morgen.

The kingpin of the Hickory House crowd, Morgen was a fast-talking Broadway-beat publicist who seemed to have wandered off from his rightful place in a production of *Guys and Dolls*. Chubby and about five foot five, topped off with a few strands of dark hair that looked to be penciled across his pate, Morgen had a reputation for gracelessness and aggression, enhanced by a thyroid condition that, in popping his eyes, created the illusion that he was even more manically obsessed than he in fact was. In conversation, Morgen liked to clean his ears with a swizzle stick. He worked for Bill Doll, the publicist for such fifties celebrities as the retired boxing champion Jack Dempsey and the director Michael Todd, although the ever-angling Morgen was always open to taking clients on the side. "Joe Morgen had the manner of a gangster and the tact of a tommy gun," said Phoebe Jacobs, the longtime head of promotion and publicity for the Basin Street East nightclub. "He knew all the ins and outs of the Walter Winchell school of celebrity PR, although I don't think he graduated from that or any school." Smelling an opportunity in Ellington, Morgen initiated a schmoozing campaign to snare the bandleader's business: he brought Ed Sullivan into the Hickory House to meet Ellington, and he landed a couple of mentions of Ellington in the Sullivan and Earl Wilson newspaper columns. ("Today's bravos: Duke Ellington's band at Birdland," noted Wilson.) Ellington put Morgen on his payroll early in 1957. Strayhorn disliked him, and Morgen felt even greater contempt for him. "Joe Morgen hated Billy with a passion that was beyond all understanding," said Jacobs. "For one thing, Morgen thought that Billy represented competition for Duke's attention, and that Joe Morgen couldn't bear. And Billy was gay, which threw Morgen completely off the deep end. Just the mention of Billy Strayhorn's name drove Joe Morgen crazy. The very idea of Billy made him nuts." Ellington retained Morgen nonetheless, in one of his purest gestures of laissez-faire management. "Pop ran his business like a family, and his family like a business," explained Mercer Ellington. "He had a certain attitude toward the people who worked for him that was like the old-fashioned attitude toward raising a family. Your sons, you let them fend for themselves—that's how they learn and how they get stronger. You get the best of them that way. You pit one against the other, really. That's the way the old man functioned as far as people like Joe Morgen and Strayhorn and myself were concerned. You let them fight it out. He hired Joe Morgen and figured he'd let the chips fall where they may and kept out of the picture. The only thing I was surprised about was that he allowed that with Strayhorn involved, since he tended to pamper Strayhorn more and protect him. That comes out of the family philosophy. You let the sons fight among themselves, but you treasure your daughters. You protect them. He was usually more that way when it came to Strayhorn."

Strayhorn, meanwhile, turned to the last of his major music projects for the year: a double LP teaming Ella Fitzgerald with the Duke Ellington Orchestra, produced by Norman Granz as an entry in Verve's Ella Fitzgerald *Songbook* series of albums dedicated to master songwriters. As usual with Ellington-related vocal projects, much of the preparation for and supervision of *Ella Fitzgerald Sings the Duke Ellington Songbook* fell to Strayhorn, who wrote a folder full of new arrangements for the sessions, including swirling new versions of "Day Dream" and "Take the 'A' Train," the latter recorded with Dizzy Gillespie as guest trumpet soloist. The folder wasn't thick enough for Granz and Fitzgerald, however. "I didn't know what was going on until we went into the studio," said Granz. "I hadn't been able to work it out with Duke. Duke was on the road. I spent more time traveling around trying to talk to Duke than we spent on the record. When we got in the studio, Strays had some arrangements, but nothing close to what we needed. Duke was supposed to do some and Strays did some, but Duke came without anything done. This was a major project, and we didn't have the arrangements we needed. Ella really was very upset, and she didn't want to do it. She wanted to walk out. Here we'd been waiting for a long time to get this together. Logistically it was a problem because Ella was traveling all the time and Duke was always on the road. And finally the day came, and Strays spent a lot of time holding Ella's hand and saying, 'There, there, it's going to be okay. Don't worry.' " Improvising a fix, Ellington supervised some recordings of Fitzgerald singing along with the band's instrumental arrangements: she hummed the saxophone parts for songs that didn't even have lyrics, such as "Chelsea Bridge." As the bassist Jimmy Woode recalled, "Ella and Billy had a rough time. That wasn't the way either one of them liked to work. They were perfectionists. They were accustomed to planning and having the work fine-tuned to perfection. The idea of faking your way through 'Chelsea Bridge' by humming along was terribly difficult for them to accept."

To fill out the multirecord project, Ellington told Granz that he and Strayhorn would compose a new instrumental suite in honor of Fitzgerald; instead, he took an existing Strayhorn ballad, "All Heart"—already recorded and credited to Strayhorn alone on a French LP by Aaron Bridgers—and added three new sections, one named "Beyond Category" (a favorite phrase of Ellington's that the jazz writer and historian Patricia Willard first applied to Ellington's own work), another a straight-ahead jam called "Total Jazz." "That was a neat Duke trick," said Granz. "Quite candidly, the suite was a way of padding the album." In the process, the suite, called "Portrait of Ella Fitzgerald," paid tribute to Strayhorn as well: Ellington's spoken introduction to the first "movement" conspicuously credits Strayhorn for his piano accompaniment ("While Billy Strayhorn sets the mood, we gather the material for our musical portrait of Ella Fitzgerald, allowing our imagination to browse through her family

album," Ellington pronounced). At the opening of the fourth section, Strayhorn took over at the mike ("Hey, Billy Strayhorn! We're
going to change piano players at this point. Would you come over
to the mike, please?"), accompanied by Ellington on piano. "I think
Duke knew the rest of the project wasn't really done right," added
Granz. "So he wanted to do something special for Ella and Billy,
and that was what he did." For variety as well as ease in the light
of Fitzgerald's frustrations, Granz chose to complete the project with
the singer accompanied by a couple of small bands of Verve stal-
warts, including Oscar Peterson, Ray Brown, and Ellington veteran
Ben Webster.

While Ellington and Strayhorn made their music, Joe Morgen
hustled to make it news, and he got stunning results: from May to
October 1957, Newsweek, Look, and the New York Times all published features about Duke Ellington's renaissance. "Duke Bounces
Back with Provocative New Work," crowed the Times; "A Living
Legend Swings On," announced the headline of the Look piece,
which declared, "Ellington and his men have burst out in a cluster
of projects as shiny as a new trumpet. . . . A whole new generation
of Americans has caught the Ellington fever. Through all the sound
and the fury, the Duke has never been in better tune." For Ellington,
this was not just a comeback but a cultural coming of age. Distinct
from his past triumphs—hit records, concert-hall performances,
praise in the music press, acceptance within academia—Ellington's
newfound acceptance as a major artist by the mainstream media was
institutional lionization. Joe Morgen's influence is impossible to
quantify, although many of the Morgen-era articles on Ellington
bear the handiwork of an old column-fodder PR man; the same
grabby "facts" reappear: Ellington has studied a thousand books on
Afro-American history, Ellington has traveled one million miles.
"All cooked up," said Phoebe Jacobs. "That was all Joe Morgen,
every bit of it. All those articles after Newport—Joe Morgen made
all of that happen. He sold everybody on Ellington."

If so, Morgen had a salable product and a prime market. Following Newport with Such Sweet Thunder and A Drum Is a Woman as
well as the Ella Fitzgerald project, Ellington (in collaboration with
Strayhorn) was clearly working at peak productivity and ambition.
These efforts coincided, significantly, with the readiness of the

mainstream to accept jazz as art and a jazz master as a cultural hero. Still, an unconventional partnership of two such heroes—both black and one gay, "composing and arranging companions," as Ellington described Strayhorn and himself—was clearly too much, at least within Joe Morgen's sphere of influence. In several hundreds of words of description and analysis of *Such Sweet Thunder* and *A Drum Is a Woman*, the name Billy Strayhorn never appeared in *Newsweek, Look,* or the *New York Times*. To the contrary, Ellington was described in detail as the works' sole creator. *Newsweek*: "Entitled 'A Drum Is a Woman,' it is the Duke's own highly personal history of jazz and 'TV's first jazz spectacular.' With Ellington billed as author, composer, lyricist, narrator, conductor, piano player, and general handy man, it [was] one of the few times a great name in jazz [had] a full hour of prime evening TV time to himself." The *Times*, describing *Such Sweet Thunder*: "This is the best work that Mr. Ellington has done in a decade. Mr. Ellington has poured greater range and variety into these sketches than in any of his earlier extended works." The credits for both *Such Sweet Thunder* and *A Drum Is a Woman* acknowledged Duke Ellington and Billy Strayhorn, but nobody seemed to be reading.

"The publicity people deemphasized Billy," recalled John S. Wilson, whose *New York Times* review of *Such Sweet Thunder* omitted Strayhorn. "We heard Ellington, Ellington." Again, according to Phoebe Jacobs, "That was all Morgen. He did everything he could to push Billy out of the picture as far as the press was concerned. Duke was Morgen's be-all and end-all." Ellington's own behavior with regard to Strayhorn was mercurial, evidently subject to conflicting personal and professional impulses. Much of the time, he served as Strayhorn's most zealous booster, lavishing him with praise on stage: "And now," announced Ellington at Carnegie Hall in 1948, "I'd like to introduce our writing and arranging companion, who we've been so much indebted to for quite a period for contributing so many of the high points of our performances, particularly in the writing." On occasions, however, he permitted Strayhorn's subordination through acquiescence. "He would let it happen," said Leonard Feather, who performed public-relations functions for Ellington in the 1940s and early 1950s. "Duke's intent was never to deny Strayhorn his due. If he allowed that to occur, it had to be a secondary effect of some effort to take advantage of a particular opportunity for promotion. I mean to say, Duke's first priority was himself. This was not unreasonable, since the lives of everyone in his organization, including Strayhorn, were tied up in Ellington's success. If *Newsweek* wanted to write about Duke Ellington the great bon vivant and scholar, Ellington gave them what they wanted. Of course, he would certainly answer any questions about Strayhorn with mighty praise, but he might not bring up Strayhorn's name unless he were asked about him. Obviously, none of this mattered to Strayhorn, who didn't appear to care one bit." Strayhorn's feelings, however, had more levels than his calmly accommodating manner suggested. In private with his intimates, Strayhorn revealed a deepening well of unease about his lack of public recognition as Ellington's prominence grew.

Honi Coles used his paternal authority over Strayhorn to pry a crack in his placid exterior in the summer of 1957—the August 20 issue of *Look* with the Ellington profile was still on the newsstands, Coles recalled. They met at the Flash Inn, an Italian restaurant near the Macombs Dam Bridge, a New York City landmark on the northern edge of Harlem. It was an ornately done-up spot, very pink and stucco, with pale blue arches along the walls that set off decorative oil paintings, originals by Castro (his full professional name) and other local artists. Strayhorn ate at the Flash Inn three or four nights a week, according to the owner, Joe Merenda, and the bartender, Cleo Hayes, both of whom considered him a friend. That night, Strayhorn ordered a bottle of Bordeaux and a Tanqueray martini to drink while the waiter was uncorking the wine. Coles had fettucine Alfredo, Strayhorn his favorite Flash Inn dish: charcoal-broiled lamb chops, extra well done. "I read Ellington's article in *Newsweek*," said Coles. "I asked him if he read it. He said, 'Yes.' I said, 'Why weren't you mentioned? You wrote every bit as much of that music they're fussing all over as Ellington, and they didn't even mention your name. Why do you let them get away with that?' We stopped eating, I believe, and we just talked. We never finished our meal. All Strayhorn could say to me was, 'Oh, Father, you know about these things. I don't care.' I said to him, 'I don't believe you. I think you do care or you wouldn't be drinking like a fucking fish every fucking time I see you.' That got him. Billy said, 'Be careful,

Father. Some day, I may get angry with you.' Then he said, 'Oh, Father, you know I don't need all that. I'm better off without all that. Let him have his articles. I'm better off this way.' I understood what he was saying. Because he wasn't a celebrity, he didn't have to answer to anybody about his lifestyle. So I said, 'I understand. The main thing is that you're happy.' And I asked him straight out, 'Are you?' And he went into his Father routine—'Oh, Father . . .' And he started to cry. I sat there with him, and Billy sat there, and he cried like a baby."

A few weeks later, the *Amsterdam News*, the Harlem daily, published a series of articles purporting to explain homosexuality. In an attempt at balance, the series provided homophobic Harlem residents a forum for commentary, including the following: "Harlem society is full of queers, both male and female. . . ." "Degenerate homosexuals know nothing of men of history." "Our main fight is against the influx of degenerate homosexuals, not just homosexuals, since there is a great difference." Clearly, Billy Strayhorn's interests were not well served by the press at the time.

Evidently frustrated and feeling vulnerable—"He didn't know where to turn," said Coles—Strayhorn found strength in the company of Francis Goldberg, the tall, outgoing one of the fraternal twins who had long been on the periphery of Strayhorn's circle of friends. "Goldie" homed straight to the center of this sphere in the late 1950s, absorbing more and more of Strayhorn's attention. Amber-skinned and trim, Goldberg had thick, wavy hair and sculpted cheekbones; he could have been a model, people told him, and he didn't dispute it. "Goldie didn't have a problem in the confidence department," said Haywood Williams. He liked to talk, which he did with his whole body; his arms were spidery, and he used them to amplify his speech, slowly waving them about in dramatic gestures that flowed from his shoulders to his hands. As an exclamation, he would jut his chin forward, arch his eyebrows and tilt his head at a side angle, something like a deer. He was considered flamboyant and, by some, overbearing. "He wasn't exactly the kind of guy you'd picture Billy going for," said Strayhorn's old Pittsburgh friend George Greenlee, who moved to New York in the 1950s to run a pharmacy in Queens. Greenlee saw some resemblance to Strayhorn's father: "He was tall and good-looking, boisterous, a very strong type of personality." Like James Strayhorn, too, Goldberg drank—every day and from early afternoon on, according to his friends (he died of cirrhosis in 1968). "You could say everybody drank in those days, but Goldie was a *drinker*," said Williams. "You'd never—never, never—see him without a drink. Billy started drinking more when he was with him, because that's what Goldie did, and they started doing everything together."

In Goldberg, Strayhorn found a companion especially eager to rove Manhattan. "They both liked the theater, they both liked museums, they both liked music," said Goldberg's sister, Gustavia Goldberg Pagan, who frequently had both her brothers and Strayhorn to her apartment on Tenth Avenue for a dinner of steaks and rice. One Sunday afternoon, Strayhorn and Goldie took Gustavia and her two children, Anna and Michael, to Coney Island; Strayhorn slipped off his shoes and walked the beach with the kids, munching on a hotdog for lunch and washing it down with something Goldie had brought in a thermos. "They took advantage of the whole city," said Pagan. "Goldie knew more about New York than anybody I've ever known. He could have been the best guide New York ever had." He was a professional chef, having learned basic skills from his father, Monticello Goldberg, a cook, while growing up in Dallas and then having trained as a cook in the navy; briefly, after he moved to New York during the war, he worked at the Ritz-Carlton, and he mentioned the fact proudly and frequently. "Goldie gave Billy a lot of cooking tips," said Frank Goldberg. "They were always in the kitchen together. Of course, Billy's favorite dish was always those beans cooked in beer. He would set out in the morning to prepare this dish, and it would take all day to get everything he needed. Billy and Goldie and I had to go to ten different stores to get everything." Between ingredients, Goldberg added, the group would break for rest stops in nine different bars.

"Billy adored Goldie heavily in a very romantic way," said Lena Horne. "It was the kind of attachment that ran very deep—it was a very needy relationship. There was something in Goldie that Billy needed very badly at that time. Strength, maybe. The booze, definitely." Strayhorn's affection for Goldberg was such that he persuaded the Copasetics to accept him as a member—at Goldberg's initiative and despite his obvious lack of show-business experience.

"He wanted to be in the Copasetics," said his twin, "and that was all Strayhorn needed to hear." As Coles recalled, Strayhorn, still the president, proposed admitting both Goldie and Frank Goldberg to defuse charges of favoritism toward his new companion, and he stressed the "administrative abilities" of Goldie, the chef, and Frank Goldberg, the postal worker, as special qualifications. "Basically, Goldie wanted to be wherever Billy was, and Billy wanted to make Goldie happy," said Coles. True to Strayhorn's argument, however, the Goldbergs served essential roles that aided the Copasetics in their expanding activities. "My brother was a doer," said Frank Goldberg. "You'd walk in and you'd say something needed to be done, and he'd do it. He'd take over. He was a doer. He was a take-charge type. 'I'll take care of it. I'll do it.' Next thing you know, he'd have it done." Francis Goldberg became treasurer. "Dancers aren't necessarily as good with money as we are with our feet. The best shuffling we do is on stage," said Phace Roberts. "Goldie was very interested in financial matters." Frank Goldberg took on a new responsibility: publication of a program—the Copasetics called it their souvenir booklet—to be distributed annually at the group's shows.

Under Strayhorn's leadership, the Copasetics were now producing full-scale musical revues, presented annually on a Monday evening near the end of September. The productions were conceived by an entertainment committee consisting of Strayhorn, Coles, Atkins, and their fellow members Pete Nugent, William "Chink" Collins, and Roy Branker; Strayhorn wrote the music—four to eight new songs related to the theme of each show—as well as big-band arrangements to be played by the Milton Larkin Orchestra, a solid Harlem affair orchestra. "The members of the entertainment committee would get together and come up with all the skits and the dialogue and whatnot. We'd put a good deal of time and work into it," said Atkins, who recalled that a few months would go into writing about forty-five minutes of material, half the show. A typical skit: the Copasetics, portraying policemen, barge into a garage to bust some crap-shooting hoodlums and their dames, but the game beckons and the cops play, joining the gamblers and their ladies for a production number. After the Copasetics' first full-scale event in 1951, which had been held at the Sudan nightclub (on the site of the original Cotton Club in Harlem), the group's location of choice was the Riviera Terrace Room, a swank banquet hall equipped with a stage on Broadway at West 73rd Street. In 1957, more than eleven hundred ticket buyers—virtually all show-business insiders and figures in black society—paid fifteen dollars apiece to attend the *Copasetics Cruise*. It was the social event of the season in Harlem and apparently was never acknowledged, even in a passing reference, in a single New York publication beyond the black press. "Anybody who was anybody had to be there," said Rachel Robinson, the wife of Jackie Robinson; the couple attended nearly every year, including 1957, when they were in the company of Lena Horne and Lennie Hayton, Miles Davis, Willie Mays, and others. (Duke Ellington never attended the Copasetics' events; "I believe he didn't want to upstage Billy," said Coles. "The Copasetics were something Billy had away from Duke, and Ellington kept it that way for him. I give him credit for that." Ellington and/or Tempo Music offered support to the organization by advertising in the souvenir booklets, however.) "People waited all year for the next Copasetics night," added Robinson. "It was important to the community—all that talent dedicated to doing something good for the community, and no profit motive. You felt wonderful being a part of it."

Strayhorn drew multiple rewards from his part in the Copasetics. In addition to the fraternal support of the group, he found the Copasetics shows a creative outlet removed from Ellingtonia: his compositions for the Copasetics reveal a side of him unheard elsewhere in his work. Nearly unidentifiable as Strayhorn's, the music is sheer play. As examples, two numbers performed at the 1957 *Copasetics Cruise*, "Welcome Aboard Blues" and "Bon Voyage" (the former with lyrics by Strayhorn and music cowritten by Strayhorn and Roy Branker, a cocktail pianist), find the author of "Grievin' " and "Passion Flower" in a state of jubilant abandon. The music to both numbers is likable, rhythmic fun as lighthearted as the words. "Welcome Aboard Blues":

> We've got frik-a-frak, apple jack
> Over the top, a little slop.
> We've even got a little razzmatazz,
> We've got luki-plu, mop-mop,

Oolya-coo, bebop
Loaded to the decks with jazz.

So welcome aboard,
The S.S. Copasetic's yours for the run of the cruise
So say adieu, *goodbye to the blues,*
And have a ball,
Because you're all
Welcome aboard.

"Bon Voyage" begins so flippantly that its fourth line hints at the conditions under which it may have been written:

Bon bon bon bon bon bon bon bon bon voyage,
Hope the crossing is fine.
Enjoy yourself and frolic ev'ry day,
Improve your health the alcoholic way,
And you'll have a wonderful time.

Indeed, said Honi Coles, "Billy had a good time when he wrote for us. He was often quite inebriated."

Several other key figures in the Ellington organization were pursuing musical projects of their own at the same time, though none as far from Ellingtonia as Strayhorn ventured with the Copasetics. In fact, like Johnny Hodges with his recent work for Verve, Ellington Orchestra members Clark Terry and Cat Anderson insured their solo efforts with the equity of Ellington's resurging appeal. They worked almost exclusively in the Ellington-Strayhorn vein and with other Ellingtonians, including Strayhorn, who was called on to compose and arrange music as well as play piano for several Ellington-oriented recordings without Ellington's participation. Terry's effort, inappropriately titled *In a Mellow Tone* (and later reissued more appropriately as *Duke with a Difference*), featured nine Ellington instrumentalists performing jam-session versions of material from the Ellington Orchestra repertoire, including "Take the 'A' Train"; Strayhorn arranged and played gracefully modernist piano on two of eight numbers, Ellington's "Come Sunday" and "In a Sentimental Mood," the latter sung by Marian Bruce, a young cabaret singer with a bright, clear contralto. "The session was a small but not insignificant example of what Billy would do without Duke," said Orrin Keepnews, who produced the album for Riverside Records. "What we were trying to do was treat the Ellington songbook in a different way, so it was a rare time when Billy got to do that music and somebody said, 'Hey, play piano, but don't be Duke. Play it like yourself.' He loved the idea, and it really comes across." The Anderson project, entitled *Ellingtonia* and credited to Cat Anderson and the Ellington All-Stars, features new Strayhorn arrangements of two of his standards, "Chelsea Bridge" and "A Flower Is a Lovesome Thing," plus a piece composed for the album, "Lovelinessence," a warmly enveloping ballad, vintage Strayhorn. Unfortunately, the low-budget Strand Records release failed to include composer credits for any of its selections; as a result, Strayhorn's contributions as composer and arranger went unacknowledged.

With Johnny Hodges, meanwhile, Strayhorn had been participating in at least an album a year since *Creamy* in 1955. The following year had seen *Ellingtonia 56*, a mixture of small-ensemble and big-band pieces (featuring the entire Ellington Orchestra, minus its leader) arranged by Strayhorn, who played gentle ensemble piano throughout and contributed the swinging "Snibor"; spelled backwards and altered, the title was a tribute to Fred Robbins, a disc jockey and the host of one of Strayhorn's favorite jazz radio programs, *Robbins Nest*. Later the same year came *Duke's in Bed* by Johnny Hodges and the Ellington All-Stars without Duke. Again, Strayhorn contributed all the arrangements, limber settings for a nine-piece band, and he played piano and wrote one new original, "Ballad for Very Tired and Very Sad Lotus Eaters," a luxurious, serious piece, its Satie-like title notwithstanding. In 1957, there was *The Big Sound* by Johnny Hodges and the Ellington Men, which Strayhorn arranged much in the style of his work with Ellington and for which he played supportive band piano but submitted only one composition, his "Johnny Come Lately" from 1941. Produced by Norman Granz, all the Hodges albums find Strayhorn at leisure; they're after-hours sessions—some friends making a little music for extra money, working without the pressures of their high-profile Ellington work. "I think those records were an important release for [Strayhorn]," said Granz. "He had a unique opportunity to play piano, for one thing, which he did wonderfully. I never told him to play like Ellington. He was great to work with. Nothing was a problem. He had a wonderful, relaxed way about him. Johnny loved him. Everybody loved him. They loved working with him, and he was very happy to do the work. I think the opportunity to do that work on his own, away from Ellington, was awfully valuable to him and good for him."

Hodges and Strayhorn seemed the most unlikely friends. Educated only through the first few grades of elementary school in the black pocket of Cambridge, Massachusetts, Hodges was a lifelong working musician, originally a drummer, then a pianist, and, by his early teens, a soprano saxophonist with the instrument's early master, Sidney Bechet. Hodges had already played in three other ensembles, including one of swing pioneer Chick Webb's bands, when he joined Ellington's budding aggregation in 1928. Embarrassed by his modest vocabulary and often shaky grammar, especially in the company of the grandiloquent Ellington, Hodges developed a protective shell of taciturnity. He declined to sign autographs, even for his most ardent fans, because he could scarcely write his name. "Everybody said Johnny was gruff. They thought he was cold," said his wife, Cue Hodges. "He was just afraid." In performance, Johnny Hodges set the shell aside and, with impeccable musical eloquence, expressed his exceptional sensitivity and good humor. Hodges and Strayhorn were a model of compatible contrasts: one, outwardly stoic, produced music of heart-swelling emotionality; the other, publicly exuberant, created works of tortured discontent. "Neither one of them guys was really who they seemed," said "Wild Bill" Davis, an organist who was a frequent partner of Hodges's for Verve. "Johnny was just as mushy inside as Strayhorn was froufrouy." Working together, Hodges and Strayhorn made complementary collaborators, gut musical feeling and conservatory acuity united in artistic fidelity.

Strayhorn so enjoyed playing with Hodges that he agreed to take one of his extremely rare live-performance engagements as 1958 began. Combining a winter vacation with work, he and Hodges accepted an offer to play the Shamrock Lounge in Miami Beach, a handsome music room with a view of the ocean and an upper-crust clientele, located in the Golden Strand Hotel on Collins Avenue, the resort strip; it was owned by Frank S. Leslie, a Toronto-based investor and jazz buff who had met Strayhorn and Hodges at his flagship hotel, a summer resort in Huntsville, Ontario, called the Bigwin Inn, where the Ellington Orchestra had performed on several occasions. Ellington released Hodges from his band temporarily, replacing him for three months with Bill Graham, a fixture at Snookie's jazz club in Manhattan who could approximate Hodges's marzipan tone. Fleshing out their group, Strayhorn and Hodges enlisted as bassist Bill Pemberton, a New York gig player, and as drummer Jimmy Grissom, who had sung with Ellington from time to time earlier in the 1950s. Leslie gave the band its name, The Indigos, to evoke the Ellington connection, which he emphasized promotionally; ads in the *Miami Herald* announced "The Indigos quartette [*sic*—a Strayhorn touch?] featuring Billy Strayhorn, Johnny Hodges from the famous Duke Ellington Band—Dancing." Booked from January 23 through the end of March, the group played Strayhorn tunes, including "Your Love Has Faded" and "Passion Flower"; Hodges vehicles from the Ellington band book such as "The Jeep Is Jumpin' "; and standards, according to Cue Hodges, who stayed with her husband in one of the Golden Strand's beachfront "villas." Strayhorn was their next-villa neighbor and lived alone, although he had a few male visitors, Cue Hodges noticed. "They had a good little group," she said. "Swinging. The people enjoyed hearing them. Johnny liked his breaks from Ellington, and so did Billy."

Duke Ellington didn't hire a sub for Billy Strayhorn. Working in Los Angeles on the first studio recording of *Black, Brown and Beige*—a revised, truncated version featuring the celebrated gospel singer Mahalia Jackson—Ellington called on Strayhorn for last-minute arrangements. "I was in Florida . . . working with Johnny Hodges," recalled Strayhorn. "We were working at a hotel, so, of course, we were off at 2:00 in the morning, Eastern Standard Time. So, I would go home, and he [Ellington] was recording at—you know, in the afternoon, at 2:00 in the afternoon [Pacific Standard Time]. So I would go home and stay up until time to call him, until the time that he was up. And we would confer over the phone about what was to be recorded that day. I was writing things [such as a new arrangement of "Come Sunday"], and I had a cab driver down there who would take the score to the airport and mail it off air special. He became very skillful at doing it, and he'd mail it off to Los Angeles. It ended up, of course, that I didn't hear anything that was recorded, even things that I had written. They were recorded, and I didn't hear them until a year later." Strayhorn was given no credit of any kind on the resulting Columbia LP, released in September 1958.

To build on his reputation as a cultural leader, Ellington needed something fresher than Ella Fitzgerald's *Songbook* of his hits and Mahalia Jackson's version of his 1943 masterpiece. Neither project advanced his redefined collaborative relationship with Strayhorn either. Fortunately, exactly the right sort of opportunity came their way while Strayhorn was working in Florida: Ellington took a commission to create the score for a serious-minded Broadway production. Based on a little-read 1955 novel, *Mine Boy*, by a black South African writer named Peter Abrahams, the proposed drama with songs would explore the theme of apartheid as it affected the lives of an all-black cast of characters. Ellington had signed on in New York after a brief pitch by the show's lyricist, Herbert Martin, and its principal producer, Christopher Manos. Both were eager newcomers in their twenties (and both white), undaunted by the challenge of mounting an all-black musical tragedy about racial oppression. Ellington haggled a bit over his compensation but agreed to contribute the score with no advance payment, and he took a copy of the script and Martin's libretto—complete lyrics for seventeen songs—to set to music. Touring with his orchestra, as always, Ellington met Strayhorn in mid-January 1958 to work on the show during a week's engagement at the Bal Masque in Miami Beach's Americana Hotel; Ellington mentioned the new project to Beatrice Washburn, a reporter for the *Miami Herald*, who wrote, a tad prematurely, "Though popular music is the stuff of his existence, two of his main achievements are *Mine Boy*, an operetta on South Africa, and *A Drum Is a Woman*, the history of jazz." In an extraordinary step for a producer, Christopher Manos had traveled south with Ellington and his orchestra. "I thought it was awfully unusual that Duke agreed to do it immediately, so I asked around, and I heard that he had a way of saying yes and then doing nothing about it," said Manos. "So I says, 'Duke, are you really going to be able to do this?' And he says, 'Well, you know, I'm very busy.' And I says, 'Well, just tell me if you can't do it.' And he says, 'Well, the only way it'll get done is if you come with me on the road and goose me.' So that's what I did."

In Miami Beach and a couple of nearby locations, where Ellington and his orchestra played through January 21, the team of Manos, Ellington, and Strayhorn worked at putting Martin's lyrics to melodies. Manos's role was counselor and spur, while Ellington's and Strayhorn's roles, seemingly interchangeable, remained mysterious to Manos. "Duke would work alone or he'd be with Strayhorn or Strayhorn would work by himself—I never knew exactly what was going on," said Manos. "At some point, Duke would play me a melody or a little thematic thing. His technique was, 'Do you like *this*? How about *that*.' I'd give him my input, and he would go away again and go over it with Strayhorn. Then the thing would get a little further along. They would work a few days on a song, and it would be finished. I never had any idea who did what, but there was no misunderstanding that Billy was every bit as involved as Duke, maybe more so when it came to the writing." Throughout the process, Ellington and Strayhorn used Martin's lyrics precisely as submitted and never proposed the slightest modification. "It was peculiar that they accepted everything that I wrote and wrote music to it," said Martin. "I couldn't complain that they were working that way and ending up with songs, but there was something missing in the lack of give and take. There are some things that could have been better had I sat down with Ellington or with Strayhorn and had we actually worked together." As Martin recalled, Ellington's interest in the show seemed to wane not long after his initial efforts with Manos and Strayhorn, whereupon Strayhorn appeared to assume control of the project. Indeed, Strayhorn's personal investment in *Mine Boy* evidently ran deeper than Ellington's. "Billy was really hoping it would work," Manos said. "Billy was, I would say, a bigger catalyst for the piece than Duke was, in that he was really hopeful that it would work. 'How's it coming?' 'Is it working?' Those kinds of questions were asked much more by him than by Duke, who sort of wanted to get something down that would work and move on with his band." Once the music for *Mine Boy* was complete—a total of twenty-two songs finished by the summer of 1958—Strayhorn's hopes for the show hung with Manos and his success at fund-raising, a laborious and uncertain task for any Broadway production, let alone a musical about apartheid.

Back in New York with Francis Goldberg, Strayhorn found some solace. Goldberg moved into Strayhorn's apartment on West 106th Street, and they set up a housekeeping system: Goldberg handled everything. "That's just how he was," said Frank Goldberg. "Strayhorn didn't have to worry about anything—my brother took care of it. Shopping, cooking, organizing things. Billy didn't have to worry anymore." Whenever friends stopped by, which some were now less likely to do, Goldberg played host. While Strayhorn had shared entertaining duties with Aaron Bridgers, cooking while Bridgers tended bar, attending to guests while Bridgers changed the records, now he lounged with a drink and chatted impassively while Goldberg scurried from room to room. Outside the house, Goldberg assumed a similarly visible and influential role in Strayhorn's life. "No matter what Billy was involved in, Goldie was suddenly there," said Bill Patterson, who frequently met the two of them late in the evening after they had attended Ellington Orchestra recording sessions or Columbia Records events together. Like Patterson, several of Strayhorn's oldest friends betrayed traces of envy. "Goldie knew Billy like a book," said Haywood Williams. "He knew how to make him happy. I think Billy needed to feel appreciated at that point, and Goldie worshiped him. He treated him like he was a god. And they lived like it too." Williams would visit on weekends; by noon, he said, Strayhorn and Goldberg were serving Bloody Marys, and in the afternoon, cocktail time, they'd have a few martinis, then a few more before dinner, an occasion for wine. "Then we'd go out drinking," said Williams. "Goldie was the leader. He made all the decisions. I don't know—maybe that's what Billy needed then. Maybe Goldie was good for him. How could you tell? How could *they* know? They were always drunk."

Thoroughly insinuated into Strayhorn's private and professional life—one of Ellington's notebooks bears the notation "Goldie" and the phone number of the apartment Goldberg shared with Strayhorn—Goldberg lobbied determinedly to accompany Strayhorn and the Ellington Orchestra on an extended European tour arranged for October and November of 1958. "We were involved in putting together our fall Copasetics event, and Strayhorn was preparing for this trip," said Honi Coles. "Goldie was very jealous that Billy was going to Europe for three months without him. Billy almost didn't go. Goldie had him feeling guilty about it. But Duke wasn't about to pay for Goldie, and Goldie wasn't going to pay his own way." In the final days of September, Coles and a few fellow Copasetics, including Cookie Cook, along with Strayhorn's old friend Bill Coleman, saw Strayhorn and the Ellington Orchestra off at a bash Ellington threw at Manhattan's Pier 88, where the Ellingtonians were sailing for Plymouth, England, on the *Ile de France*; Goldberg stayed at home. "It was quite an elegant affair," said Coleman. "Billy seemed to be having a great time." Whatever the nature of Strayhorn's conflict with Goldberg, he kept it private. "Everyone was toasting each other farewell. Billy was quite in his element," continued Coleman. As the ship headed across the Atlantic, Strayhorn remained in the festive spirit: "He was toasting day and night," recalled the trombonist Britt Woodman. Strayhorn stopped, however, on the last evening of the voyage, October 2. At Ellington's recommendation, Strayhorn was named guest of honor at the trip's climactic captain's party, a lavish ceremonial dinner traditionally held in tribute to the ship's most celebrated passenger. More than a hundred passengers gathered to offer Strayhorn his grandest toast, but he didn't attend. Early the next morning, he was found nattily dressed and asleep on the floor in a corner of the ship's mess, where he had passed out, apparently while looking for something to eat.

At the home of wealthy friends of Herbert Martin's in Hartford, Christopher Manos was running backers' auditions for *Mine Boy*, now titled *Saturday Laughter* ("sounded like more fun than a mine," said Manos), while the composers played one-nighters across Europe. From October 5 through November 20, the Ellington Orchestra gave thirty-seven concerts in thirty-three cities, from Berlin to Oslo. Strayhorn had little to do and put his all into it. "He wasn't writing anything at the time," said Jimmy Woode. "During many of the days, we enjoyed restaurants together. Billy did a good deal of shopping. He came to our shows to hear the band. After the performances, several of us generally went out to hear the local music over cocktails." In London, the British baritone saxophonist Joe Temperley, then playing with the trumpeter Humphrey Lyttelton's swing-style band (one of England's most popular jazz groups), went pubbing with his idol, Harry Carney, after one of the Ellington Orchestra's shows; Strayhorn joined them and attracted some attention by drinking gin and tonics, straight up, in pint glasses. "Pubbing, cabareting, clubbing—all those things. That was how Billy spent his time," said Woode. "He was enjoying himself."

Christopher Manos, meanwhile, was not. For readings of select scenes and musical numbers from the show, he had retained a musical director, Abba Bogin, and a working cast, which included Ellington's occasional vocalist Joya Sherrill, Strayhorn's friend Brock Peters, Thelma Carpenter (formerly with Basie), and new faces Diahann Carroll and Ivan Dixon; all donated their time on the understanding that they would be hired for the anticipated Broadway production. "The music we got from Ellington, whether he wrote it or did it with Strayhorn or Strayhorn did it, whatever, needed some work to be usable in auditions, let alone in an actual production," said Bogin. "What we got very often would be a sketch of a thirty-two- or sixty-four-bar tune in a very straight, commercial form. It might have to be extended or have to be shortened or changed around at various points. The singers had difficulties with some sections, and there was no composer there. So we'd figure something out ourselves and just do it; we had no choice. Strangely enough, I don't think Ellington cared one way or another what we did. I met him early on before he left with his band, and he said to me, 'I'm sure you know your business. Whatever you guys do is fine. I don't have the time to be with you. If the show gets produced, I'll try to stop in and see what you did. Until then, do whatever you want.' I got the distinct impression that he had no concept of what it took to write a show, in terms of knowing what the play is all about or doing what a Richard Rodgers or any composer working for the theater would do to be involved with the play and try to make a song work as part of a show." Another possibility is that Ellington's show-business experience, rather than naïveté, prompted him to practice artistic triage. Having already expended his and Strayhorn's creative resources on the project, which was one with notable artistic merit but little apparent commercial potential, he gave priority to his orchestra, the lifeline of his career. As Manos acknowledged, the very nature of *Saturday Laughter* was its undoing. "This was right at the beginning of the civil rights movement in this country, and we were trying to stage a Broadway show based on the black point of view on apartheid in South Africa," said Manos. "We were young and idealistic. But the money people weren't." By late November, when Strayhorn returned to New York with Ellington and the orchestra, *Saturday Laughter* had been disbanded for lack of funds.

In the absence of a high-profile new project, Ellington agreed to revive another of his neglected early efforts, much as he had the previous year with the Mahalia Jackson version of *Black, Brown and Beige*. "Originally, see, Duke had big, big hopes for *Jump for Joy*," recalled Sid Kuller, the principal lyricist of the 1941 production. "He thought it really should have made it to Broadway like we had planned, but we were way ahead of our time." With civil rights so much in the news, Kuller urged Ellington to resurrect their satirical take on Uncle Tomism, a decidedly more accessible approach to black consciousness than *Saturday Laughter*. "Duke liked the idea of showing people what they missed, see. Right an old wrong," added Kuller. Opportunely, the booking agent Joe Glaser wanted the Ellington Orchestra for an extended run at the Copa City dinner theater in Miami Beach. Acceding to Kuller's overtures, Ellington offered Glaser an update of *Jump for Joy* and headed to Chicago, where he was booked to play the Blue Note nightclub from December 17 to January 4, a holiday-season tradition for the Ellington Orchestra. Immediately after Christmas, Strayhorn joined Kuller in Miami Beach; Goldberg stayed home again, to his distress ("Goldie couldn't leave his job, but he couldn't understand that Billy had to leave New York for *his* job," Honi Coles recalled), and the two old collaborators set out to write a new show in less than three weeks' time.

When Ellington got to Florida in the second week of January, about a week before the updated edition of *Jump for Joy* was due to open, Strayhorn and Kuller had written several new songs, including a gospel number, "So the Good Book Says"; a misplaced piece of xenophobia called "If We Were Any More British, We Couldn't Talk at All"; and an ode to the cool-jazz attitude, "Walk It Off." "That one was totally Billy's idea, the title and even some of the words," said Kuller. "It was his philosophy. You got a problem? Walk it off." On Ellington's arrival, the trio hammered out nearly a dozen additional tunes, from the sultry vamp showcase "Three Shows

Nightly," designed for the nightclub singer Barbara McNair, to the burlesque novelty "Show 'Em You Got Class," performed by the comedian Timmie Rogers. "All I had to do was think about Strayhorn," said Rogers. "He *was* class." Kuller, Strayhorn, and Ellington kept writing new songs for the show more than a week after it opened on January 20. Produced by Kuller and choreographed by Nick Castle, a veteran Hollywood dance director whom Kuller had met at MGM, the one-set production jammed a cast of nearly thirty singers and dancers, including the vocalists Lil Greenwood and Jimmie Randolph, Talley Beatty, and the comic dance duo Stump and Stumpy (James Cross and Harold Cromer), onto Copa City's modest stage. The music was credited to Ellington alone; Strayhorn was acknowledged, along with Ellington, as one of the arrangers. (In copyright registrations filed by the show's publisher, Robbins Music, Ellington and Strayhorn were cited as co-composers of three songs: "If We Were Any More British, We Couldn't Talk at All," "So the Good Book Says," and "Walk It Off." None of the music written for the production was recorded.) Although ads in the *Miami Herald* announced, "Pre-Broadway Engagement . . . The World's Greatest Musical Extravaganza of All Time," the production was scattered and formless. Kuller cut and added songs and skits nightly in a frazzled, ultimately futile effort to stimulate attendance. *Variety* reported "extensive revisions since first night in an attempt to come up with a staging that can overcome the negative results on patron pull." Frustrated, Kuller and Ellington struggled to salvage the show. "We loved the thing," said Kuller. "We would do anything to save it, and we tried. The thing is, see, we finally realized people don't go on vacation to Miami Beach to become socially enlightened. We were giving it to them with sugarcoating. But it was still medicine. The resort crowd didn't want it." Some hundred thousand dollars in the red, *Jump for Joy* closed abruptly on February 8, and Copa City shut down for the duration of Miami's peak vacation season.

Strayhorn appeared to take the production's failure in stride. "Let me put it to you this way," said Kuller. "Billy wasn't as personally excited about the show as he was when we did it in 1941. His work was fantastic. When he sat down to write music, he was 100 percent involved. He was a master at his craft. But I mean, he didn't seem to be overly concerned personally if the show made it or not.

As soon as he was done writing, he was off. He and Paul Gonsalves went out partying. Man, when they were around, the booze was flowing. This was a different guy than the peaceful kid I took to the wine country in 1941, let me tell you." As Talley Beatty noted, "Billy was *flying*. It was party time for him. His attitude was, 'This is Duke's thing. Good for him. I've done my work. I hope you like it. Now, goodbye, I'm going to have a drink now.' "

Strayhorn returned home by the second week of February 1959, nearly two months before *Jump for Joy* had been scheduled to end its run, to find Francis Goldberg charging abandonment. They were in the middle of an ugly squabble when a musician friend of Strayhorn's stopped by their apartment to pick Strayhorn up for an Ellington Orchestra recording session. Strayhorn opened the door for his colleague, who lingered in the living room while Strayhorn hustled into the kitchen to talk to Goldberg. "He didn't even offer me a drink," said Strayhorn's fellow musician, "so I knew there was something serious happening." Only Goldberg's voice carried through the kitchen door. "The guy was out of control, screaming, carrying on. 'You're always going somewhere without me,' this and that about going to Florida. It was not pretty, man." About twenty minutes later, Strayhorn glided through the door pleasantly, and he and his friend cabbed downtown. "We went down to the date, and he said to me, 'I have to apologize to you for what you were just exposed to.' I said, 'No, man, that's all right. Are you okay?' That's all *I* was concerned about—was *he* okay. He said, 'I'm fine, thank you. *He* is a *very vulgar* person. And I don't like that very much.' The way he said that, 'He is a *very vulgar* person'—that was Strayhorn, man."

Several of Strayhorn's other friends were seeing signs of growing conflict. As Bill Patterson observed, "Billy had always let Goldie do everything for him. Everybody always knew that. But Goldie took it too far. He dominated Strayhorn, and Billy went along with it; he seemed to want it. But Goldie got abusive." According to Haywood Williams, "Goldie couldn't control his emotions. All of his feelings were strong feelings, and when he was upset, he really took it out on Billy." At least once or twice a week, Strayhorn was meeting friends for drinks without Goldberg and leaking hints of mounting distress. "Billy had one or two more than he should have and he let it out more than he would have any other time," recalled one of his best friends. "He said, 'You know, he can really hurt a person when he wants to. I don't know how much of it I care to take.' " Initially a boost to Strayhorn's self-esteem, Goldberg's force of personality had hardened into a tool of diminution.

Ellington's stature as a composer grew, unimpeded by the failure of *Saturday Laughter* and the disappointing revival of *Jump for Joy*. Branching into yet another medium, he accepted a commission to score his first feature film, exactly the kind of venture beyond the jazz world that helped validate a jazz artist as a real composer in the eyes of the mainstream. The producer and director Otto Preminger, a radical by Hollywood standards—he had defied censorship rules by allowing words like *virgin* and *pregnant* in his 1953 film *The Moon Is Blue*, and had produced two all-black films, the 1954 *Carmen Jones* and *Porgy and Bess*, released early in 1959—asked Ellington to compose the score for his screen adaptation of the best-selling courtroom novel *Anatomy of a Murder*. Written by Michigan Supreme Court Justice John D. Voelker under the pseudonym Robert Traver, the book told the story of a country lawyer (portrayed by James Stewart) defending a jealous husband (Ben Gazzara) accused of killing a suspected rapist of his flirtatious wife (Lee Remick). "Otto chose Duke because Duke would be a talked-about choice, and Otto valued that," explained his wife, Hope, who worked on *Anatomy of a Murder* as a costume designer before their marriage. "And he liked to use people who really wanted to score a film. Otto was quite unusual because he insisted on having the composer on the set during the production. He felt that they got closer to the picture that way. Therefore, he said he liked to use composers eager to prove themselves, because nobody else would sit for spending all that time on the set."

True to custom, Ellington had Strayhorn fill in for him as *Anatomy of a Murder* began production in the third week of March. With almost gimmicky veracity, Preminger was shooting entirely on location in the actual settings in rural Ishpeming, Michigan, that Voelker had depicted in his book. (As an exception, Voelker's own Victorian house was used as the defense attorney's residence.) The entire cast and crew of about 120 were put up at the one hotel in the area, the Marquette Mather Inn, a rough-hewn old place where

Strayhorn stayed while he watched rehearsals, jotting notes for the music by day and reading Voelker's novel over sips of cognac in the hotel lounge through the evening. A cozy hotel with a bar that closed promptly at 11:00 p.m., it brought out Strayhorn's convivial grace. "Billy was an utter delight, wonderful company," said Lee Remick, with whom Strayhorn took a few late-night walks along the dirt paths leading into the surrounding woods. "He told me all the names of the trees and the things he thought were beautiful about them." Strayhorn would occasionally drift to the lounge piano and play requests or snippets of classical pieces. More than once, James Stewart joined him for four-hand duets. "He was a fine gentleman and a heck of a pianist. I never sounded so good," said Stewart, who had studied piano and sung (and recorded) with a New Orleans–style jazz band during his undergraduate years at Princeton. Ellington arrived the first week of May, some two months after Strayhorn but early enough in the production to spend a couple of weeks living with the cast and crew; he so valued the commission that he postponed his usual summer stint at the Blue Note in Chicago until mid-July. Less willing to sacrifice his usual Chicago steaks, he had beef shipped in from the Sutherland Hotel's butcher to be prepared at the inn. "Between the fish that Voelker caught in the morning and the steaks that Duke had flown in, we ate very well," Hope Preminger recalled.

For all his controlling devices, Otto Preminger had little influence on the music composed for *Anatomy of a Murder:* it's pure Ellingtonia and, as such, a most unconventional movie score, thematically bracing, hardly subordinate mood music. Strayhorn contributed a few touches, including a couple of lyrical bars in the main theme and a pretty part for celeste, which he also played for the soundtrack; he performed as well the tender piano solo seemingly played on screen by Stewart in a pensive moment at home. "He asked me to play something I liked," explained Stewart. "What I think he did, you see, was write something for me that I would have played myself. It was very interesting the way he did it." When not composing on the inn's piano in Ishpeming, Ellington and Strayhorn worked up arrangements for the Ellington Orchestra and oversaw the soundtrack recording at the Radio Recorders studios in Los Angeles; holed up in a four-room suite at the Chateau

Marmont for several days of intensive arranging and recording, Strayhorn increased their efficiency by preparing the meals. "He became the official cook, because we had a great big kitchen with lots of pots and pans. He would not allow anyone else to enter the kitchen, and he used to cook some great dishes. He even got himself a chef's hat," wrote Ellington in his 1973 memoir, *Music Is My Mistress*.

Though Preminger used only a fraction of the music composed for the film, he got his news value: the score was widely noted as a breakthrough for Ellington and celebrated, especially by the jazz press. As Nat Hentoff wrote in the *Saturday Review*, "This is one of [Ellington's] most satisfying collections of new themes in recent years. There is . . . evident in the score Ellington's unique capacity to create quickly evocative, impressionistic moods; and there is, above all, his commanding ability to use his orchestra as his own instrument. The result is film writing that sounds much more personal than most, since it has been, in effect, performed as well as written by one man." Ellington himself characterized the score as a learning experience. "Music in pictures should say something without being obviously music, you know, and this was all new to me," he said in an interview for the *American Weekly Entertainment Guide*. "I'll try another one and then I'll show them." Strayhorn kept his distance from the project: although he attended the film's preview screening at the Stanley Warner Theater in New York on June 19, 1959, he sat with a friend, a concert pianist, apart from Preminger, Ellington, and the stars (and Joe Morgen), and he passed up the premiere party for a quiet dinner for two in Greenwich Village. "Billy said, 'Let's have spaghetti,' " recalled his companion, the pianist. "I said, 'Well, maybe we should at least make an appearance at the party. Aren't they expecting you?' And Billy said, 'Oh, let Edward have his fun. I could use a drink.' "

9

UP AND

DOWN,

UP AND

DOWN

Saturdays used to be Goldie's. Initiating the weekend with cosmopolitan fervor, Strayhorn and Goldberg would typically catch the matinee revue at the Apollo or an afternoon concert at Carnegie Hall and try a new restaurant the New York chefs were talking about. Frank or Gustavia might come along. It was a surface mark of the corrosion of his relationship with Goldberg that as the 1950s ended, Strayhorn entered into a new Saturday routine with another group of friends. He started socializing regularly with a prosperous black couple, Marian and Arthur Logan, whose brownstone at 121 West 88th Street on Manhattan's Upper West Side was becoming a social center for New York's black elite. Strayhorn had met Marian Logan professionally when she was Marian Bruce, the nightclub singer he accompanied on Clark Terry's *In a Mellow Tone* album. Since her marriage to Logan, a doctor, in March 1958, she had largely ceded her musical career to a role as one of black society's grand hostesses. A handsome woman and self-assuredly possessed, she wore her good looks like an object to be coveted; because of her high, sculpted cheekbones and flowing, waved shoulder-length hair, she resembled Marlene Dietrich, and, like her, she would never stand or sit—she would lounge. She chain-smoked Kents with her left hand and held her drink, usually champagne—"my bubbly"—in her right. Marian Logan was particular: she preferred Dom Perignon, talked about favorite vintages impressively, and served them in fluted French crystal from Tiffany's. She had a light, throaty speaking voice and carried on conversations in a disarming blend of formal language, softly and carefully articulated, and slang, spit out. Describing her home's interior design, she said, "We requested that an open staircase be constructed, leading to the second floor. Arthur and I thought it might bring a sense of mystery to the room, although it allowed all the men to look up at my ass." Gutted to the beams and renovated to their specifications, the main floor of the nineteenth-century townhouse the Logans bought early in 1960 was thoroughly as inviting as the exposed walnut stairway that served as its centerpiece. All the old interior walls were removed, creating one room the length of the building, a party space. There was a grand piano at the front end of the floor and a small bar in the back; dark woods and muted earth tones shrank the space and warmed it. "Marian's parlor was one of the real 'in' places of black society," said Rachel Robinson, the wife of Jackie Robinson. "Marian was an extraordinary hostess. She had cocktail parties that were like a Who's Who." In the late 1950s, Logan played hostess to the likes of the Robinsons, Lena Horne, Harry Belafonte, and Sarah Vaughan, as well as Duke Ellington and Billy Strayhorn.

Neither man gravitated to the Logans' for social status. While Strayhorn was inching into Marian Logan's inner circle, Ellington became close to her husband, his personal physician—an admitted hypochondriac's best friend. Reared in Tuskegee, Alabama, and educated at Williams College in Massachusetts and the Columbia College of Physicians and Surgeons, Logan had the cordial warmth of a country gentleman and a professional authority that engendered trust among the most privacy-conscious patients, public figures such as the Reverend Dr. Martin Luther King, Jr., and the Robinsons, in addition to Ellington and Strayhorn and many of their friends, including most of the Copasetics. (In 1956, Strayhorn had titled a surging, bop-oriented piece he composed for the Ellington Orchestra after the institution where the Copasetics received medical attention and Dr. Logan practiced, "Upper Manhattan Medical Group," or "U.M.M.G.") Logan had a finely groomed mustache and a furrowed pompadour, both silver. Fair-skinned and delicately featured with olive eyes, he was frequently mistaken for white. "I got used to the dirty looks from people who thought I was hanging on a white man, and a doctor, yet," said Marian Logan. When Logan spoke, which he did with the slightest Alabama accent, he would steadily increase both the speed and the pitch of his voice, then clip off the last word of a sentence, leaving an instant of sudden silence; this infused the most casual remarks with dramatic impact. Ellington, now over sixty, treasured his association with Logan and not only because the doctor carried weight with Ellington's most fearsome antagonist, his mortality. "Of course, Edward needed Arthur. Arthur kept him healthy, so he could make his music," said Marian Logan. "Edward also loved the *idea* of Arthur. He thought it was magnificent to have his personal physician with him all the time, like some sort of ancient potentate. He loved to have Arthur and I at recording sessions, and we'd go to all of the shows—he'd see to it that we never had to pay—so he could have his personal physician on hand. He would call Arthur at the most ungodly hours—four in the morning, five in the morning—just to make sure Arthur would pick up the phone in case he might *really* need him for something if he weren't perfectly healthy, which Edward usually was. Edward knew he was a hypochondriac—lots of people are. Big deal. That doesn't mean anything. Edward liked the idea of having his doctor at his beck and call, anywhere, anytime, and Arthur was complicit in it. Arthur went along for the ride. You know why? He loved it, too. He loved the idea of being Duke Ellington's doctor. It was all a big, fabulous charade, two grown men playing dress-up."

Early on Saturday afternoons, Strayhorn called Marian Logan from one of the pay phones by the escalators in Macy's basement, where the store sold imported foods and gourmet specialties. Ever fond of nicknames, Strayhorn had taken up Arthur Logan's pet name for his wife, Doll Baby; she usually called him Strays but sometimes Itty Bitty Buddy or Bitty for short. Strayhorn usually addressed Dr. Logan as Arturo. "Strays said, 'Good afternoon, Doll

Baby. I'm at Macy's. What are you fixing for dinner?' " Marian Logan recalled. "I said, 'I don't know. What do you have in mind?' Strays said, 'Don't do a thing. I'll be right there.' " An hour later Strayhorn ceremoniously unpacked two overloaded brown shopping bags onto the Logans' dining-room table, displaying all the ingredients for paella. "I took the job of mixing cocktails while Strays made dinner. Arthur chopped the vegetables and such," said Logan. "There was so much food cooking, my goodness. We called some friends [including Strayhorn's colleague Felrath Hines from the Neal Salon, who lived behind the Logans on West 89th Street], and a few hours later, we were properly looped and having a party." With minor variations in ingredients—the recipe and the friends would vary, according to availability—this became a weekly ritual for Strayhorn and the Logans. "Strays would say, 'I'll make the pot,' and he'd be off. It would be like somebody would call a stew. But when he got finished with the wine and the seasonings and everything, oh, it would be ambrosia, I'm telling you."

Within a couple of months, no one needed to be invited; overlapping groups of Strayhorn's and the Logans' friends—Hines, Luther Henderson, Bill Coleman, the Neals, the Robinsons—knew to come by the Logans' house on Saturdays for Strayhorn's pot. "We all took turns cutting up the ingredients and everything. Strayhorn had us all working for him," said Hines in mock outrage. Francis Goldberg came just once or twice. "Strays finally brought Goldie down. He was bugging him to come," said Marian Logan. "He was very presentable and good-looking. He made a very good impression. But he was a pain in everybody's ass. He had to be the center of the attention. He tried to take over the cooking and make it a professional production, and it was supposed to be a fun thing, a thing for the whole group." At dinnertime, Goldberg situated himself at the head of the Logans' table and waited to be served rather than make his own plate, like everyone else. "Goldie was terribly emotional, and that got under Strays' skin something awful. Anybody joke around with him and say something anywhere teasing, Goldie went into a fit. 'How *dare* you talk to me that way?' He'd be out of his chair and standing there at attention, the big baby. You'd look over at Strays, and he'd be gone. Strays was in the kitchen, stirring his pot. Goldie embarrassed him; we hardly saw him. When Strays started coming around regularly, Goldie was nothing but trouble. Strays was trying to get away from him."

Like Strayhorn and some of those most dear to him since his childhood, from his mother and Harry Herforth to Aaron Bridgers and Lena Horne, Marian Logan loved nature and books. Logan made it known that she was fond of white flowers, and Strayhorn made it a habit to bring her one—just one and of any variety, but white only—every time he saw her. Since they were sometimes difficult to find, Strayhorn had a standing order with a neighborhood florist, the Academy Floral Company on Broadway and 107th Street, to set aside white flowers, and he gave them to Logan with such frequency that she kept an opal teardrop vase on the piano just for Strayhorn's gifts; she would usually replace each one before it had time to die. Logan, in a position of some leisure, bought and read about a dozen books a year, predominantly biographies and popular fiction, as well as some poetry (her favorite poet was e. e. cummings), which she shared with Strayhorn. "Not every book. One out of every four or five I read, if it was really interesting," she said. "Strays didn't care for escapism. He liked to read something stimulating whenever possible"—that is, virtually anytime. Some Saturdays, the Logans and Strayhorn broke their cooking-party routine and took a drive north on the Taconic Parkway into the Catskills, Arthur Logan behind the wheel of his sleek, immense black Impala convertible, his wife alternately chatting and napping, Strayhorn reclining side-long in the back, reading a book. In order to vary his stimulants, Strayhorn would also bring a portable bar: a wicker-and-leather attaché-style case equipped with various mixological accessories, glasses, and bottles filled with gin and tonic water. "He'd lie there in the back with a cocktail, and he'd read away," said Marian Logan. "Arthur would be looking at the countryside and say, 'Strays, there's a beautiful farmhouse,' or whatever. Strays would say, 'Wonderful, Arturo, wonderful! Describe it to me.' And he'd keep reading and sipping on his cocktail." When the three venturers dallied off the highway onto local roads around Phoenicia in New York State, country stores and roadside stands—rural shopping opportunities— would get Strayhorn engaged. He loved buying farm-grown fruits and vegetables and once, impressed by a harvest of cabbage, bought a whole bushel basket of it; back in the city, he called his friends and invited them to come and each take a head. "We stopped into one little store somewhere, and Strays said, 'Ooooh, this is what I've always wanted!' " said Marian Logan. "It was one of those old-fashioned ice-cream makers that you have to crank. Strays just had to have it, so he bought it, and we brought it home, and the next weekend, Strays made ice cream. Peach. We called everybody, and he laid down the law: everybody had to take a turn cranking the goddamn thing or they couldn't eat any of the ice cream. Except he wasn't about to do any cranking. Oh my goodness, no. Of course, naturally, we wouldn't let him eat any of his own ice cream. My God, oh, they were good times.

"But Strays wasn't always in very good shape," Logan said. "He had his good days, but he had his bad days, believe me, the poor thing. You had to see him. Some days he came by, and he would stay here and he would be great. He loved to play the piano. He played for me. Always classical. Never jazz—never, most of the time, unless I asked him to. His favorite thing, when he was here, was we would stay up all night and talk. Arthur went to bed. Strays said, 'Good night, Arturo. I'll tuck your Doll Baby in.' We'd stay up all night. Five, six in the morning, we'd still be yapping. That was his favorite time in the world. The phrase he used for it was *halfway to dawn*. He said, the way he saw it—he had such a wonderful mind, a brilliant mind, the way he saw things—he said he liked the fact that it was a kind of in-between state. It wasn't day and it wasn't night. What day was it? You're half asleep. You're half awake. Your resistance is gone—it's like a truth serum. Your feelings just pour out. You don't even realize what you're saying. He loved that, loved it. He told me, he said, 'I think *everything* should happen at halfway to dawn. That's when all the heads of government should meet. I think everybody would fall in love.'

"We talked about civil rights. Strays was very aware of what was going on in the world. The man was politically aware. He wanted to do something for the movement—we both did—and we would talk all night about the situation and the things we thought had to be done. He knew every single person involved in the movement by name. His interest was not casual. The man was as serious as shit. Then, half the time, he was a wasted man. He couldn't talk. He was drinking day and night. Half the time, he wasn't really there. He was a shell. But nobody could tell unless you really knew him. If you didn't know him extremely well . . . I mean, like family, and there weren't that many people who really knew him like that. He didn't allow it. If you really knew him, you knew what a bad state he was in. He always had the same expression. He had a beautiful smile, like a baby. Half the time, he would be so out of it that he literally couldn't speak. You had to put your ear right up to his mouth to hear what he was saying. He couldn't make sounds. You never knew how he was going to be. He drank just constantly, in every imaginable situation. He wasn't looking for reasons to drink. It was beyond reasons. He just drank. If he was down, he drank to drown it, and if he was up, he drank to celebrate. He drank for relaxation. He drank for fun."

One afternoon that spring, Strayhorn called his friend Bill Coleman. "Why don't you come on by, and we'll have breakfast," Strayhorn suggested. "I have bacon!" Coleman came over out of curiosity. "It was funny, like he had some exotic thing, bacon! Like it was a rare delicacy that was impossible to get. 'I have bacon!'" Coleman opened up Strayhorn's refrigerator to see the bacon for himself, and there was indeed a package of bacon on a shelf and a bottle of gin on another, and nothing else.

Professionally, Strayhorn bobbed between fervent engagement and resigned inertia. He continued to take on projects outside his ongoing work with Ellington, most often with Johnny Hodges, but he was functioning, at times, from a dilatory remove. In April 1959, he accepted an offer from Stanley Dance, the English jazz writer and record producer, to serve as musical director and pianist on a small-band Hodges showcase with fellow Ellingtonians Quentin Jackson on trombone, Harold "Shorty" Baker on trumpet, and Russell Procope on clarinet, as well as session players Al Hall (founder of Wax Records, a 78 label) on bass and Oliver Jackson on drums. A long-time Ellington enthusiast, Dance had once written a withering critique of Strayhorn's early contribution to the Ellington Orchestra canon: "Mr. Strayhorn is an example of today's youth in jazz. He throws tradition overboard. He will have originality at the expense of beauty. . . . Listen to 'Chelsea Bridge,' an example of an obsession for tone colour and voicing which excludes everything else that matters," wrote Dance in the English journal *Jazz Music* in 1943.

After Dance moved to the United States and married the producer Helen Oakley, he slipped into Ellington's inner circle and he and Strayhorn achieved a gentlemanly concord. "I wouldn't say we were best friends, but Billy was always perfectly gracious. I don't know if he ever read a word I wrote about him. He never brought it up, and I didn't either, certainly," said Dance, a tall, soft-spoken fellow with a Ronald Colman mustache and the temperate charm of a palace official, which is essentially what he was. "That [recording] date, Stanley and Billy, you know, I'd say kept away from each other," recalled Oliver Jackson. "Billy and Rab [Hodges] were so close, man, that's the only reason Billy did the date."

The one-day session, conducted at the RCA Records studios in Manhattan on April 14, yielded seven blowing-session numbers: five standards and two originals attributed jointly to Hodges and Strayhorn. Both of the new pieces, "Cue's Blue Now" and "Watch Your Cue," were jam-opportunity riffs entitled in honor of Hodges's wife, who nevertheless saw the project as short of a high point for either Hodges or Strayhorn. "I don't think Billy put very much into it. It was more like Johnny's kind of record," she said. Since Hodges was under contract with Norman Granz to record exclusively for Verve Records, Dance found himself prohibited from releasing the album under Hodges's name. As an out, he titled it *Cue for Saxophone*, a hint at the featured player's identity, and issued the record in the name of Billy Strayhorn's Septet. "Billy didn't care," said Dance. Indeed, as Jackson explained, Strayhorn seemed to exert a minimum of creative effort on the project. "He showed up late, and he didn't have anything planned," said Jackson. "He knocked off whatever arrangements we used off the top of his head. He didn't seem to give much of a damn, and the thing had his name on it. It was *sad*, man. This great musician, and this record had his name on it—there were songs there with his name on them—and he didn't give a damn about it." Nonetheless, the Hot Club de France, a society of French jazz professionals, fans, and scholars, awarded the album its Grand Prix du Disque de Jazz pour Petit Orchestre, an honor likely influenced, at least in part, by Strayhorn's reputation in Paris.

"I said, 'Hey, Strays, isn't this something, man? All those things you did for Duke, and all the people think Duke did 'em? And here there's finally a record with your own name on it, and it's really

Rab's! Isn't that something?' And Billy said, 'Oh yes, Oliver. I'm sure there'll be an uprising.' Man, he didn't think nobody cared. The way he said that—'I'm sure there'll be an uprising'—it hit me like a brick. His own name didn't mean nothing to him no more. Like, fuck it—nobody cares. Why should I?"

Jackson and Strayhorn, who lived only a few blocks from each other, became friendly after recording *Cue for Saxophone*. The father of two young daughters, Jackson liked to walk with his children through Riverside Park, a strip of playgrounds, blacktop paths, and greenery along the Hudson River, where he'd sometimes find Strayhorn on a park bench, writing music or reading the *New York Times*. "I'd sit on the bench with him, and we'd talk while the kids were playing," recalled Jackson. "I'd love that. We would talk about current events, the problems in the world. We would talk about music, music and dance, music and singing, music and drums. He had a lot of thoughts about drums and harmony, how the sounds of the drums at each point should complement the instrumentation and colors of the band. One day I saw him in the park with a big sheet of music paper, and I asked him what he was writing. He said, 'Oh, something for strings.' I said, 'What?' And he said, 'Oh, just something for myself. Just for me.' I looked down at the music paper, and it was a complete orchestral score. He was writing a symphonic piece right there in his head, sitting in the park. Another time, he would be stone-drunk, sitting on the same park bench smoking cigarettes. Ten, eleven in the morning. The kids and I would just be going out, and he looked like he hadn't been home yet from the night before. I'd see him from a distance, and I never knew what I would find that day."

Before *Cue for Saxophone* made the record stores in the spring of 1960, another album preempted it as the first full-length LP bearing Billy Strayhorn's name. It wasn't, however, a genuine Strayhorn solo project. Titled *Billy Strayhorn/Live!!!*, the Roulette Records release was a recording of the Ellington Orchestra in performance at the Blue Note in Chicago on August 9, 1959, with Ellington leading the band and playing the piano. According to the unsigned liner notes, "Billy has no intentions of leading a band on a permanent basis, but on this album he took the nucleus of Duke's great band and went into the Blue Note." In truth, Strayhorn had had no involvement with *Billy Strayhorn/Live!!!* other than being the composer of one of the record's eight selections ("Passion Flower") and arranger of several others (including the pop songs "All of Me" and "On the Sunny Side of the Street"). As with Stanley Dance and his Hodges record, Roulette found that Ellington's contract with Columbia Records prohibited the company from using the band-leader's name. "So they put Strayhorn's name on it," said Teo Macero, one of Ellington's three principal producers at Columbia. "Technically, they didn't need permission, not even from Billy, because Billy didn't have a record contract with anybody." Though legal, the move raised obvious ethical questions: How did Billy Strayhorn feel about it? Did he consider his own identity interchangeable with that of Duke Ellington? "The two records came out just a little while apart—our studio record and the live one—and we talked about it," said Oliver Jackson. "Billy said, 'Oliver, haven't you heard? Duke and I have changed jobs. I've taken over the orchestra, and Duke is writing the music.' That was the only answer you'd get out of him. He had the greatest poker face in the world, you know. It was impossible to figure out how Billy Strayhorn really felt. That was all he would say on the subject, this joke—he and Duke had changed jobs. So I said, 'Oh. There's gonna be an uprising.' And we laughed our fool heads off. My kids were *staring* at us. I thought we were both going to piss in our pants right there in Riverside Park."

At home, meanwhile, Goldberg finally pushed Strayhorn's tolerance to its limit. He had met someone new, a young black artist (from western Pennsylvania, like Strayhorn) whom he was seeing surreptitiously while leaving signals in a trail evidently intended for discovery—and conflict. "Goldie had the sensitivity of a shark," said Talley Beatty, who had dinner with Strayhorn at the Flash Inn several times (and once at the West 106th Street apartment, accompanied by choreographer Alvin Ailey) in the final weeks of the year. Beatty was developing a dance piece using recorded works by Ellington and Strayhorn. (Its music drawn primarily from the Ellington catalog, the work would take form several years later as *Road of the Phoebe Snow*, named for the Lackawanna Railroad line where Beatty set this ballet of love, suicide, rape, and gang violence; it would premiere, to critical acclaim, at the Delacorte Theatre in

Central Park in the last week of August 1964.) "Billy couldn't take any more shit from Goldie anymore. That was it," said Beatty. "Goldie didn't have to do it that way. He found some young boy and carried on behind Billy's back but arranged it so Billy would find him out. Little hints and weak excuses, bad lies. He was just hurting him. Goldie really knew how to be hurtful." Before Thanksgiving, Goldberg moved out of the apartment. He took most of the kitchen supplies, a painting by Felrath Hines, and the contents of the liquor cabinet.

Seeking comfort in the constancy of home and family, Strayhorn made an extended visit to Pittsburgh, staying at his parents' house through New Year's 1960. George Greenlee and his brother Bluford were driving and offered Strayhorn a ride. The trip was always long, at least nine hours along the two-lane roads that curl and drip around the Tuscarora Mountains, and half again as long in the kind of snowstorm the Greenlees and Strayhorn found themselves burrowing into. Strayhorn, in the back seat, mixed cocktails with his briefcase kit. George Greenlee drove until the car was thoroughly cocooned in ice; the windshield wipers polished a thickening coat of crystal. "I said, 'I can't drive anymore. We're not going to make it,'" he recalled. "We pulled over and stopped the car. I turned to Billy, and he was sitting there with a drink. I said, 'Wait a minute—alcohol! We can use the booze and deice the windshield.' Billy said, 'You must be joking.' He was horrified. I said, 'No, that'll do it. Lemme have the booze. I'll go out and pour it on the windshield, and we should be okay. We can't just sit here all night.' Billy said, 'Oh, don't be dramatic. Let's just wait a while. The storm will stop.' He thought we could just sit there and sip our drinks and everything would be fine. I reached back and started to grab the bottle. Billy said, 'Oh, don't *grab*. Here, take it!' He handed the bottle over to me; I think it was scotch. Good scotch, I think Johnny Walker Black. I went out and poured it on the windshield, and it worked like a charm. But Billy was mad as hell. We drove along, about one mile an hour, and kept looking out the window for a liquor store. When we finally found one, he said, 'Stop! Stop! Stop!' and he went out in the storm and bought two bottles—another bottle of Johnny Black and something cheap in case of emergency."

Safe in Pittsburgh, nearly twenty-four hours after leaving New

York, Strayhorn found change: his nieces and nephews numbered twenty-three now. Johnny and his wife, Susan, had David, Kenneth, John, Douglas, Darryl, and Linda; Jimmy and his wife, Helen, had Helen, Carole, James, Lawrence, Donna, William, and Deborah; Georgia and Robert Conaway had Adrienne, Cheryll, Michael, and the twins Keith and Kevin (both mentally handicapped), in addition to Georgia's sons Gregory and Albert from her first marriage, to Albert Morris; and Lillian and her husband, Jesse, had Leslie, Gary, and Galen. (Teddy was still a bachelor, and he was drinking hard.) There was decrement: Georgia and Robert had recently separated, Georgia moving somewhere in surburban New Jersey, where she was living with friends. And, at the center, equilibrium: Lillian and James, their anger dissipated and their bodies tired, rested together in a benign union of acceptance.

Duke Ellington kept touring as always, fielding pitches on the phones backstage to appear at jazz festivals sprouting up all over the country in Newport's image. For the upcoming summer of 1960, the Duke Ellington Orchestra was booked to appear at seven festivals, including the Saugatuck Jazz Festival in Michigan, the Randalls Island Jazz Festival in New York, the Quaker City Jazz Festival in Philadelphia, and the Monterey Jazz Festival in California. Promoters of the highest-profile and best-paying festivals, such as Jimmy Lyons of Monterey, solicited Ellington to premiere long-form compositions befitting Ellington's standing as a composer and, by association, the stature of their festivals. Ellington acceded discriminatively, accepting one "commission" in early spring of 1960 to compose a piece for the Monterey event to be conducted that September. (Though Lyons did not compensate Ellington for the composition per se, the value of the premiere was factored into the fee for the orchestra's appearance, according to Lyons.) "Ellington and Strayhorn talked the thing over," said Lyons, "and Duke said, 'Jimmy, Billy has a wonderful idea. We'll compose a new suite inspired by the John Steinbeck book.' He meant *Sweet Thursday*, which deals with our area. Billy knew about it and had read it, so that's what they decided to do." In mid-March, Strayhorn flew to Las Vegas, where Ellington was playing a twelve-week engagement (doubled, by demand, from a planned six weeks) at the Starlight Lounge in the Riviera Hotel and where Irving Townsend of Columbia was due to discuss prospective recording projects, including the Steinbeck piece. There was little work for Strayhorn. "He and Duke did some talking about the music they were going to do for Monterey," recalled the bassist Jimmy Woode, "but the festival was so far off that they didn't apply themselves to it excessively. We decided to have a contest—Strayhorn, Gonsalves, myself, and a few others at first, but they dropped out early. We wanted to see if any of us could outdrink Strayhorn. We identified him as the epitome, of course. The rest of us could only aspire to approach his ability." The competition went on for three straight days and two nights, unimpeded by sleep or intervention by Ellington. Gonsalves and Woode broke away only to work, playing four shows over two evenings in the midst of their drinking heat. They stopped to eat each day, and on the third afternoon lunched at the Riviera coffee shop, where Woode watched Strayhorn slowly slide down the front of his banquette seat and under the table. Benevolent in victory, Woode and Gonsalves spun a few chairs around and slid the backs against the tabletop, devising a nest for their friend to rest on the floor, and they asked the waitress to leave Strayhorn alone, kindly, until he awoke.

When Irving Townsend arrived from Columbia's Los Angeles office, he joined Ellington for steaks at the Riviera with Strayhorn (who was rested), the orchestra's road manager, Al Celley, and band members Harry Carney, Ray Nance, and Jimmy Hamilton, along with a couple of female guests. Townsend was eager to issue an attention-grabbing new addition to the Ellington catalog but seemed only halfheartedly responsive to the Steinbeck project, as Hamilton observed. "Duke told Billy to speak up. 'Strayhorn, why don't you explain your latest idea? It's quite an idea,'" Hamilton recalled. "That's when Billy told everybody about *The Nutcracker Suite*, which we did in the band shortly after that. Billy had a way with words when he talked. He talked that thing up. That's when it was decided, there, that we would do it, *The Nutcracker Suite*." The notion was to adapt Tchaikovsky's ballet score for jazz orchestra, a venturesome project that appealed to Strayhorn, Ellington, and Townsend alike: it could rekindle the conservatory-trained collaborator's youthful passion for classicism (and, in the process, enliven his spirits) while heightening Ellington's stature and, perhaps, expanding his audience. The link to a nineteenth-century Russian composer would enhance not only Ellington but also his favorite concert form, the suite; one of the most beloved works of one of the world's most popular orchestral composers is a group of tuneful dance pieces, just like what Duke Ellington wrote (often with Billy Strayhorn). Jazz composers and arrangers had long drawn from classical sources, of course. Ellington himself had vamped on Franz Liszt's second *Hungarian Rhapsody* in his version of Arthur Johnston and Sam Coslow's "Ebony Rhapsody" in the *Rape of the Rhapsody* segment of the 1934 Paramount movie *Murder at the Vanities* (an Ellington performance that Strayhorn said inspired him as a young man in Pittsburgh); indeed, the swing bandleader Larry Clinton had recorded "jazzed-up" versions of a few movements of the *Nutcracker* in 1940. Still, the task of rethinking a complete long-form classical masterwork in a new idiom remained a formidable challenge. "It was a struggle," said Strayhorn; with Townsend's support, he dove into the jazz *Nutcracker* in New York, consulting with Ellington by phone. "It's always a struggle, you know, to present someone of the stature of Peter Ilych Tchaikovsky and adapting it to our flavor without distorting him. It entailed a lot of conversation. Long-distance calls back and forth between New York and California and records, listening to the actual, the way that the originals were actually played and discussions and this and that and the other. Tchaikovsky wasn't available. Actually, it sort of felt like we were talking to him, because we didn't want him turning over any more than he already was." Strayhorn reveled in his chimerical company and applied himself to their collaboration with much of his old zeal. "Doing the Tchaikovsky suite was like a tonic," said Marian Logan, who spent most of one weekend in her apartment watching Strayhorn write, hum, whistle, and occasionally dance a few steps to the emerging music. "It was a beautiful springtime, but you would have thought it was Christmas, he was carrying on so with that *Nutcracker*. He loved that so. I said, 'Bitty, you were born at the wrong time. I think you're really an old Russian.' 'Oh really? Do you really think so?' I said, 'Well, you're certainly acting like one.' Strays said, 'Well, then, I think I should have a vodka.' And he did. We toasted

Tchaikovsky and had a grand old time. But he really worked on that music. He loved doing that music." According to Logan, "Strays liked to have a collaborator. He liked somebody to hide behind. Now he had the greatest collaborator of them all, a dead man. Duke was always removed—he was never around, and when he was, he never told Strays what to do—but he was still there." Obscured by shadow over shadow, Tchaikovsky's over Ellington's, Strayhorn busied himself in security.

He took a flight to Columbia's Radio Recorders studio in Los Angeles and, working closely with Ellington, began recording on June 3, ten days after the Ellington Orchestra concluded its Las Vegas run; the sessions were animated. "Billy was very, very greatly involved in the recording," recalled Jimmy Hamilton. "He had quite a few unusual ideas all prepared for us, and we had to do them very exactly. [Russell] Procope was supposed to play this strange little bamboo whistle. [Juan] Tizol played the tambourine. It was his ideas, and everybody was very happy with the results—I mean, Duke and everybody who was involved." Indeed, in an unprecedented demonstration of the project's debt to Strayhorn, Irving Townsend decided to feature him prominently on all the album credits and artwork, commissioning the photojournalist Gordon Parks to do the photography. "The record company told me this was a collaboration between Billy and Duke—and Tchaikovsky—and I tried to capture the uniqueness of that partnership, Billy and Duke's," said Parks, whose cover portrait of Ellington and Strayhorn does evoke partnership, although something less than collaborative equality: Ellington and Strayhorn wear identical clothing (white polo-style sweaters casually unbuttoned at the neck); Ellington, his chin resting suavely on the knuckles of his left hand, gazes squarely into the lens, while Strayhorn, snuggling body-to-body behind Ellington, his head nodding forward and his eyes heavy, peers at the ground.*

Strayhorn's name was linked with Ellington's throughout Townsend's liner notes, whose concluding paragraph reads, "Duke Elling-

* On CD, the Ellington-Strayhorn *Nutcracker* was issued as one of three works (along with the Ellington-Strayhorn arrangement of Grieg's *Peer Gynt Suite* and the Ellington-Strayhorn composition *Suite Thursday*) on a release entitled *Duke Ellington: Three Suites*. Strayhorn's name does not appear on the front or the back of the CD package, and only Ellington is depicted in the cover artwork.

ton's first brush with the classics is successfully completed. It is a tribute, I think, to Duke and Billy and to Tchaikovsky." But Strayhorn's role was virtually lost in the press, which generally described the project as Ellington's alone. To some extent, Joe Morgen continued to exert influence on the coverage of Ellington in the major New York–based publications, particularly the trade papers and the gossip columns; Ellington's place in the American consciousness, however, transcended publicity. "Morgen was forever promoting Ellington to anyone who would listen and ignoring Billy, naturally," Leonard Feather said. "The number of those in the know who listened to Joe Morgen was diminishing. However, so was the number of those whose conceptions of Ellington were about to change very greatly. The general public had just come to accept him as a serious composer. Now, the same public was not quite ready to have that perception adjusted to accommodate the reality of Strayhorn—by that I mean that they were both great composers but often working hand in hand. The *Nutcracker* LP serves as the perfect case in point. There, we have Ellington and Strayhorn promoted equally, quite remarkably—and quite a testament to the record company, at that. But only Ellington registered in the mind of the public. One couldn't be surprised by the manner in which Billy responded to this occurring time after time. He truly invested himself only when the work inspired him. He could turn out a great deal of music, and he was literally incapable of producing anything less than excellent and interesting. But it became known that he was becoming prone to periods of isolation and delay unless he found a particular musical project inspiring."

Sam Shaw, an independent film producer who knew Ellington through his brother Eddie Shaw's music-publishing business and had met Strayhorn at Luckey Roberts's joint years earlier, was developing a feature, his first, that explored thematic territory close to home for Strayhorn: a story of black artists in Paris "struggling with the world and within themselves to be accepted as the people they were," in Shaw's description. Initially, Shaw conceived of the film in the mid-1950s as a veiled biography of the black collagist Romare Bearden, a friend of Shaw's through New York gallery circles. (Shaw had a second career as a still photographer; many of his photographs depict artists at work, and the images are kinetic and instinctive, moments of emotion slapped down onto paper.) Shaw's backers at United Artists, however, deemed a fine artist's conflicts "too internal for their bankbooks," according to Shaw. He was a beefy and tough little man with a floor-brush mustache and a good liberal's discomfort in neckties; he liked corduroy jackets and tweed caps, even in the summer, and might be mistaken on a film set for an extra in period Warsaw peasant garb. Shifting the story to jazz musicians, Shaw optioned the rights to an earnest 1957 novel by his acquaintance Harold Flender, *Paris Blues*, about a black tenor saxophonist named Eddie Jones. (Flender had a bit of firsthand experience with jazz as a writer on a TV variety series, *The Eddie Condon Floor Show*.) For the film, Shaw lined up a tag team of writers—credited, Walter Bernstein, Irene Kamp, and Jack Sher; uncredited, Ring Lardner, Jr., Ted Allen, and Flender—and devised a script about two American musicians, one white, now the main character, and one black, his friend, who move to Paris and, while finding their creative voices and debating the relationship between refined and vernacular music, fall for a pair of tourist women, one black, one white. That both romances were mixed-race matches was an element of the film that contributed significantly to Ellington's agreement to take on the project. "Duke thought that was an important statement to make at that time. He liked the idea of expressing racial equality in romantic terms. That's the way he thought himself," said Shaw. "That aspect of the film appealed to Billy, too, metaphorically for a gay relationship. Billy was also interested in the artistic struggle. One of the guys wanted to compose concert music but wasn't accepted by the classical establishment. This issue was of great importance to Billy, and also to Duke, of course."

At the insistence of United Artists, the romantic story lines were untangled and rewoven: white trombonist Ram Bowen (to be portrayed by Paul Newman) and his black band mate, renamed Eddie Cook (Sidney Poitier), pair up with white schoolteacher Lillian Cornell (Joanne Woodward) and her black colleague, Connie Lampson (Diahann Carroll), respectively. Nonetheless, both Ellington and Strayhorn found more areas of commonality in *Paris Blues* than they had in *Anatomy of a Murder*. "They felt close to the characters, like they were part of them—black artists in a foreign, white world," said Shaw.

At the outset of rehearsals for *Paris Blues*, which was to be produced entirely in France, Strayhorn heard from his sister Georgia. Since he would be in Europe anyway, he offered to let her stay in his apartment in Manhattan if need be. He gave a set of keys to Bill Coleman, asked him to collect the mail, and filled him in on Georgia. Strayhorn took a day flight into Le Bourget airport in the first week of October and checked into the Hôtel de la Trémoille, a warm little four-star hotel in the eighth arrondissement, where the Pennebaker Production coordinators had arranged for Ellington and Strayhorn to work in adjoining suites. Ellington remained stateside, however, to honor concert and studio commitments (including a session to record *Suite Thursday* for a Columbia LP) through the end of November. On Strayhorn's first evening in Paris, he went, alone, to hear Aaron Bridgers play at the Mars Club. "When we saw each other again, it was like we had never been away again. We always had that kind of feeling. That never changed," said Bridgers. "We spent most of our free time together. However, I was working at nights and Billy was busy during the day, writing music. So we got together whenever we could find a way to do so." Strayhorn arranged a most effective way, introducing Bridgers to Shaw, who was looking for someone to portray an expatriate black pianist in the film and agreed to cast Bridgers; the role had few lines (and those few were cut before the film's release). "Billy took me out to meet Aaron, where he was playing, and I was impressed. I thought he had a great look, very strong, very handsome," said Shaw. "Billy was very proud of him. There was a real connection between the two of them. You felt it across the room when they were together. Billy was a very complicated guy, very deep. And he wasn't always happy. He was the most delightful and charming man you'd ever meet, but he could slide into a deep seriousness, and you'd see it. When Aaron was there, Billy was a little more at peace. Everybody in the cast accepted Aaron. It wasn't like, 'Oh, there comes Strayhorn's guy' or a thing like that. Aaron held his own. You could see why Billy loved the guy. He was a good soul. But he could be very, very serious, just as serious as Billy. The two of them went through a lot, and you could tell it." When Ellington arrived—overcoming his lifelong fear of flying, he took his first transatlantic flight on December 8—Strayhorn brought Bridgers to many of the sessions at Ellington's Trémoille suite. "Billy had some of the music outlined before Duke arrived," said Bridgers. "Then Billy would write something and play it for Duke, and Duke would nod and say something like, 'Yeah, man, I like that.' Or Duke would play his parts for Billy, and Billy would encourage him. Back and forth—it was like that when I was there." Strayhorn's weakness for Paris life, however, often overcame the strength of his professionalism, and Ellington was left to work alone.

Strayhorn had an address book with the names and addresses of friends and colleagues around the globe and one book just for Paris, a separate world for him since the after-school meetings of the Cercle Français at Westinghouse High. His Paris book was a checklist, and every evening a friendship flourished over food and drink: with the music writer Claude Carrière at Gaby and Haynes's soul-food restaurant, with the jazz buff Alexandre Rado at the Club Saint-Germain, with the expatriate American saxophonist Johnny Griffin at the Montana bar. ("Where did you learn to write music the way you do?" Griffin asked Strayhorn. "In high school," he said.) The one Parisian friend with whom he couldn't revel this time was Jean Berdin, who was laid up in bed with multiple bone fractures from an accident. Strayhorn called him a few times, however, and offered advice on handling his plight. "One day I told him how much I was suffering and that I had had a horrible night, because I had many parts of my body broken, and I was suffering very much. And Billy said, he said, 'Suffer.' I said, 'What?' 'Suffer'—that's what he said. I was furious at him. I hung up the phone very angry with him. I suppose he meant that suffering, pain, can be good for you. I don't know."

To serve as a musical adviser and French translator for Ellington and other Americans involved in the movie's music, Shaw hired the expatriate American jazz trombonist and arranger Billy Byers. "They hired me to be general music supervisor and Duke Ellington's translator. However, Duke Ellington needed no translator, because everybody spoke to him in English, so I wound up hanging out a lot with Strays," recalled Byers, a tubby, roundheaded little fellow with a boyish nimbleness of musical style and of mind. "Duke worked all the time. He was a very organized man. Every day, he got up and wrote for about four hours, no matter how late he had been up or how heavy the cabareting the night before. Billy's role was this: he did what he could when he could. But he was always out getting drunk in the Mars Club. I was with Strays almost every night, with Aaron when he wasn't working his club, otherwise the two of us or the two of us and one of Strays's friends. I love to drink too. However, I couldn't keep up with him. I had a habit of going to bed every night. He went on to the next day." Early one morning Byers, drunk, drove Strayhorn, drunker, to his hotel on a borrowed motor scooter. "There is no justification for our survival," said Byers.

"After working and living with them like that, so closely, my perception of Ellington and Strayhorn completely reversed. It turned upside down," Byers added. "Now, I had always understood that Duke was a free creative spirit and a bon vivant, and I had always pictured him with a bottle of champagne in one arm and a blonde on the other, gliding through the club car and saying to Strays, 'I just got an inspiration: Da da da-da da da [the melody of the lyric "missed the Saturday dance"]! Go and do something with it.' Nothing could have been further from the truth. It turned out that Strays was the indulgent artist and Ellington was the professional; Ellington worked like a dog, and Strayhorn was the playboy. He was drunk and hanging out all the time. They were both great composers, but Duke was a professional and a crowd pleaser, and the essence of his pieces was to please the crowd. Strayhorn wasn't: the essence of his work was to satisfy himself. He didn't always have a lot of output. Duke kept Strayhorn around knowing the output might be small and getting smaller, but wanting it *all*."

If the cocktails were overwhelming the jazz in Strayhorn's life at the time of *Paris Blues*, Aaron Bridgers did not see it. "He was simply having a good time, that was all," Bridgers declared. "He was very happy, very content. Very content. Very content. I'm sure of it. Billy was very happy. That's the only reason he would drink. He was celebrating." Members of the film's cast and crew were struck by something grayer when they met Strayhorn away from Bridgers. "He seemed like quite a sad little man to me," remarked Paul Newman. "Billy was not really with you, even when he was with you," said Ted Allen. Diahann Carroll, who turned to Strayhorn for company between takes, saw anguish in his reserve. "Spending that time with Strayhorn was something I could never forget," she said. "He was a beautiful, delicate little flower, just, you know, a genius, but a tortured genius. He was an unhappy person. His genius was so overwhelming that being in his presence was something you could never forget. You know, there's such a thing as feeling too much and hearing too much. He suffered from that. I got exactly the same feeling being in the presence of James Baldwin. Strayhorn had the ability to perceive other people better than most of us, and what he perceived wasn't always kind, particularly in relation to himself and the life he chose for himself. Strayhorn and Baldwin both knew the cruelness of the world, and that's what I thought was part of the enormous sadness beneath their exteriors."

Aesthetically, what Strayhorn contributed to *Paris Blues* helped advance its underscore beyond the level of the *Anatomy of a Murder* music, which was essentially a song score. The several sections of the *Paris Blues* music that bear Strayhorn's stamp work not only as jazz miniatures but as organic musical complements to the scenes for which they were devised. As the critic John Tynan noted in *Down Beat*, "Most of the genuine musical interest in the picture lies in the Ellington-Strayhorn underscore. [It has] unique appeal both as music and as the means of heightening dramatic impact. It is clear that Ellington and Strayhorn have learned a lot since *Anatomy of a Murder*." Once again, however, Strayhorn was not acknowledged in the film's credits, even though the first music in the movie is "Take the 'A' Train."

In the early hours of a cold January morning in 1961, Alan Douglas, a young American record producer, approached Strayhorn at the Mars Club, having met him a few times at the Barclay Studios during the *Paris Blues* soundtrack recording sessions. Strayhorn was gregarious now that he had finished working on the movie, and Douglas was solicitous, scouting projects to record efficiently in Europe for release in the States by United Artists' new jazz label. "I said, 'Billy, when are you going to sit down and record something yourself? We know how your stuff sounds when Duke plays it. Why not let us hear how it sounds when you play it? Why not?' And he didn't even think about it, really. He just said, 'Why not?' I didn't know if he was serious or he was drunk. He just said, 'Why not?' Like nobody ever asked him before." Firming up their serendipitous deal by phone that afternoon, Douglas and Strayhorn arranged to record in a pair of back-to-back three-hour sessions at Barclay, beginning at midnight (when studio rates were lower) two days later.

With some logistical guidance and financial support from Douglas, Strayhorn scurried to develop a theme for the project, write the necessary arrangements, and line up musicians. It would be an intimate album: Strayhorn's favorite pieces among his own compositions, performed as piano solos or piano and bass duets, occasionally accompanied by a string quartet or abstract voices in harmony. "Billy decided what he wanted to do," said Douglas. "It was an incredibly personal album. He conceived it as something very introspective. He wanted to create an atmosphere and a mood and a place to go that was just quiet and alone but still complex and intelligent and mysterious." Most of the songs came from Strayhorn's first decade as a composer, and all had been performed or recorded by Ellington or Ellingtonians: "Something to Live For," "Lush Life," "Take the 'A' Train," "Day Dream," "Chelsea Bridge," "Passion Flower," "Just A-Sittin' and A-Rockin'," "A Flower Is a Lovesome Thing," "Multicolored Blue" ("Violet Blue"), and "Strange Feeling" (from the Ellington-Strayhorn *Perfume Suite*). Strayhorn's performances, however, redefine many of the compositions in singular terms: " 'A' Train" is a graceful ballad with whispered strings; the densely orchestral "Chelsea Bridge" is a spare piano solo; "Just A-Sittin' and A-Rockin' " rocks pensively. "The idea wasn't meant to be definitive," explained Douglas. "He was saying, 'Here are these songs that mean a lot to me, and this is what they happen to mean at this particular point.' " If so, the album expresses a sweeping melancholy, its tempos lonesome strolls, its harmonies variations on moans and sighs. Entitled *The Peaceful Side*, it evokes an uneasy rest. "It was my title, and it never was right," said Douglas. "It was really the *inside* of Billy Strayhorn. What was really peaceful was the actual recording."

Conducted overnight and completed shortly after 5:00 a.m.—Strayhorn's beloved "halfway to dawn" time—the sessions were memorable for their absence of incident, according to the engineer, Gerhart Lehner. "The ambiance, it was like a dream," said Lehner. "Billy's music just poured out, like the recordings already existed and he was miming to a tape." Strayhorn and the bassist Michel Gaudry sipped wine and played, rarely needing more than one or two takes; during the break, they talked about French linen. They snacked on cake. "He was serious but nice and easy," recalled Gaudry, who, like Douglas, had got to know Strayhorn at the Mars Club. "That was his secret—he made you feel comfortable. He was so honest. His playing was so honest, and it was so emotional. It just happened. He gave me a little advice, like colors he wanted, some moods. Then, 'Okay, play! Play!' No problem! And it came out like pure emotion." Mimi Perrin, the leader of the jazz "vocalese" groups the Blue Stars and the Double Six of Paris, directed the chorus, dubbed the Paris Blue Notes. "We didn't sing any words; we sang 'Aaaah . . . ' " said Perrin. "And that was what Billy Strayhorn was like, making his record. Aaaah . . ."

Strayhorn himself was critical of his piano performance. "In Paris I made an album, and . . . it sounded all right when I heard it there, but that was some months ago. I don't play much anymore. . . . Ellington's very fortunate because he has a band, and he plays with the band and writes too. But in order to play and write, he's unique really, because you either do one or you do the other. It's like Nat Cole when he started singing—he stopped playing, because you really can't—playing requires—you've got to—it's a thing itself, and when you play *and* write, it's a different thing. I mean, you can do it. If you know how to play the piano, you can play forever once you learn it. But I mean to really *play*—and that was Nat's thing—that's why he doesn't play anymore. I don't feel that I'm *playing*. It sounds great to somebody else, but it doesn't sound great to him, his conception of how he should play. He has high standards of what he should sound like."

If *The Peaceful Side* fell short of Strayhorn's standards, he took enough pride in his first major solo effort to give a copy to each of his close friends in New York. He paid for the gifts himself (at artist's cost), and the album needed the sales boost: it sold "maybe a couple of thousand" copies, according to Douglas, who attributed the lackluster sales to United Artists' inexperience with both music promotion and the arcane machinery of record distribution. (The few reviews of the record were good: "After more than 20 years as an inextricable element in the musical complex that is Duke Ellington, Strayhorn emerges in these performances, recorded in Paris, as a personality in his own right. This is a lovely, low-keyed set," wrote

John S. Wilson in *Down Beat*.) "But it never got a chance to find its audience," Douglas said. "People weren't used to seeing Billy's name out there, so nobody knew what they were going to get. And what they got from that album was so very different from Ellington. It was a whole different sound and feeling—on songs you had a certain conception of, from Ellington. It was pure Billy. He did it the way he wanted to do it. It was his concept of who he was." There was an error on the credits printed on the back of the LP jacket (in addition to a misspelling of Gaudry's name as Goudret): "Passion Flower" was mistakenly attributed to E. Coates and G. Wiskin, who had composed a song with the same title. On each of the copies he gave away, Strayhorn block-printed his own name next to the "Passion Flower" listing, and he spelled it Strayhorne, just as he had twice earlier, before he met Duke Ellington and when he tried to leave him.

Arriving back in New York in mid-March, Strayhorn called a limo for the ride from Idlewild Airport to West 106th Street. (His favorite service was Bermuda Limousine, at which he was so well known that for years drivers passed on stories about how Billy Strayhorn would request a limousine: instead of ordering a car for precisely the time and place he required, as other customers might, Strayhorn would ask for it deferentially, saying something like, "If you have a driver available, could you please see if he could pick me up when it's convenient?"—or so went the drivers' tales.) While Strayhorn was in France, Georgia Conaway had moved from New Jersey to Corona, Queens, and worked for a while as a waitress until the restaurant owner's German shepherd attacked her; a patron beat away the dog with a garbage-can lid, but Georgia sustained twelve bites, which were treated with antibiotics that set off a severe allergic reaction that required hospitalization. Taking her brother up on his offer, she relocated to Strayhorn's apartment in Manhattan and looked for work. "I think she always wanted to end up in New York," said her son Michael Conaway. "I think she wanted to go there, and hopefully her brother would introduce her to friends who would be wowed, and maybe [she would] start a business, something where she could display her talents. I think that had always been a problem for her: what do you do when you're a very, very bright and talented woman, and you're black and your husband is a millworker, and you have five kids to raise? She finally just went for it."

In Pittsburgh, meanwhile, child-welfare agency authorities challenged Robert Conaway's ability to raise a family of five—including mentally handicapped twins—while working full time, and they initiated steps to place the children in foster care. Stepping in, Georgia's eldest son, Gregory, who was twenty-three and out of the house, packed up the children and bused them all to be with their mother on West 106th Street. Hoping to help, Gregory's aunt Lillian, also estranged from her husband, followed with her own two children. All nine of them—Georgia; her daughters, Adrienne and Cheryll; her sons Michael, Kevin, and Keith; Lillian; her daughter, Leslie, and her son Gary—were living in Strayhorn's one-bedroom apartment when he came home from Paris. "I guess we had kind of trashed the place," recalled Georgia's daughter Cheryll Conaway Chakrabarti. "Remember, there were nine of us in that little place. All the girls in the bedroom, all the boys in the living room. We were just kids. We wanted to run around and play and get a little wild sometimes, and we didn't have very much room."

Abandoning his place to his sisters and their families, Strayhorn took a residential apartment in the Master Apartments on Riverside Drive at 103rd Street, an elegant Art Deco tower overlooking Riverside Park and the Hudson River. Most of the residents were monied and white, and many were show-business professionals, owing to the Master's reputation for thick walls, supposedly designed specifically for the convenience of working musicians and actors. On the ground floor, there was a 500-seat theater and a small museum called the Corona Mundi Art Center. In April 1961, Strayhorn moved permanently into a one-bedroom apartment with a terrace facing the park and the river; in the living room stood a new Steinway grand piano, a housewarming gift from Ellington. Aesthetically and socioeconomically, the apartment was several steps above West 106th Street. "His new apartment was much more appropriate to his maturity and sophistication," said Cheryll Chakrabarti. As one of the building's doormen, Jimmy Monici, recalled, "Billy Strayhorn? That was a classic old Masters tenant, a perfect gentleman, extremely elegant, always gracious. Quiet. Quite a tipper."

The Conaway kids grew impressed with Strayhorn's generosity on more than one level. Several assumed that he had continued to carry the lease on West 106th Street and to pay the rent (or Ellington did—none of Strayhorn's closest friends or family members ever knew which of his bills he handled himself and which went straight to the Ellington organization); however, both Georgia and Lillian worked on and off, and Robert Conaway was sending a portion of his steel-mill pay from Pittsburgh. Strayhorn evidently covered some grocery bills for his sisters' families through an account he kept at Jack's, a market near Broadway and West 106th Street. "We knew we could go there and get anything we needed and he would pay for it or the bill went to Duke. We just knew we could get whatever we needed," said Michael Conaway.

Most memorably to his nieces and nephews, Strayhorn shared what he valued most, music. He played for the kids when they visited him at the Masters, asking their opinions of compositions in progress. "I used to sit and watch him, and he'd play a little thing and say, 'How does it sound? What do you think?' " recalled Adrienne Conaway Claerbaut. "I'd say something, and he listened to me, he really did. At least he made me feel like he did. He'd write a little more, and I came away seeing what it took to write music and feeling like my opinion was worthwhile." Encouraging development of their own musical interests beyond jazz, Strayhorn prompted discussions about their favorites. "All music is beautiful" was his decree. In a proof of his own faith in it, Strayhorn was an attentive audience as the kids took up their own music studies. "I joined the high school chorus [at Charles Evans Hughes High School on West 18th Street], and I said, 'You have to come to the school and hear our chorus and hear this jazz version of "Chopsticks" that we do,' " said Claerbaut (who took up music seriously as an adult). "And he came and spent a lot of time. I introduced him all around the school. That support meant everything to me." Much the same way, Strayhorn supported Michael Conaway's interest in the trumpet. "I wanted a trumpet, and he bought me a trumpet," said Conaway. "I had seen it in a pawnshop, and I told him about it. He gave me the money, and I went out and bought it—sixty bucks. I loved it. It's funny. We all took the challenge that Uncle

Billy gave us and got something out of it, even if we didn't become professionals." (Conaway became a mathematician in the aerospace industry but kept music as a pastime.)

In December 1961, the producer Creed Taylor signed Strayhorn as musical director of yet another Johnny Hodges date for Verve, this one with a difference: Strayhorn would be billed as the session's leader. "There were two elements to what we wanted to do," recalled Taylor, a small red-headed man with an ear for beauty and a reputation for commercial savvy. "One, obviously, was Johnny Hodges's unmistakable sound. And two was Billy Strayhorn's compositional and arranging colors, those gorgeous, liquid, dreamlike colors. I thought he should be a marquee name. I gave him free rein, and he produced a beautiful record. All beauty, no ego." Untitled, the record was billed as *Johnny Hodges, Soloist, Billy Strayhorn and the Orchestra*. The "the" meant Duke Ellington's: recorded in two late-night sessions at the Van Gelder studios in Hackensack, New Jersey, on December 11 and 12, 1961, the album featured a big band made up entirely of Ellingtonians performing Ellington compositions ("Gal from Joe's," "I'm Just a Lucky So and So"), along with a few Hodges riff tunes ("Jeep's Blues," "Juice A-Plenty") and Strayhorn pieces ("Your Love Has Faded," "Day Dream"), plus one standard (Hoagy Carmichael and Mitchell Parrish's "Star Dust"). "It was like an Ellington session, only the music was ready," said the trombonist Chuck Connors. "Billy handed out the music, and we played it, and it was amazingly gorgeous—one, two, three." According to the engineer, Rudy Van Gelder, who owned the studios, it "was just like everybody wished they could always work. Billy was the dream leader. The guys loved to play his music and they knew what he wanted. He didn't have to say a word to anybody—I don't think he did." The result was a casual album of appealing tunes expertly played, warming like a favorite sweater. It sold modestly, almost solely to Ellington fans, Taylor presumed. "Although Strayhorn's name was on the record, it was still a kind of Ellingtonia," said Taylor. "If you really thought about it, you'd realize that what the record showed was how much Billy Strayhorn defined what we think of as Ellingtonia. But nobody really thought of it that way. They saw Strayhorn's name but still thought Ellington. I think that's one of the reasons Duke didn't mind that Johnny and Billy made that kind of record. It made his people happy, and it made him look good. He had nothing to lose."

Just weeks later, in the early days of 1962, Strayhorn was offered an arranging opportunity that posed a larger threat to the Ellington organization. Frank Sinatra had founded his own record label, Reprise, in 1959 and had recorded Al Hibbler in May 1961. (In a come-fly-with-me tribute to Hibbler, Sinatra called the former Ellington vocalist "my pilot.") When the time came to plan a follow-up album for Hibbler, Sinatra used the project to lure Strayhorn to Reprise. "Sinatra wanted Strayhorn to come over to his label," recalled Hibbler. "He said, 'Listen, Hib, can't you get Strayhorn to come work for me?' I said, 'That's your department.' So he called up Strayhorn, and they talked it over." Strayhorn's old friend Haywood Williams was at his apartment during one call from Sinatra. "Billy said, 'That was Frank Sinatra. He wants me to work for him.' I said, 'Really? What are you going to do?' And he said, 'Oh, I don't know. I'll hear what the man has to say.' " Ellington, however, already knew what was up. "When Duke found out, he blew his fuckin' top," said Hibbler. "I heard about it from Frank. He said, 'Duke won't let me have Strayhorn. [Ellington said] "You already have my singer. Now you want my arranger? I won't allow it!" ' I don't know what Duke did, but that was the end of that. He was damn pissed off at Sinatra, and I know he gave Strayhorn a talking-to." Honi Coles heard from Strayhorn shortly after he and Ellington spoke about Sinatra's overtures. "Billy told me quite simply that Duke wouldn't permit it," said Coles. "He said, 'Strays, haven't you heard about the prodigal son? He can't go home again.' "

His Columbia contract expired, Duke Ellington signed with Reprise Records himself on November 28, 1962, in a deal meant to capitalize on his skill not only at making music of his own but at recognizing talent in others. Ellington's contract granted him license to sign artists and supervise recordings for the "Ellington Jazz Wing" of Reprise; Down Beat reported, "Ellington will have carte blanche to record whomever and whenever he desires." He started overseas: booked for a thirty-six-date tour of Europe under Norman Granz from January 12 through March 1, Ellington took up talent scouting between engagements, accompanied by Strayhorn, who seemed in good spirits. "He was like the old Billy. He drank—oh, yeah—but he was happy," said Jimmy Hamilton. Working together, Strayhorn and Ellington mended their conflict over Sinatra. Seeking out artists and brainstorming record projects, they clubbed in Manchester and had breakfast (in midafternoon) at a sidewalk place in Piccadilly. Strayhorn even appeared on stage—and on camera—with Ellington and the orchestra in a studio concert program taped at the Granada TV studios in Chelsea on January 22, 1963. Sitting in for one number, Strayhorn performed a gentle new composition, "Angu" (credited to Ellington). At the conclusion of the piece, he played a simple, pretty figure, and the camera closed in on the star sapphire ring Lena Horne had given him, wiggling on his left pinky.

Under Ellington's direction, Strayhorn worked on a flurry of recordings at the Barclay Studios in Paris during the last week of February. "He was very busy and he was laughing and smiling," said Gerhart Lehner, the engineer for all the sessions. On a showcase for Alice Babs, a Swedish singer Ellington had first met in Stockholm twenty-four years earlier (when she was fifteen), Strayhorn contributed arrangements (some songs were scored for four French horns), played piano on several numbers (including "Take the 'A' Train" and "Something to Live For"), and coached her in developing a composition of her own, "Babsie." "This was really nice for me," said Babs, "because I had been wondering over the years, since I had many, many Ellington recordings, why he attacked the piano with so much power and was, you know, more mild and soft at other times. After I worked with Billy and Duke I knew the secret." Babs saw Ellington and Strayhorn trade off piano duties, sometimes in the midst of recording a song, a technique they had employed since their early years together. "It was a fantastic experience to see this," Babs continued. "On that occasion also, Billy really helped me work out my song. He and I sat alone in a room next to the studio, and we worked it out. He was a fantastic help to me. He had a certain way of making me sound more like me than I knew how to."

Backing another singer—a young South African, Bea Benjamin—Ellington and Strayhorn shared piano duties with Benjamin's lover, the pianist Dollar Brand (later well known as Abdullah Ibrahim), whom Ellington also recorded the same evening for an instrumental album. (Strayhorn played his own "Your Love Has

Faded" as well as several vocal standards, including "I Could Write a Book," "Darn That Dream," and "A Nightingale Sang in Berkeley Square.") "I was very nervous," Benjamin recalled. "This was my first record, and there I was with Duke Ellington. Billy kept me calm. He helped me along with my singing—he coached me and changed things to fit my voice—and just the look in his eyes made me feel better. He seemed to be able to feel what I was feeling." Seeking fresh musical touches, Ellington and Strayhorn had Svend Asmussen, the Danish jazz violinist, accompany Benjamin with improvised pizzicato work. "I got blisters from playing so much pizzicato that night, but Duke and Billy were fascinated by the sound," said Asmussen. "Duke had the time of his life in those sessions, producing the records. Billy's job was to keep everything together, musically. Duke very rarely bothered to go into the booth and listen to a take. After a number, he'd say, 'Wonderful! Next number—what do we have? Bea, darling, what do you want to sing?' 'In My Solitude,' she said. 'Marvelous,' he said. 'What key?' 'B-natural,' she said. And then Duke said, 'Uh-mmm . . . Mis-ter Strayhorn . . . that's where you take over.' He would have no business playing in B-natural. Billy would laugh and sit down and play anything in the world in any key, perfectly. One take. And Duke would say, 'Marvelous! Wonderful! What should we do next?' " Focusing more deeply on the possibilities of jazz for string instruments, Ellington and Strayhorn followed up Asmussen's Benjamin sessions with an album featuring the trio of Asmussen on viola and Stephane Grappelli and Ray Nance on violin. In addition to playing piano on some cuts, Strayhorn pitched in a new composition, the aptly titled "Pretty Little One." "He understood the violin as well as he understood jazz, and he wrote for the violin as a violin," said Grappelli, who felt a kinship with Strayhorn and arranged to spend time with him the day after the string sessions. (The Bea Benjamin sessions have never been issued in any recording format. Some of the string recordings were released on LP in 1976, two years after Ellington's death, as *Duke Ellington's Jazz Violin Session.*)

"We became friendly very quickly," Grappelli recounted. "He was very fond of learning. He was very intelligent. I took him to museums in Paris. We spent an entire day in the Louvre marveling at the artworks and talking about them. He was very interested in the French painters, the impressionists, and he studied them very closely. I remember he said that many people talk only of color when they talk of the impressionists. Billy saw much more in their work. He talked about the shapes and the lines and the feelings—everything. I showed him the old streets. He was full of questions. He wanted to learn everything. We walked along the Seine. I was telling him how much I loved the river and how I loved to look at it as it ran through the city. We were talking about the water running through the city. Billy said it seemed to him to be the essence of life. It carried life through the city and beyond it, he said. He was very thoughtful. He looked sad, and I said, 'Billy, what are you thinking?' He said, 'I think when I die I want my ashes thrown into the river by my house in New York City.' "

10

BLOOD

COUNT

As a park-bench news buff, Billy Strayhorn had a reputation for political awareness among his friends and in jazz quarters. "Strayhorn was ahead of me in terms of what he knew—how the white world operated, who had the power, how they used it," said Dick Gregory, the comedian and activist, who performed at the annual Copasetics shows in the early 1960s. With the civil rights movement intensifying, Strayhorn spoke increasingly about channeling his passion for the cause into action, and he found the forum in the Logans' parlor. The Reverend Dr. Martin Luther King, Jr., a close acquaintance of theirs, visited the Logans a few times a year during his frequent visits to New York; in the Logan's circle of prosperous black New Yorkers, he saw a hub of influence and money, the latter an especially precious resource in his efforts. At several small gatherings of the Logans' most prominent friends, including the Robinsons (but not Ellington, owing to his road schedule), Strayhorn and King talked together at length. "I saw the two of them shuffle off into the kitchen," recalled Marian Logan, "and I said to myself, 'There goes Strays. He's going to have Martin cookin' up a pot.' I waited a few minutes, then went into the kitchen alone, like I needed to get something, and they were off in the back of the kitchen, face to face, talking a mile a minute about some aspect of civil rights law. After that, every time Martin was coming, he asked about Strays."

At King's appeal and with his guidance, the Logans began sponsoring fund-raising events in their apartment, inviting a hundred or so of their most affluent friends and acquaintances to shake hands with King. "Everybody wanted to meet Martin and have their picture taken with him, and we gave them a good evening. Catered. Good champagne—not the best, but good. We didn't want to be extravagant," said Marian Logan. "Strays always helped me plan the whole thing, the menu and such. And he always played piano. *And* he always gave a big check. After a couple of hours, I would tell everybody, 'Okay now, it's time to be quiet, because we have something to say. And the purpose of the gathering is: Freedom is *not* free. Now, cough up.'" From a few steps up the Logans' stairway, King would give a short inspirational speech while Marian Logan collected donations. Strayhorn would play "Why Don't You Do Right"; its chorus, though he didn't sing it, ends with the lyrics "Get out of here and get me some money too."

"Martin called once on a Saturday," said Marian Logan. "Strays was here and I was in the kitchen, and the phone rang. Martin said, 'Marian, we're having trouble.' I said, 'Leader, what's wrong?' He said, 'Well, we're running back and forth from Selma to Montgomery, and we can't take the buses. We need some cars.' I said, 'I don't know what I can do about that, Martin.' And Strays came in, and I put my hand over the phone, and I told him what was going on with Martin, and he got on the phone. He said, 'I've got an idea, Martin. Let's run a raffle. We'll get somebody to contribute a station wagon.' Well, that turned out not to be necessary—somebody else donated a couple of cars. But until then, for a few days Strays and Martin were working on their raffle. Working for the movement made Strays stronger. It brought out the best in him. Of course, he always brought out the best in other people, and he gave me the strength I needed to work for the cause. I went to Atlanta to help Martin integrate a hotel, and not everybody thought it was a smart idea, including Ellington. He was afraid I was going to get hurt. He was truly worried for me. He said, 'Bridie Mae, what the fuck are you doing going to Atlanta? You're going to get your ass killed.' But Strays never criticized. He was always supportive. 'If that's what you want to do, Baby Doll, go ahead and do it.' I did, and Strays called me every single night to make sure I was all right."

Assuming his most-practiced role, a quiet source of others' strength, Strayhorn offered the same kind of support to his dear friend Lena Horne as she strove to develop her own voice on behalf of black consciousness. Derided by some black activists for her "white" appearance and her dormancy in the early days of the civil rights movement, she recovered self-confidence through Strayhorn's empathy. "It was a big upheaval in my life," recalled Horne. "Billy was the source of my consciousness raising, not about being black but about being me and understanding that I was somebody who both blacks and whites could accept in some ways but could not accept in others, because of who I was. I had to learn to accept myself first, and that's what Billy helped me do. He taught me not to hate myself, not to feel a lot of guilt. Billy was like a piece of me, and he knew how wretched I felt. Stokely Carmichael and some others had talked terribly about 'blue-eyed black folks' and how rotten they were, and my son had great blue-green eyes. It was a time of making middle-class blacks feel like shit. Billy soothed me—'I know what you're like. You know what you're like. What you've done, what you've done without. This too will pass.' He was marvelous. He was there as my backbone. He knew that I was suffering for my people. They didn't know, because they had been separated from me by MGM and the record companies, by people who said, 'Oh, she's not really black. She's different.' Billy knew my insides. He knew that I had to expose myself. He knew I had to be unafraid. He knew me and knew my hunger, and he sorted the whole thing out for me." Bolstered by Strayhorn, Lena Horne decided to undertake her first initiative of public acclamation for black rights early in 1963. "When I said, 'I've got to go, I've got to go South, I have to,' he said, 'Yes, of course you have.' He said he'd go with me, and he helped me make the plans."

On Easter Sunday, April 14, 1963, James Strayhorn died of a heart attack at age seventy-four. He had suffered from arteriosclerosis, likely accelerated by years of cigarettes and liquor. Billy flew in for the memorial services and sat on his mother's right, his older brother, Jimmy, on her left, in the front row of folding metal chairs arranged before the casket at Hopewell's Funeral Home on Tioga Street in Homewood. Within the natural effusion of grief, there was a strain of content in this loss, however. "That man put Mama and everybody through an awful lot," Lillian Strayhorn Dicks said. "Everybody sort of let go a big sigh when it was all over." Billy stayed in town a few days to help comfort his mother and, with Jimmy, to attend to the legal and financial details. On his return to New York, Strayhorn seemed little affected by his father's death; he didn't even tell most of his friends. Among those he did, such as Cookie Cook and Honi Coles (his other "Father"), Strayhorn seemed nonplussed. "I don't think he had felt anything for his father for years," said Coles. "I would be exaggerating to say [the death] was a crucial event in his life. I have read, yes, that that is what happens for many homosexual men—when their father dies, they let loose. Strayhorn wasn't that way. He wasn't that way. He let go of his father a long time before I met him. He had other father figures—Duke, I was one of them. If Duke had died, now that would have been a different thing."

Ready after months of planning, Lena Horne and Billy Strayhorn left for the South on June 5, 1963. They traveled by train to Atlanta, first for a meeting with the twenty-three-year-old protest organizer Julian Bond; both Horne and Strayhorn made donations to his organization, the Student Non-Violent Coordinating Committee. "Julian, Julian—he had such a mind," said Horne. "He and Billy talked so deeply, without emotion yet completely from the heart." The following morning, Horne and Strayhorn flew to their primary destination, Jackson, Mississippi, where the National Association for the Advancement of Colored People was preparing to stage its largest rally to date, in defiance of a state court injunction barring racial protests. They were greeted at Hawkins Field airport by the NAACP's Jackson representative, Medgar Evers, a thirty-seven-year-old former insurance salesman. "We met with Medgar, and we said, 'What can we do?' And he said, 'Well, we're having a big rally tomorrow. Will you come?' I said, 'Yes.' 'Will you sing?' And Billy said, 'Yes.' He made the commitment to Medgar. He made me do it, and he taught me how because I didn't know what to sing. I didn't know the songs. Billy had to teach me 'Amazing Grace' and tell me how to do it." Evers arranged for Horne and Strayhorn to stay overnight in one of his friends' homes, apologizing for not welcoming them into his own house, which, he told them, had been damaged by firebombs. "He felt terrible that we couldn't stay with them," said Horne. "He said there was debris everywhere, and he felt bad about the impression it would make on us." On the evening of June 7 at the Jackson County fairground, its perimeter outlined with barbed wire, some two thousand supporters applauded as the regional secretary of the NAACP, Ruby Hurley, introduced Lena Horne. Strayhorn gave her a squeeze of the hand, and Horne walked up to the microphone to sing, a cappella. (Evers, noticing three white men smoking cigarettes in the front of the audience, handed Hurley a note instructing her to ask the men to refrain from smoking while Horne was singing; rather than comply, all three walked away.) Five days later, President Kennedy gave his first nationally televised address on civil rights. "We face a moral crisis," Kennedy pronounced. "It cannot be met by police action. It cannot be met by increased demonstrations in the streets. It cannot be quieted by token moves or talk. It is time to act in the Congress, in your state and local legislative bodies, and in all our daily lives." Shortly after the conclusion of the president's address, just after midnight, Medgar Evers was shot in the back on his front lawn by a salesman named Byron De La Beckwith, an outspoken segregationist (and one of the three smokers who had walked out on Horne).

"He [Evers] left Billy and me with such a good, strong feeling that weekend. I was horrified when they told me," recalled Horne, who heard about the murder while she was having her makeup applied moments before an appearance on the *Today* show; unbridled, Horne revealed the depth of her rage on the air, live. "The whole experience was a turning point in my life," she said. "I think Medgar's death signaled a change for many, many people. Medgar, the dear, sweet man, gave the movement a sad human face." At the same time, participation by a broadly popular black celebrity like Horne helped expand the movement's reach, according to Evers's widow, Merlie Evers. (A year after De La Beckwith's conviction in 1994, more than three decades after his crime, she was elected president of the NAACP.) "Lena Horne was very, very special to our population at that time," she said. "She was a role model. With her participation, she showed that people who have obtained celebrity status can and do still relate to the salt of the earth, as Medgar used to call his ground troops—that theirs was a just cause. It served another purpose as well. People who were afraid to venture out—there was an awful lot of fear then, and a lot of it was justified. When the word got out that they attended one of the rallies, some people's mortgages were called in the next day, in full. People suddenly lost their jobs. So people were afraid to come and we needed them there, and Lena brought them out."

Duke Ellington, who had always protested racial inequity through the defiant, proudly African eloquence of his music as well as in his public role as a cultural leader, was offered a chance to make a timely new contribution to black consciousness as the Southern summer and the civil rights movement approached a boil. For the theatrical attraction of an exhibition entitled *Century of Negro Progress* at Chicago's McCormick Place convention center, Ellington was commissioned to write an original stage production as a demonstration of black pride. Enthusiastically and virtually single-handedly, Ellington created *My People*, a potpourri of old and new songs and tone poems (some sung by Joya Sherrill and Jimmy McPhail) produced twice daily in the 5,000-seat Arie Crown Theatre. (Although Ellington wrote the lyrics and most of the arrangements himself, there were two notable exceptions: "Strange Feeling" from the Ellington-Strayhorn *Perfume Suite* and the novelty number "Purple People," which was copyrighted as a Strayhorn composition and used in *My People* but not included in the album of the music or released on any other record.) Ellington's usual touring schedule kept him from directing the show's jazz orchestra. That task fell to Strayhorn, assisted by the pianist Jimmy Jones; as a result, the seventeen-piece ensemble was billed as the Billy Strayhorn Orchestra despite his relatively minor involvement. "Billy was happy to do it because it was a good thing to do, a statement against racism," said Jimmy McPhail. Although it was received somewhat lukewarmly by the press, *My People* played its full run, until September 2, to responsive audiences. "Obviously the time was ripe for the thing," said McPhail.

Handing off his duties to Jones, Strayhorn took a brief break from the show for another demonstration of black pride, the 200,000-strong March on Washington on August 28, 1963. Arriving two days early to offer help in the preparations, Strayhorn rendezvoused with Marian and Arthur Logan at the Willard Hotel, where the Southern Christian Leadership Conference had reserved a block of rooms for King and his friends, including the Logans and Strayhorn. "Strays spent most of his time in our room," said Marian Logan, "because we decided we would be the room with the booze. Everybody congregated there. Martin and Strays got together again, and Strays talked off his ear about Ellington's show and how wonderful it was. Martin promised to go see it, and after that, he did. Arthur and I took him, and that was where he met Edward for the first time. They saw each other and hugged like they were old friends." On the day of the march, Strayhorn declined to walk but sat in the third row of the seats, alongside the Logans, and listened to all the speakers and the singers. "I mentioned to Arthur, 'Isn't that funny? Itty Bitty Buddy came all the way here to the march, and then he didn't march.' And Arthur said, 'He might not be feeling well. I'll talk to him about it'—which he did, and Strays said, 'I'm fine, Arturo. Just a little tired. That's all.'"

Social consciousness so pervaded the era that it overtook the Copasetics that year. Although each of the organization's past several shows had been more thoroughly conceived and better produced than the last, the fall 1963 event surpassed them all in its topicality. For the 1961 production, *On the Riviera,* Strayhorn and Roy Branker, a cocktail pianist, had written numbers with French themes, including a cancan performed in drag and a spoof of pretentious painters featuring the Copasetics dancing in berets and smocks (to choreography by Cholly Atkins and Pete Nugent). In 1962, the group put on *Anchors Aweigh,* a marginally nautical romp written by Strayhorn with the help of Honi Coles. "There were stowaways and beautiful girl sailors—it was all very realistic," said Coles dryly. "But it was *fuuunnnn.*" This time, in a twist, the Copasetics produced a show with a touch of seriousness, though that touch was gentle. Entitled *Down There,* the production was a joyful ride on the "freedom train" of civil rights. With both music and lyrics by Strayhorn, *Down There* followed a group of nameless characters—the Copasetics in their usual onstage personas—from a day at hard labor to a wild night of liberation. "We wanted to do something that was in keeping with what was happening," said fellow Copasetic member LeRoy Myers, who ranked the show as his favorite. "There was a lot of feeling all around for that show. We had a lot to feel good about, and it was meaningful. Billy did the right thing there." (As usual with the Copasetics shows, the music was not recorded, and Strayhorn never had it published. Virtually none of the music from *On the Riviera, Anchors Aweigh,* and *Down There* is known to exist.)

"Strayhorn was going through a good period," remembered Honi Coles. "The civil rights activities gave him something to work for. He was a fighter, and he was even more of a minority than most of us, because of his lifestyle orientation. He kept the drinking under control or he was hiding it very well—you never know. But it was a pretty good time for him."

That year the traditional September event had been bumped up to the last Monday in August to accommodate Strayhorn, who was accompanying Ellington and the orchestra on its most exotic overseas jaunt yet: a fourteen-week goodwill tour of the Near and Middle East sponsored by the "New Frontier" State Department of the Kennedy administration. Ellington and Strayhorn were hoping to draw inspiration for a new suite. Strayhorn was soon called, however, into more rigorous service. Immediately on landing in Damascus, the orchestra's first destination, Ellington fell ill and called Arthur Logan, who said the malady sounded like air sickness, since the band had been flying on a DC-3, a small, outdated, unpressurized propeller plane. But Ellington's condition worsened over the ensuing week, and at his patient's insistence, Logan agreed to meet Ellington in East Pakistan and travel with him on the rest of the tour; Marian Logan would meet them soon after that, in Baghdad. As Arthur Logan recalled, "I found him there physically in pretty good shape but pretty badly depressed": Ellington said he had never seen such a level of poverty.

Strayhorn filled in as pianist for the orchestra, sharing conducting duties with Harry Carney. In a concert at the Scheherazade Grand Hotel in Calcutta on October 14, Strayhorn played and sang "Lush Life." "That was a little strange, hearing Strayhorn do 'Lush

Life' in Calcutta," said Rolf Ericson, the Swedish-born trumpeter, who had temporarily joined the Ellington Orchestra for the tour. Feeling better, Ellington soon reclaimed his place on the bandstand, only to encounter larger problems. In Baghdad on the evening of November 12, Iraqi air force jets attacked a government palace in an attempted coup d'etat while the Ellington Orchestra performed at the Khuld Hall, just a few hundred yards away. The bandleader and his musicians were escorted to their rooms, where they were instructed to remain, lights off and blinds down. Meantime, Strayhorn and Arthur Logan found their way up onto the hall's roof, and Strayhorn snapped pictures of the jets' fire. "They were shooting all over the palace," recalled Herbie Jones, the trumpeter called over from the States to replace Ray Nance. (The reasons for Nance's departure are unclear.) "A little later, we were in Turkey," Jones continued, "and they had a special dinner for the band, with the diplomats and everybody around. Somebody came in and yelled out, 'The president's been shot.' And I'm thinking, 'Yeah. Well, okay. Everybody's always getting shot around here.' The guy says, '*Our* president.' And you hear about a dozen plates fall on the table." The tour was cut short on the spot, and Ellington and his company were hustled home. "Edward was beside being beside himself," said Marian Logan. "The whole tour was strange, and now the president went and died on him. He had a big problem with death—not just his own, anybody's. He couldn't deal with it. It scared the daylights out of him. So he blocked it out. He just wouldn't deal with it."

In the right corner of the landing at the top of the steps that led from the ground floor of the Logans' building on West 88th Street to their living-room entrance, there was a straight-backed wooden chair. It was intended to be used for putting on and taking off boots, but since neither of the Logans wore boots the seat of the chair was covered with at least a week's worth of newspapers, amassed until someone got around to lugging them down to the trash. On a cold Saturday early in 1964, Arthur Logan poked onto the landing to greet Strayhorn and noticed his friend sitting precariously on top of the newspapers; he was not removing boots. Strayhorn was huffing to catch his breath after having climbed the Logans' stairs. His eyes were slightly popped, and he looked pale. Marian Logan watched from behind her husband as he quickly knelt in front of Strayhorn and studied his face. "Arthur said, 'If I were a doctor, I'd say you could use a checkup,'" recalled Marian Logan. "Strays nodded his head, and Arthur reached out his hand to help him get up and go into the house." Four or five days later, late on an afternoon at the end of the week, Logan came home a couple of hours earlier than usual and sat down in front of Marian at their dining table. "He said, 'Oh, the worst news in the world, doll.' I said, 'What?' And he said, 'Itty Bitty Buddy is sick.' I said, 'What's the matter?' He said, 'He has cancer—of the esophagus. And it's bad, Doll Baby. It's bad.' He was just brokenhearted. He just sat there. He put his head on the table, and he cried like a baby."

Marian Logan let her husband weep, holding his hand. "After he was all calmed down, I asked him, '*How* bad?' He said, 'Very advanced, probably terminal. But I'm going to send him to some specialists. We'll see what they can do. I said, '*Why?* What causes that? Cigarettes?' Arthur said, 'Smoke, drink—either one. Maybe neither. It's cancer. We don't know. And it doesn't matter now.'"*

Logan hadn't yet shared his diagnosis with Strayhorn; he wanted to tell him privately on their next Saturday, friend to friend. "Arthur said, 'Well, I'm going to get Strays.' They drove into the country and talked. This is when he told him what to expect, what was going to happen, and all that kind of information. They were gone three or four hours. Arthur always believed that you should tell the patient the truth, no matter what it was. He said, 'If you lie to people, they'll know you're lying, and they'll think of something even worse.' They came back, and Strays walked through the door with a smile on his face. Strays felt very secure because he loved Arthur and he believed in him and had known him for years. He said, 'Now, I'm all right, Doll Baby. I'm all right. We're going to manage through it. Arturo said I can drink, so let's have a Sterling martini.'"

Bill Coleman stopped by Strayhorn's house later that evening

---

* Cancers of the esophagus, pharynx, and mouth are strongly associated with both alcohol consumption and the use of tobacco products, according to various studies recorded by the National Institute on Alcohol Abuse and Alcoholism.

and heard the news. Startled and distraught, Coleman found his friend collected. "He discussed it matter-of-factly, in very measured tones. 'Arthur says I have cancer.' He kept that even temper. He talked about dying possibly and was completely cool and calm as he talked about it. He was resigned and obviously had been resigned about important matters before and knew how to handle it."

Ellington, less accustomed to resignation, responded to the diagnosis of his partner of twenty-five years in an eruption of emotion. "Arthur called Edward and told him. He was on the road somewhere," Marian Logan recounted. "Arthur said, 'Edward is terribly, terribly angry. I think he blames me. 'How can you tell me this? Do you know what you're saying? Why didn't you tell me this before?' 'I said I just diagnosed him.' Edward said, 'What kind of doctor are you? Why didn't you see this coming?' He was irrational. And he was pissed off." Perry Watkins, a theatrical producer traveling with the orchestra at the time, saw Ellington's rage nearly deplete his renowned patience. "I think Billy's illness upset him. I know it did, because I was on the road with the band," said Watkins. "We did twenty-seven gigs in thirty-one days, and we really had no time to think very much, and during that time the news of Billy's illness came. Mercer and I were adjacent to each other [in the hotel], and he [Ellington] called Mercer, and I went into the room, and he said, 'I'm very upset, and I don't want any nonsense tonight. You tell the cats.' The gentlemen in the band act up variously from time to time, and he was in no mood that night for any foolishness at all. And on top of that, he lost a pair of gold cufflinks, which also made him pretty angry, too. So he was in no mood that night. He said, 'You know, this thing distresses me no end.' He said, 'Why Billy? Why Billy, of all . . . ' He said, 'This thing shouldn't happen to me.' "

There's no knowing exactly what Duke Ellington and Billy Strayhorn said to each other. Was Strayhorn as contained with Ellington, his closest collaborator, as he was with his personal friend Bill Coleman? Would Ellington have vented his frustrations to Strayhorn or provided stolid support? Using the same wording with many of his friends, Strayhorn would only say, "Edward told me not to worry about a thing."

In their work together through the mid-1960s, Ellington and Strayhorn lost a bit of creative momentum, producing two albums of contemporary hits arranged in the Ellington style (including "Moon River," "Red Roses for a Blue Lady," the Beatles' "I Want to Hold Your Hand," and the like) and an Ellingtonian version of the Sherman Brothers' score to the Walt Disney musical *Mary Poppins*. Playfully imaginative, the new treatments and performances generally transcended the music's origins: the work is artful, if not always art on a scale with the Ellington and Strayhorn masterworks. "A lot of the arrangements of those pop tunes were done on the spot in the studio," said Buster Cooper, a trombonist. "Duke hummed the sections or Billy scribbled ideas down, and Tom Whaley copied the parts right there. The ink on the sheet music would still be wet when we were cutting the record." If the course of the Ellington and Strayhorn collaboration was in a level stage, it also had impressive spikes, most notably the suite inspired by cultures the composers had encountered in the Middle East. Performed (in incomplete form) as early as February 1964 and refined over the following year, the mistitled *Far East Suite* evoked, translated, filtered, intermingled, and reinvented the sounds of a complexity of Eastern cultures with a loving sense of wonder, even though one of its highlights—"Isfahan," named after the city in Iran—had been composed by Strayhorn long before the trip (and was originally titled "Elf"). The work (not released commercially until early 1967) represented a return to form for Ellington and Strayhorn, as Dan Morgenstern raved in *Down Beat:* "If you have been saving a vintage bottle of Chateau Lafitte Rothschild or some other kind of ambrosia, the advent of this chapter in Ellingtonia provides that special occasion you have been waiting for. . . . Hail, then, to the Duke of Ellington, who has added the colors and textures of the Orient to his brilliant palette, and has given us new riches on top of riches. Hail, also, to Billy Strayhorn, who has enriched his legacy. It is encouraging that music of such strength and beauty can be created in our troublesome times; music that fulfills the uplifting purport of true art."

"Billy became much more serious after his diagnosis for cancer— more serious about music, more serious in general," recalled Bill Coleman. "He didn't seem to want to put as much of himself into the less artistic projects for Ellington. He started talking about writing classical music again. We talked about his writing a work of variations on some jazz themes. He had more gravity." For his Riverside Park reading, Strayhorn switched from the newspaper to books, Oliver Jackson noticed. (His library at the time included Dylan Thomas's *Me and My Bike*; *Picasso's Picassos*, a book of prints; Robert Laffont's *Il ne m'est Paris*, in French; and Mary McCarthy's *The Stones of Florence*.) He laughed less at Ernest Brown's jokes, his fellow Copasetics member thought. "I guess he never thought I was funny, but he stopped pretending," said Brown. He brushed up on art, calling Felrath Hines to recommend favorite books and exhibits. His conversations with Martin Luther King at the Logans' seemed to Marian Logan longer and more heated; the two men moved from the kitchen into the parlor, facing off in the cushioned chairs. In the second week of December 1964, when King was awarded the Nobel Peace Prize, the Logans brought Strayhorn to see their celebrated friend off to Stockholm. Euphoric activists celebrated with King in a lounge at Kennedy Airport as Strayhorn watched from his swivel chair and punctuated the encomiums with an occasional "Bravo!"

That winter, he began nurturing a close relationship with an acquaintance of Frank Neal's and Charles Sebree's from their days at the Art Institute of Chicago, Bill Grove, a graphic designer long on the periphery of Strayhorn's social circle. Two years younger than Strayhorn, Grove, who was white, was quiet to a point that unnerved some and serious to the verge of humorlessness. "He never said anything, so you never knew what he was thinking," said Haywood Williams. Grove's was an expressionless, unchanging face, handsome as it was. He had a trim row of light brown hair scalloping a vast forehead. Raised in moderate comfort outside of Chicago, Grove had studied piano as a boy and painted watercolors; he despised his father, his sister Madeline Grove Williams recalled. "He was always very reserved," she said. "When he was young, he was extremely shy, painfully shy. He was a very timid person. He was always extremely vain, a very fancy dresser. Not flashy, but he took pride in wearing beautiful clothes." Since young adulthood, Bill Grove had socialized primarily with black men, his sister said. One of his longtime intimates in New York, the black pianist Dwike

Mitchell said of him, "He is the one person—and I say person, not white person—who I've ever met in my life who didn't have an ounce of prejudice in him." Grove, who moved to New York in 1939, the same year as Strayhorn, valued order and precision. He spent virtually all his professional life at the same job, as art director of the magazine *Consumer Reports*, where the staff knew him as proper and detail-oriented. "We were located in a slum of Mount Vernon, New York, and people dressed and behaved for the occasion, but not Bill," recalled the magazine's editor, Irwin Landau. "Bill was always elegantly dressed, very well-mannered. Besides being a good designer, he was a very good editor and an expert on the nuts and bolts of things like our ratings tables and what was right and what was wrong and where we used a period. I think everyone remembers visits from Bill where he would say, 'Are you sure this is correct?' "

Neighbors on Manhattan's Upper West Side (Grove lived on Central Park West, a few blocks south of Strayhorn's old place on West 106th Street), Strayhorn and Grove started meeting regularly for dinner at the Flash Inn, cocktails at the Showman's. "Strays' whole gang knew, 'Okay, now they're a couple,' " said Marian Logan. "At first, people did a little double take, you know, because he was white. But that wasn't what that relationship was about—it wasn't any black-white thing. It was a thing about compatibility. Strays found just what he needed right then with Grove. They both drank like it was water, but they talked a lot and Grove listened to Strays. He was a listener; Goldie was a talker. They went to movies. They read magazines and books." (Strayhorn's copy of *The Stones of Florence* was inscribed "BS/BG.") With Bill Grove, Billy Strayhorn slowed down, as if to stretch the time.

Among the few who knew of Strayhorn's illness, its symptoms still inconspicuous, Honi Coles urged his friend to expend his creative energy more judiciously. "I told him, 'Do your own stuff—write a symphony,' " said Coles. " 'Put together your own band, make your own records. You put yourself second long enough. Time to put yourself out there.' " With the venues for tap dancing diminishing, Coles had taken a nonperforming job as stage manager of the Apollo Theater; without Strayhorn's assent, he was already planning to produce a concert showcasing Strayhorn as a performer. "I had the date allocated, and I was ready to talk him into it. Then somebody beat me to the punch." In March 1965, three representatives from the Duke Ellington Jazz Society, a six-year-old organization of Ellington enthusiasts, offered Strayhorn the opportunity to be featured in the first solo concert of his lifetime. The fact that they had no knowledge of his illness served to persuade Strayhorn to give the performance. "He was very happy to be recognized," said Marian Logan. "He didn't want it out of pity." Strayhorn was indeed well recognized within the clubby realm of the eighty-member society. "Our approach as a matter of principle was always Ellington-hyphen-Strayhorn—that those two men were to be treated as absolute equals, and it was established as a matter of great importance," said Douglas Bray, president of the society and chair of its concert committee. Encouraged by Ellington's sister Ruth, who passed along Strayhorn's unlisted home phone number, Bray called Strayhorn to discuss the prospect of his performing; it took four phone calls over two weeks, Strayhorn hedging and postponing, until Bray—accompanied by fellow Ellington Jazz Society members Tom Detienne and Tom Harris—met Strayhorn to discuss the concert. They convened at six o'clock on a weekday in the lounge of the new New York Hilton in midtown Manhattan, a swinging-sixties atmosphere; suited businessmen arched hungrily in plush-cushioned, chrome-tube chairs that shifted about in a swamp of shag carpeting. Making small talk, Bray brought up a parallel he saw in Strayhorn's association with Ellington and the mentor-protégé relationship between Goethe and Schiller; Strayhorn knew his Goethe well enough to chat on the subject and promised to catch up on Schiller. "Good," Bray recalled Strayhorn's saying, "now I can learn about me."

As the group shifted to its agenda, however, Strayhorn withdrew. "He just did not want to do it," recalled Harris. "He expressed great reservation about whether an audience would come to hear him. 'Why would anybody pay money to come and listen to me for an hour and a half? They want to hear Duke and not me.' And we reiterated over and over again that he was greatly beloved in Ellington circles, [among] Ellington people, and pointed out that this was who the audience was. I remember we reassured him that this was like an extended family. I think he felt reassured when we focused on this extended-family aspect—this would not be an audience off the street. These would be people who were prepared to love him because they already knew what he had done, and they were prepared to enjoy and to love whatever he wanted to do. We put it on the basis 'Pretend you're just playing for friends, Billy.' In the course of giving all the reasons why he couldn't do it, shouldn't do it, didn't want to do it, he said, 'Don't forget, Dukie Boy is out there all the time. I play in my apartment and in recording studios. But it's not the same thing. I don't play in public. I'm not a public artist or performer.' " Frustrated, Bray finally offered Strayhorn an out. "All right, Billy," he said, "Let's talk about it again another time. Maybe you'll feel differently about it next year," and, taking a long draw on a cigarette, Strayhorn abandoned his objections. "You know," he said, as Bray recalled, "it sounds like fun."

Once committed, Strayhorn tackled his concert debut with youthful vigor. He planned out a three-part program made up entirely of his own compositions and co-compositions with Ellington: first a recital-style segment of unaccompanied piano, then a few trio performances and a set featuring a small group with somewhat unusual instrumentation. He lined up trumpeter Clark Terry, who had left the Ellington Orchestra in 1959; clarinetist and alto saxophonist Bob Wilber; French horn player Willie Ruff; bassist Wendell Marshall; and drummer Dave Bailey, along with Ozzie Bailey for a few vocal numbers. A week before the concert, scheduled for the afternoon of Sunday, June 6, at the New School on West 12th Street in Greenwich Village, Strayhorn called a rehearsal in his apartment; he had written new arrangements for the whole second half of the concert, vigorous charts of old and relatively recent pieces, such as "Passion Flower" (reconceived as a soaring up-tempo number), "Chelsea Bridge," "Rain Check," and "Upper Manhattan Medical Group." The band ran through the tunes for about four hours, with breaks for cocktails and hors d'oeuvres. "He had worked out every detail—the harmonics, everything he wanted us to play," recalled Ruff. "He even had worked out, very precisely, the dynamics, which nobody, nobody bothers with in jazz. If he didn't hear what he wanted to hear, he hadn't written what he wanted to hear—the writing was like that. That day, when we were rehearsing, he made a few changes on things he didn't like, or, more likely, if somebody had trouble playing something. One horn passage of mine was tricky. He said, 'I can rewrite that, you know.' And I said, 'No, Billy, I like the way it lays. Let me get used to it.' It was just a hard phrase to make. He really knew the French horn. But he never, ever used clichés. His writing was so unusual it could catch you by surprise the first time." In honor of the group's rehearsal site, Strayhorn dubbed his first band in nearly thirty years the Riverside Drive Five.

A group of friends—an extended family indeed—the sold-out audience of jazz fans in the 450-seat New School auditorium gave Strayhorn an explosive ovation as soon as he walked on stage, dolled up in a new, bright-white suit. He beamed and laughed out loud, still giggling as he started playing a set of meticulous piano solos, including chamber-jazz renditions of pieces from throughout his career: "Hear Say" (his modernist segment of the Ellington-Strayhorn *Deep South Suite*), "Orson" (a tribute to Welles), "All Heart" (a ballad of his incorporated into the Ellington-Strayhorn *Portrait of Ella Fitzgerald* suite), and the buoyant Ellington Orchestra dance tune "Clementine." "I had known he was good, but I didn't know he was *that* fantastic a pianist until that concert. He blew the hall away," said the pianist Randy Weston, one of the many musicians, including Ray Nance, Billy Eckstine, and the drummer Jo Jones, who attended the show. Strayhorn charmed the place with his nonchalant humor. "He had a graceful confidence that was overwhelming," said Dave Bailey. "From the moment that he tiptoed to the piano, everybody just knew, okay, here comes a genius. Swee' Pea was a very demure person and a very mysterious person, meaning you didn't know whether to take him seriously or not. But he used that fact as a performer. He handled the audience very deftly." Tom Harris recalled that Strayhorn introduced a new song (untitled and unknown) with a slyly mocking story, announcing, "I have a friend. And this friend has an orchestra, and this friend travels with this orchestra fifty-two weeks a year. He refuses to take a vacation, and this has been going on for years. Every once in a while, this friend calls me from some place I've never heard of, from some distant part of the world, and says, 'Billy, I'm working on a song, but I'm stuck, can't finish it. Now, the first part goes like this: Bah bah bah bee boo bee bee bah bah, bah bah bah bah bee bee boo bah boo. I want you to finish it for me. Call me back tomorrow morning. Or in ten minutes. And tell me how you finished it.' " Pause and laughter. "Now, I'm going to let you in on a secret. I didn't call him back yet, but I'm going to play it for you now." According to Tom Detienne, "the audience went bananas, completely bananas."

Reviewing the performance in the *New York Times*, John S. Wilson noted, "Mr. Strayhorn is a small, dapper man with a flair for elegance and a mocking wit." Musically, Strayhorn was equally well received by the press; Dan Morgenstern wrote in *Down Beat*, "This concert . . . afforded a rare and welcome opportunity to hear and see Strayhorn in a full-fledged showcase of his multiple talents. It indicated, among other things, that Strayhorn is much more than Ellington's alter ego (although that in itself would be no mean accomplishment). . . . Everything he plays is invested with a rare sense of form and development, and there is none of the empty rhapsodizing to which some of his melodies and harmonies lend themselves in lesser hands."

Ellington, out of town again, missed the concert but heard such glowing reports from his sister that he arranged for Strayhorn and his Riverside Drive Five to record their numbers for an album. The week after the concert, Ellington himself produced—and paid for—the sessions, recorded at the RCA Records studios. "The day after the concert, I got a call," said Bob Wilber, a reed player. "It was Billy, and he says, 'Well, we're going to record the concert because it went so well.' And I showed up, and the first thing I notice is—I look into the control booth—and there's Duke. Duke was sort of the producer for the date. With Billy, you sensed a very firm sense of purpose behind the work. With Duke, it was fun." As they wrapped up all the band's numbers, Ellington announced that he wanted to tape one more. "We got some time. Let's fool around," he said, as Wilber recalled. "So he sat down at the piano with Billy," Wilber said, "and Duke said, 'Anybody got a riff? Guys?' And Clark came up with some little figure and played it for Duke. Duke said, 'Okay, let's go,' and they rolled the tape, and they recorded it. The number was done, and Duke said, 'That's the way to do it.' " (Ellington, Strayhorn, and the Riverside Drive Five recorded two tunes created this way, "Oink" and "Pig Sty." Both derived from riffs contributed by Terry, and the songs were copyrighted by Tempo

Music in the name of Terry's wife, Pauline Reddon. On CD, "Pig Sty" has been mistakenly entitled "Pick Side" and inaccurately attributed to Strayhorn.)

Strayhorn seemed radically energized by the whole stream of events, optimistic, confident, altogether upbeat, even about his health. He talked about taking the Riverside Drive Five on a national tour. Looking back as he planned forward, he offered George Greenlee, the man who had introduced him to Ellington, the job of managing the tour. "He said, 'George, I'd really like you to do this,' " said Greenlee. "Obviously, he was thinking his time might be limited, and he wanted to pay me back in some way. He was wrapping up. But I didn't know anything about managing a tour. Frankly, it was a strange job to offer me. But that's what he had."

Discussing the prospective tour with Willie Ruff, Strayhorn brought up his illness, which Ruff had heard something about through his longtime duo partner, Dwike Mitchell; Bill Grove and Mitchell were still close friends. "He said he wanted to keep playing and he thought he'd be able to keep going for a while longer because Dr. Logan found a surgeon to operate on his throat," said Ruff. "He said Dr. Logan got this big Japanese surgeon who commuted between Tokyo, New York, and Boston to do this one operation. He said esophageal problems were very common in Japan because they drink very, very hot things, like boiling; it has to be bubbling when it goes down, he said. So they had some advanced treatments, and was going to have this thing done." The surgery Strayhorn underwent, relatively common in the United States as well as Japan, was a tracheostomy, in which an incision is made in the windpipe, between the Adam's apple and the collarbones; the thyroid gland is severed, and a metal (or plastic) tube is inserted for breathing. In Strayhorn's case, the voice box wasn't affected, so his speech was unimpaired.

The silken chic of Strayhorn's ascots, puffed between starched and pressed collars, obscured the severity of his condition only among casual company. "You could tell in his eyes—he was more shaken up than he wanted people to think," said Haywood Williams. "He tried to put on a happy front. 'Everything's fine. I feel great.' You knew better, if you knew him at all." Among close friends and in the solace of a fifth or sixth drink, Strayhorn showed signs of a steadily darkening state. Slumped at the Logans' dining table late one night, he rolled a wax apple out of a lazy Susan and stared at it for a few minutes, declaring matter-of-factly, "A fruit that only looks like it's alive. That makes two of us." With Lena Horne, whom he could see just once every few months since she was living in Palm Springs and touring the nightclub circuit, Strayhorn poured out his distress. "I had never seen Billy like that," recalled Horne. "I had seen him depressed before. We had both gone through terrible low points and helped each other ride it out. This time, he didn't think this was one you could ride out. This was it. He knew it, and I knew it. And all I could do is let him feel and let the feelings out. Oh, he cried. He cried, and he drank, and he cried some more. I couldn't be around as much as I wanted to be. I wanted to be with him all the time."

As he had always revealed his feelings through his music, Strayhorn started venting his anguish creatively. He composed a straightahead blues piece and titled it "Boo-Lose," combining his fondness for wordplay with open self-pity. Venturing several steps further, he took on one of the lightest assignments Ellington had ever given him and twisted it into a message of fatalistic discontent. On a trip along the West Coast, Ellington had heard Gerald Wilson's Los Angeles–based big band perform a Wilson tune called "When I'm Feeling Kinda Blue," a backbeat-driven dance number in the vein of late-1950s rock and roll. Ellington "smelled a hit," said Wilson, and asked for the music. "Duke took the arrangement I did for my band, which I gave him happily," said Wilson. "Duke said he wanted Strayhorn to add lyrics, which he did. Strayhorn came up with a new title, and he wrote a set of lyrics, and he called me up. He had just called Duke and read them to Duke, and Duke loved them. Duke wrote them down over the phone, and we had a song: my music and Billy's lyrics." Strayhorn's new title was "Imagine My Frustration," and the lyrics use a banal old rock-song theme, the wallflower pining for acceptance. By the end of most such songs, the protagonist is at last appreciated for his or her (traditionally, her) unseen or unconventional virtues and finds happiness. Not so in Strayhorn's subverted variant, a cynical story of hopelessness. This time, despite her proud persistence, the wallflower remains unredeemed and unappreciated:

Went down to the dance,
Sat down by the wall,
Invited to dance
By no one at all.

The couples danced by
So charming and gay
But nobody once
Looked over my way.

So awfully sad,
Dissatisfied
And hurt so bad,
I almost cried.

Imagine my frustration
With no invitation to dance.

Head high, standing tall,
Who else could I be
But belle of the ball
Who likes what they see,

And then in my ear
Someone said to me,
Wallflower, my dear,
How come you can't see?

They couldn't care less,
They're not impressed.
As you might guess,
You're in excess.

Imagine my frustration
With no invitation to dance.

A smile to the crowd,
Tiptoe and alert,

The band blew and bowed
But nixed on the flirt.

A voice said to me,
Wallflower, my dear,
You're sweet as can be
But how come you're here?

They couldn't care less
About your dress,
You're in a mess
And in excess.

Imagine my frustration
With no invitation to dance.

Recorded by Ella Fitzgerald with the Ellington Orchestra in October 1965, "Imagine My Frustration" appeared on the album entitled *Ella at Duke's Place*, the first Ellington Orchestra vocal project without Strayhorn on hand since Ellington and Strayhorn had met.

Strayhorn's cancer spread. Under Arthur Logan's orders, the weakening patient began a regimen of high-dosage radiation treatments once a week at St. Clare's Hospital on 52nd Street and Lexington Avenue; though nonintrusive, each of the sessions left Strayhorn dispirited for several days. He wasn't eating and, for the first time in his fifty years, looked his age. His deep cherry-bark skin turned a thin gray. The radiation failed to slow the disease's momentum, however, and Strayhorn required additional surgery to excise cancer cells. His esophagus was removed, necessitating a gastrostomy, wherein the stomach is severed and attached to a feeding tube with an external cap under the chest. Strayhorn could now consume liquids only, by opening an "abdominal tap" and pouring the fluids directly into his stomach. Though further consumption of alcohol would scarcely aid Strayhorn's condition, Logan assessed the trauma of changing Strayhorn's habits at this point as more detrimental to his patient than the alcohol itself. "Mix the martinis," Strayhorn told Marian Logan when she visited him at home after

т : **Strayhorn and Lena Horne**
acation at Horne's house in
Springs in the early 1960s.
ᴼᴹ : **Lennie Hayton, Horne,**
Strayhorn at a mid-1960s
asetics show

ABOVE: **The Copasetics, including Strayhorn, fifth from left, standing, in an unfinished painting by member Eddie West.** BELOW: **The Strayhorns at an early-1950s reunion in Pittsburgh: standing, from left, are mother Lillian, James Jr., Billy, Lillian, Georgia, Theodore, and James; John, who took the picture, is kneeling in front.**

TOP: In the Logans' parlor for the baptism of the couple's son: Martin Luther King, Jr., Marian Logan, Warren Arthur "Chip" Logan, Arthur Logan, Rachel Robinson, Strayhorn, Marguerite Gill, Dick Thomas. BOTTOM: Bill Grove and Strayhorn in Strayhorn's apartment at the Masters in the early 1960s

CLOCKWISE, FROM TOP LEFT: Strayhorn supervised a big band of Ellingtonians for the Verve LP entitled <u>Johnny Hodges, Soloist, Billy Strayhorn and the Orchestra</u>; <u>The Peaceful Side</u> was the only Strayhorn solo album released during his lifetime; Strayhorn's name was substituted for Ellington's on <u>Billy Strayhorn Live!!!</u>; the Billy Strayhorn Trio's version of "Johnny Come Lately" on a 78 rpm for Mercer Records was a two-piano performance featuring Strayhorn and Ellington

*May the new year
be as good to you
as you were kind
to me during my illness*

Billy Strayhorn

Strayhorn in the studio and at the Showman's Cafe in his final years.
TOM: In December 1966, Strayhorn had holiday postcards printed with regards
his well-wishers

After Strayhorn's tracheostomy and abdominal surgery, Ellington gives him his customary four kisses on the cheeks

his surgery. "Arturo said I can drink. And I know when Arturo tells me I can't drink I'm in trouble."

Too ill to carry his traditional workload for Ellington (who continued his financial support), Strayhorn was husbanding his creative energy for unusual projects that appealed to him. At Ellington's urging, he composed part of an exceptional suite entitled *A Blue Mural from Two Perspectives* for Ellington to perform as part of Lincoln Center's *Great Performances at Philharmonic Hall* concert series. Premiered on December 12, 1965, the piece was written for four saxophones, piano, bass, and drums and is, in part, a classically inspired "mirror" composition: the sheet music is designed to be read forward first, then backward. (Called "retrograde," the technique originated in the Middle Ages and was adopted in the twentieth century by twelve-tone composers.) The work took the musicians, including Ellington, aback. "It was weird, really. That was pure Strayhorn," said Louie Bellson, the drummer for the performance. "I had never heard of anything like that, but Billy explained it to me. He said, 'Bach liked to do it, Lou. Try it. You'll like it too. Just read the music down till you get to the end, then read it backwards. You'll have fun.' And you know what? I really did." The bassist, John Lamb, conservatory trained, had some experience with the technique in performances of chamber music, which he mentioned with some pride to Ellington during rehearsal the afternoon of the piece's premiere. "I told Duke, 'You find this in a fugue.' " "Naturally," replied Ellington, determinedly repeating his piano part to master the piece. Though its title evokes its design, Ellington didn't mention the piece's conception in his introductory remarks, and the critics missed it, though *A Blue Mural from Two Perspectives* was well received. "The suite is not merely a matter of magic sounds," wrote critic Dan Morgenstern in *Down Beat*. "It is also substantially structured and plumbs a wide range of moods and feelings. The opening section is a prime example of Ellington's and Strayhorn's ability to create with a minimum of instrumental resources and, one might add, to create music beyond categorization." (It was never again performed or recorded in its entirety.) Strayhorn, watching from a box with a small group of musicians, including the pianist Jimmy Jones and Bill Berry, an Ellington Orchestra trumpeter, smiled delightedly throughout the performance and at its conclusion pulled a flask of cognac out of an inside pocket of his sports jacket for a celebratory toast. Berry tried to pretend he wasn't looking as Strayhorn unbuttoned his shirt, popped open his abdominal tap, and poured cognac into his stomach.

"Strayhorn was definitely trying to do a classical thing with a jazz touch, instead of a jazz piece with classical sophistication. That's the way he explained it," recalled Bellson. It was Strayhorn-Ellington rather than Ellington-Strayhorn. As Strayhorn told Marian Logan, "I can't be Edward anymore, Doll Baby. I hardly have the strength to be me."

Ellington, at the same time, was pursuing a growing creative passion of his own: he started becoming absorbed with composing religiously themed music for performances with his orchestra in houses of worship such as Grace Cathedral in San Francisco, where his first "Concert of Sacred Music" took place on September 16, 1965. The shift in Ellington's focus at this point, more than four decades after he put together his first band, seemed to many of those nearest to him to be one of the most personal steps of his career. "Edward felt that was his most important work," said Ruth Ellington Boatwright. "He felt very deeply about it. He applied himself to it completely." Though some of Ellington's past music had evoked the spiritual tradition (notably "Come Sunday" from *Black, Brown and Beige* and the "Sunday Morning" finale of *A Tone Parallel to Harlem*), Ellington began creating whole programs of pieces invoking God and propagating faith. Some of the music was drawn or adapted from early Ellington efforts, including *My People* and his 1945 rhapsody *New World A-Comin'*, as well as *Black, Brown and Beige*. Like those projects, his new devotional music was unmistakably his own although, at his request, Strayhorn offered some advice on arrangements, an occasional melodic idea, and the basis for one of Ellington's narrative interludes, a rumination on what Ellington called "the four freedoms by which I think Billy Strayhorn lived: freedom from hate, unconditionally; freedom from self-pity; freedom from fear of doing something that would help someone more than it does him; and freedom from the kind of pride that could make a man feel that he was better than his brother."

Strayhorn's influence on Ellington's religious work may have been more personal than musical. As Mercer Ellington saw this phase of his father's life, confronting Strayhorn's mortality shocked Ellington into dealing with his own place in the eternal scheme. "His first reaction was 'How could that happen to Strayhorn?'" said Mercer Ellington. "That went into 'Hey, then, why couldn't that happen to me?' and that started him thinking more deeply about God and everything. He always believed in God his whole life. That was always there. It came more to the forefront when Strayhorn got sick. The old man didn't like the whole idea of death or any kind of ending of anything." Strayhorn participated personally in only one of Ellington's "sacred concerts," a revised version of the Grace Cathedral event conducted at the Fifth Avenue Presbyterian Church in lower Manhattan at 8:00 p.m. and midnight the day after Christmas 1965. "And now there will be a change in programming," Ellington announced midway through the concert. "Billy Strayhorn and his pretty little friend." Lena Horne, demurely gorgeous, her hair wrapped in a white silk scarf, snuggled alongside Strayhorn on the piano bench and sang a new Christmas ballad (lyrics by the Reverend Dean Barlett, the pastor of Grace Cathedral) to Strayhorn's plaintive piano.*

Strayhorn and Bill Grove kept separate apartments, but as Strayhorn grew more seriously ill, they were rarely seen apart. At the Flash Inn, Joe Merenda started having two place settings prepared every time Strayhorn called to say that he was on his way. Grove joined Strayhorn at the Copasetics meetings, a de facto member. "If Billy was there, Bill Grove was there," said Honi Coles. "As far as everybody was concerned, he was one of us." It was Strayhorn and Grove at the Logans' ("He sat and kept quiet, but he was there— and Martin liked him. He gave a bunch of big checks," said Marian Logan), at the Neals' ("There weren't a lot of white faces in the lot, but he was one of them. Grove didn't mind at all. You might say he liked it," said Dorcas Neal), and most everywhere else Strayhorn used to go alone, including his families' homes in Pittsburgh. On a summer weekend in 1966, Strayhorn brought Grove around to meet his brothers. "Bill Grove was the only one of Uncle Bill's companions that I ever remember him bringing home to the family," said

---

* The music to this composition, known as "Christmas Surprise" or "A Song for Christmas," is credited jointly to Ellington and Strayhorn in Ellington's memoirs. The piece has not been copyrighted and is not included in the published folios of Ellington's sacred music.

Jimmy Strayhorn's son Larry, who was twenty-six at the time. Jimmy and Grove talked outdoors while the Strayhorn kids watched; they seemed to chat easily, and Grove admired the concrete flower boxes Jimmy had crafted from handmade castings.

Every weekend, as a rule, Strayhorn and Grove called a limo and took a ride out of Manhattan, sometimes with friends, including Dwike Mitchell. "Billy would say, 'We're going to New Jersey,'" recalled Mitchell. "And he and Grove—I might come, but they usually went alone—Billy and Grove would spend the day driving god-knows-where together all over New Jersey. They'd stop along the roads and shop for fruits and herbs and all kinds of things. And you know Grove was a drinker, like Billy. So you know that by the time they'd come back at the end of the day, they'd be flying, crawling out of the limo with bags of things from New Jersey, rolling out onto the curb." Strayhorn and Grove had a "thing," Mitchell said. Over the months, their friends noticed a new theme emerging in both their apartments: Grove gave Strayhorn an original oil painting of the sun and a ceramic serving dish glazed like the sun; Strayhorn gave Grove gold cufflinks with engravings of the sun and a sun-shaped wall clock. "They developed this just between them," said Mitchell. "They became enamored of the sun and its radiance and powers of life-giving. Light and illumination and how it gave life. This became like the symbol of something that they had between them." Amid this collection of vivifying symbols, Strayhorn found a real source of rejuvenation in Grove's companionship.

"The other side of that coin," said Marian Logan, "was that Strays finally looked like he had the kind of thing he really wanted, but he knew it wouldn't be for long. He knew damn well it would be all over soon and he couldn't get everything out of it that he should have. 'Isn't he great?' He used to say that. 'Isn't he great? He's so *great*.' He said to me over and over toward the end, 'Bill's so great. If they had white boys like that in Pittsburgh, Doll Baby, you wouldn't *know* me.' He would never have left! 'I'm going to miss that boy.' He meant, you know, after he was gone."

Strayhorn had had a will drawn up on July 30, 1965, naming as executor of his estate his sister Georgia's eldest son, Gregory Morris, a public school teacher whom Strayhorn respected as a peer. The stipulations were few. Among them: there were to be two memorial services, one private and one public; he was to be cremated, his remains to be cast into the Hudson River; his black star sapphire ring would go to the Copasetics; a 72"-by-36" Frank Neal painting of two Haitian women would go to Francis Goldberg, who had already taken it when he left Strayhorn's apartment; the balance of his property, both professional and personal, would go to his mother, Lillian Strayhorn. On October 19, 1966, however, Lillian Strayhorn died suddenly at age seventy-four of arteriosclerosis. Though his grief compounded his own grave condition, Strayhorn summoned the strength to fly home for his mother's services. He had become so frail that Gregory Morris didn't recognize him at the Pittsburgh airport and drove past him several times. With his sister Lillian's assistance, Strayhorn selected the clothes his mother would be buried in and planned virtually every detail of her memorial at Hopewell's in Homewood, the same site as his father's service. He held up better than his family expected. "Although he was saddened by her loss," said Morris, "I believe that he was definitely relieved that she would not have to endure his death." Strayhorn told his sister Lillian, "Now I don't have to worry." "What he meant," she said, "was Now I can go in peace." Through her death, Strayhorn's mother eased his own.

That holiday season, Strayhorn felt too weak to visit Pittsburgh. "It's not Christmas without Mama, anyway," he told Marian Logan. "So Arthur said, 'Let's go somewhere—doctor's orders.'" Logan handled the arrangements, and Strayhorn and Grove spent the eight days from Christmas 1966 through New Year's Day 1967 with the Logans (including their three-and-a-half-year-old son Chip, Strayhorn's godson) on St. Vincent, in the Caribbean. At a recently built two-bedroom house on the Villa Beach, Strayhorn spent the afternoons on a wicker lounge chair in a firsthand test of the life-giving powers of the sun. Grove, fair-skinned and prone to sunburn, tended to stay indoors reading; he would walk outside a few times a day to be with Strayhorn or bring him a drink: each morning Strayhorn mixed a half-gallon batch of rum punch and stored it in a wide-mouth jar in the kitchen refrigerator, and each afternoon he mixed another to replenish it. Lena Horne called every night. There was a fully equipped kitchen, and Arthur Logan and Grove took to it as if it were a clubhouse. Every few days, they'd stock up on chicken, fresh fish, and local vegetables, then improvise meals. Strayhorn had his liquified in a blender the Logans brought. At the table, Strayhorn sat before an array of drinking glasses, each filled with a different preparation: a milky glass of stuffed crab, a speckled glass of salad greens. "Grove would bring out his dishes in those glasses, and Strays would smile, and he'd say, 'Lovely! Oh, that looks wonderful!' " said Marian Logan. "He'd pour his filet of fish or his fettuccine into his stomach, and he'd say, 'Oh, that's delicious, Arturo! You must give me the recipe.' He pretended it was a great, gay party, but there was an angry undertone, the dryest sarcasm you'd ever hear." On New Year's Eve, the group threw a small party, inviting a few locals they had met in the markets and around town. For entertainment, Arthur Logan paid someone he and Strayhorn had encountered in a nearby bar twenty-five dollars; the man had explained that he was a bandleader, like Duke Ellington, and he showed up with his four sons, one of whom played the guitar while the others sang and struck percussion instruments. They knew six songs, which they repeated all night with changes in mood and tempo. Strayhorn joined in on one number, rattling maracas over his head. "Aren't they wonderful?" he asked no one in particular, grinning with all the enthusiasm he showed for dinner.

Rested from his trip to St. Vincent, Strayhorn felt strong enough to work on and off during the first few weeks of the new year, and he harnessed his strength with care: for the first time since his score for the all-black, gay-oriented production of *The Love of Don Perlimplín for Belisa in Their Garden* in 1953, he tapped some of his deepest creative resources to compose a work for non-Ellingtonians. Stimulated by a performance of the Dwike Mitchell–Willie Ruff duo at the Hickory House, Strayhorn composed a suite for piano and French horn, and he asked Mitchell and Ruff to perform it for him privately. "It was something he wanted to write for himself and hear himself, something he had in him that he had to do," said Mitchell. A through-composed twelve-minute work in three organically related movements, the suite takes the raw-nerve emotionality of pieces like "Passion Flower" to a level so intimate and infused with pain that hearing it is an act of voyeurism. If "Something to Live For" was a wishful sigh and "Lush Life" a cynical moan, Strayhorn's suite for piano and French horn is his dying scream. "It takes so much, it's so emotionally involved, that I was drained for days after playing it," said Ruff, who discussed the piece with Strayhorn at the composer's apartment, where he and Mitchell performed it. "Its meaning is so strong. It's really Billy's autobiography. It's really the last words from a great genius shutting down before his time. It's all about frustration and anger—lost chances, missed opportunities. He's saying, 'I'm mad! Goddamn it!' He's mad because he's checking out and he wasn't done. You know, he could have done anything. He could have been the biggest of the big. He could have done it, man. His genius is right there in his music. But there he was, checking out, and nobody except the musicians and few of the writers in the jazz magazines knew who Billy Strayhorn was. He looked back at his own life and he couldn't find himself." (Strayhorn never copyrighted the piece, which was recorded by Mitchell and Ruff in 1969 as *Suite for the Duo* on an album of Strayhorn compositions.)

With Bill Grove's help, Strayhorn held on. He had the walls of his apartment repainted in light, bright colors, and Grove hung a set of sheer, pale yellow curtains, as if to magnify the sunlight. Felrath Hines, who visited in the midst of the redecorating, offered his counsel on the psychology of the new decor. "Billy said he wanted the apartment to brighten him, like an afternoon outdoors," recalled Hines. "He was choosing light, natural colors for everything. I said something about doing something in white, to open up the space, and he said, 'Oh no, Fel, too much like a hospital. I'll be living there soon enough.' " Remaking his own appearance in the same spirit of renewal, Strayhorn switched to his summer wardrobe half a year early, and he bought a pink cotton seaman's cap that he took to wearing everywhere. He looked eccentric—out of time and place, lost in clothes a couple of sizes too big for his undernourished frame. Fighting the lethargy and the discomfort that came with his cancer, he sought distraction in a semblance of his old social schedule, though this grew difficult. He planned on going to the Showman's one afternoon and set out to hail a cab on Broadway but had to call his niece Adrienne for help to walk the two blocks east. "He was very emaciated from the cancer, and his clothes were hanging off of him, and that sailor hat of his was down over his face," recalled Adrienne Conaway Claerbaut. "We made it over to Broadway, and Uncle Bill said, 'Just hail me a cab, because I want to get to Harlem.'

And I hailed a cab, and the cab driver looked at him and said he wouldn't have a bum like him in his cab and drove away. He was so upset. He was so dejected. He felt just terrible." Strayhorn pared his social life down to an occasional dinner with Grove at the Flash Inn. Noticing his absence from the Hickory House, Willie Ruff dropped by Strayhorn's apartment before his set one evening. "His place was darkened and all," remembered Ruff. "I said, 'Billy, how are you doing?' He said, 'No good, baby.' He said, 'Whatever you do, don't get this thing. This thing is a motherfucker.' " Ruff brought Strayhorn up on the latest talk among his musician friends—"this and that about people, various people we knew in our field"—while Strayhorn sat quietly in the dark until he fell asleep.

"He was in bad shape," said Lena Horne. "So I said, 'All right, we're going to take you to Palm Springs.' " Horne and Lennie Hayton had a vacation home there, and they drove Strayhorn, along with Grove, cross-country to rest in the Western sun. "We'd lie outdoors. Sometimes we'd talk. Sometimes we didn't," said Horne. "Bill Grove did everything for him. He couldn't do very much anymore. He hadn't mentioned anything about what he wanted to do now— he knew he was dying. We didn't have to talk about it. He didn't say anything about what he wanted, and this began to worry me. So Bill Grove and I talked about it, because we didn't know what to do. And one day Billy said, 'Well, I think I better go to my family.' Grove had to get back to that magazine he worked for, and I had a tour to do. So my friend Elois [Davis] took him to Los Angeles— that's where she lived—and they went to the airport, and he went home to say good-bye."

Though George Greenlee had recommended seeing a Pittsburgh attorney, Silvestri Silvestri, to revise his will in the light of his mother's death, Strayhorn cut short his visit to Pittsburgh and returned to New York gravely ill. "He was too sick, although he really should have done it," recalled Silvestri. The day after Strayhorn arrived back in New York, he saw Arthur Logan, who sent him straight to the Hospital for Joint Diseases on Madison Avenue in East Harlem. "Arthur came home and said, 'Go see your Itty Bitty Buddy, Doll Baby. He needs you now,' " recalled Marian Logan. His disillusionment dissolved into resignation, Strayhorn rejected sympathy. "I went to visit him frequently," recalled the Reverend John Gensel, a Lutheran minister and music enthusiast who made the New York jazz community his personal mission. "As soon as I came in, instead of saying, 'Oh, John, I feel so terrible,' he didn't say anything like that. He turned to his friend Bill, who was sitting at his bedside, and he said, 'Oh, Bill, see if the pastor wants a glass of orange juice.' There he was, so thin and so small, and he was immediately concerned that I was taken care of." There was an arrangement of spring wildflowers on Strayhorn's dresser, ordered by Lena Horne, and she had it replaced every few days. Ellington ordered baskets of fruit for Strayhorn's guests to eat while they visited and, in an elaborate (and costly) get-well gesture, sent a musical gift. He arranged for several pianists working in Paris at the time (including Aaron Bridgers, Claude Bolling, Raymond Fol, and Joe Turner) to record solo performances on a tape that Ellington had shipped to the hospital. "Duke asked a number of us to do this. I was very happy to, being very fond of Billy," said Bolling. "I said to Duke, 'What should I play? I don't know what to play.' Duke said, 'Give him some James P. [Johnson].' Duke loved James P." Ellington himself phoned Strayhorn at least once a day. "He couldn't visit him," said Marian Logan. "Edward couldn't see him like that. He couldn't take that."

Strayhorn spent the day napping, looking through magazines, and, as he found the strength on a few good days, working on a partially composed three-part piece, *The North by Southwest Suite*. He had completed an orchestration of the first movement, "Blue Cloud," before his hospitalization and had sent it to Ellington, who was already performing it around Europe. Retitled "Blood Count," the piece, in its final form, is a wrenching moan, its pedal-point bass line evoking the rhythmic drip of intravenous fluid. And Strayhorn put away his music paper. "He didn't write anymore after 'Blood Count'," said Marian Logan. "That was the last thing he had to say. And it wasn't 'Good-bye' or 'Thank you' or anything phony like that. It was 'This is how I feel,' and he felt like shit—'Like it or leave it.'"

Every evening, Bill Grove took the commuter train from Mount Vernon to the 125th Street stop and walked directly to the Hospital for Joint Diseases. "Grove took good care of Strays," said Marian Logan. "Arthur couldn't do as much for him as that boy did for him. But it got to where there was only so much anybody could do." On

Tuesday, May 30, Strayhorn told Grove, "You don't have to come tomorrow."

A little past halfway to dawn, at 4:45 a.m. on May 31, 1967, Billy Strayhorn died of esophageal cancer at the age of fifty-one. He was with Bill Grove.* Lena Horne heard in Europe, where she was honoring a tour commitment. "It tore me apart that I couldn't be with him. I was heartbroken about it," she said. Marian Logan was vacationing with her son at the Montreal World's Fair, Expo '67, when her husband called with the news. "I said, 'It can't be. I'd just talked to him, and he was telling me to go to the park there and watch the Saint Lawrence River go by." Both Arthur Logan and Ruth Ellington phoned Duke, who was one week into a three-week engagement at Harrah's Casino Cabaret in Reno. "Arthur said Edward just cried," Marian Logan recounted. "He said, 'This is too much for me, Arthur.' And he just cried. Arthur said, 'Are you going to be all right?' And Edward said, 'Fuck no, I'm not going to be all right! Nothing is all right now.' And Edward just cried." As Ellington wrote in *Music Is My Mistress*, "I started sniffling and whimpering, crying, banging my head up against the wall, and talking to myself about the virtues of Billy Strayhorn. Why Billy Strayhorn, I asked? Why? Subconsciously, I sat down and started writing what I was thinking, and as I got deeper and deeper into thinking about my favorite human being, I realized that I was not crying any more. It seemed that what I was doing was more important than anything, so on and on I wrote."

Margieriete Pharr, the wife of the painter Nye Pharr and a friend of Ruth Ellington's and Aaron Bridgers's, called Bridgers. "I was expecting it but I wasn't, you know what I mean?" said Bridgers, who, when he heard the news, slipped off the silver Juvenia watch that Strayhorn had given him and tucked it in a box. George Greenlee, in Paris for a conference, found out from Bridgers at the Living Room, where he had gone to see Bridgers perform, only to find him arranging a leave of absence with the club manager. "Aaron was trying to keep his cool with the club owner," said Greenlee, "but

---

* It has been widely reported in articles and books, including the biography *Sweet Man: The Real Duke Ellington*, by Don George (G. P. Putnam's Sons, 1981), that Strayhorn died in Lena Horne's arms, but Horne was out of the country at the time. The source of the apparent effort to obscure Strayhorn's homosexuality is unknown.

he was literally shaking. The club owner said to him, 'Go, say good-bye to Billy. We'll wait for you.' " Cookie Cook called Honi Coles. "He loved that man dearly—we all did," said Coles. "That's why we decided then and there to retire the title of president of the Copasetics in Billy's honor. After Billy, there would never be another president." The next morning, Luther Henderson was riding the crosstown bus to visit Strayhorn in the hospital when he learned Strayhorn had already died. In its obituary, the *New York Times* reported: "Billy Strayhorn, jazz composer, arranger, lyricist and pianist, who was often called Duke Ellington's alter ego, died of cancer yesterday at the Hospital for Joint Diseases. . . . According to [the *Times's* jazz critic, John S.] Wilson, Mr. Strayhorn was 'a small, stately man' who observed the world with 'benign amusement' through dark-rimmed glasses. His friends emphasized his modesty, his humility and his desire to stay in the background among the Ellington contingent."

Strayhorn's family members met in New York to plan a public memorial service, with suggestions from Lena Horne, Ruth Ellington, and members of the Copasetics, while Bill Grove hosted a private gathering of mourners among Strayhorn's gay friends and others close to the two of them. Bill Coleman's old coworker Frederick Brewington, who lived near Kennedy Airport, was assigned to pick Aaron Bridgers up and drive him to Grove's apartment. "He was completely distraught," Brewington recalled. "We stopped by my house and I stupidly showed him the new Baldwin piano I had just bought for my son and asked Aaron if he wanted to play it. He looked at me like he didn't remember what a piano *was*." At Grove's place, Francis Goldberg had taken on cooking duties. "Goldie tried to make it *his* production, all about *him* and his *wonderful food*," said one of Strayhorn's friends. Grove, though closest to Strayhorn over the past decade, grieved with collected grace and with empathy for Strayhorn's other intimates. "Grove ached for Billy then and every day for the rest of his life," said Dwike Mitchell. "But he didn't play Camille." Bridgers, Goldberg, and Grove—the three men Strayhorn loved most, Ellington excepted—mourned together. "There was no competition, apart from some attitude from Goldie," said one of their friends. "Everybody loved that man so much, there was just all kinds of crying everywhere. You have to remember, a lot of individuals felt like he was the most important person in their life. Of, I don't know, thirty, forty people who came in and out of the house that day, twenty-five of them just lost their best friend."

Ellington was virtually paralyzed with despair. There was to be a private viewing of Strayhorn's body and a brief memorial service for family and close friends at the Frank E. Campbell Funeral Chapel on Madison Avenue on Saturday, June 3; a public service at John Gensel's church, St. Peter's, would follow on the morning of the fifth. Ellington, booked with his orchestra in Reno, made no plans to attend either service. "Arthur kept calling Edward every day," recalled Marian Logan. "Arthur said, 'You got to come to New York.' Edward said, 'I can't.' Finally, on the morning of the [public] funeral, Edward called. He was in town. But he said he still wasn't going to the funeral. So Arthur went to see him. Arthur said he was lying in the bed, buck-naked. He said, 'I can't go to the service.' 'What do you mean, you can't go?' He said, 'Because I don't have anything but my kissy-blue shirts.' That's what he called his favorite blue shirts. He said, 'I don't have a white shirt.' So Arthur said, 'Don't worry, Strays is laying out there in a kissy-blue shirt too. He doesn't have a white shirt on.' Edward said, 'Really?' And he jumped out of bed and threw his clothes on."

Some 350 mourners were seated for the 10:30 a.m. service as Ellington arrived and marched purposefully to a roped-off pew in the second row of the nineteenth-century Lutheran church; he sat alone. Before him, the altar was decorated with twenty floral arrangements sent by Strayhorn's family members, friends, admirers, and colleagues like Louis Armstrong and ASCAP; behind him, the congregation included Lena Horne, the Robinsons, Otto Preminger, Benny Goodman, Carmen McRae, Milt Jackson, and Sylvia Syms, in addition to more than a dozen of Strayhorn's family members, in from Pittsburgh. As a prelude to the service, Randy Weston performed a brooding piano rendition of his composition "Blues for Strayhorn"; at the piece's conclusion, Weston told the assemblage, "I wrote the song for Billy two years ago. I never thought I'd end up playing it at his funeral. It was difficult for me." There were brief Bible readings by the Reverend Ralph E. Peterson of St. Peter's and a meditation by Gensel. Scheduled to give the service's only eulogy,

Ellington braced the front of his pew with two hands as he rose slowly and, gathering himself, walked up and took the pulpit. He had horror in his eyes and a nervous smile. Ellington read what he had written in his hotel room in Reno when he first heard of Strayhorn's death:

> *Poor little Swee' Pea, Billy Strayhorn, William Thomas Strayhorn, the biggest human being who ever lived, a man with the greatest courage, the most majestic artistic stature, a highly skilled musician whose impeccable taste commanded the respect of all musicians and the admiration of all listeners.*
>
> *His audiences at home and abroad marveled at the grandeur of his talent and the mantle of tonal supremacy that he wore only with grace. He was a beautiful human being, adored by a wide range of friends, rich, poor, famous, and unknown. Great artists pay homage to Billy Strayhorn's God-given ability and mastery of his craft.*
>
> *Because he had a rare sensitivity and applied himself to his gifts, Billy Strayhorn successfully married melody, words, and harmony, equating the fitting with happiness. His greatest virtue, I think, was his honesty, not only to others, but to himself. His listening-hearing self was totally intolerant of his writing-playing self when, or if, any compromise was expected, or considered expedient.*
>
> *He spoke English perfectly and French very well, but condescension did not enter into his mind. He demanded freedom of expression and lived in what we consider the most important and moral of freedoms: freedom from hate, unconditionally; freedom from self-pity (even throughout all the pain and bad news); freedom from fear of possibly doing something that might help another more than it might himself; and freedom from the kind of pride that could make a man feel he was better than his brother or neighbor.*
>
> *His patience was incomparable and unlimited. He had no aspirations to enter into any kind of competition, yet the legacy he leaves, his oeuvre, will never be less than the ultimate on the highest plateau of culture (whether by comparison or not).*
>
> *God bless Billy Strayhorn.*

Father Norman J. O'Connor, a Catholic priest active in the jazz world, said a prayer, and the service ended with Billy Taylor and Ray Nance, on piano and violin, performing "Take the 'A' Train" as a dirge. At Aaron Bridgers's initiation, a small group—Grove, Cook, the Logans, and a few others—walked to the West Side and took the A train up to Harlem for a round of toasts to Strayhorn at the Showman's.

As he had stipulated in his will, Strayhorn's body was cremated. On the Saturday morning following the public memorial, his closest intimates, except Ellington, who was back on the road, gathered at the 79th Street boat basin at the foot of Riverside Park, where Strayhorn used to take his morning strolls. It was a balmy, still summer morning, sunless. A sluggish breeze drifted off the Hudson. A few houseboats rocked on their moorings as Strayhorn's friends—among them, Bill Grove, Marian and Arthur Logan, Ruth Ellington, Honi Coles, Cookie Cook, and Bill Coleman—huddled uneasily on the macadam waterway. The Reverend John Gensel, his back to the river, led the assemblage in prayer. "I read a few words," said Gensel, "and everyone closed his eyes, and I remember thinking about the weather. It was so warm and calm, exactly like Strayhorn's music." He turned and emptied Strayhorn's ashes into the air over the water, and a breeze lifted them away.

Fulfilling his uncle's request, Gregory Morris took over Strayhorn's estate. Valued at under fifty thousand dollars in cash, property, and royalties (as they were estimated at the time), Strayhorn's equity was divided among his family members by a formula they agreed on. None of Strayhorn's male partners, including Bill Grove, sought or received anything, though rumors spread that Strayhorn had willed the rights to "Take the 'A' Train" to Aaron Bridgers. "Somehow, a lot of people got the impression that Billy had set me up," said Bridgers. "All the way back to Paris, people were saying that they heard Billy had willed me ' "A" Train.' I had to call Ruth and tell her, 'Please put a stop to this. Please tell everybody that Billy didn't will me anything and I don't want anything." A bit of conflict sparked between the Strayhorns and Ruth Ellington (representing Tempo Music) over ownership of the music manuscripts and other papers related to Strayhorn's work left in his apartment at the time of his death, some half-dozen boxes of original manuscripts, copyists' scores, band parts, published sheet music, and so on. "She [Ruth Ellington] said, 'That music was Billy's. It belongs to us,' " said Gregory Morris. "In other words, 'Billy belonged to us.' We had a big problem with that point of view." As Ruth Ellington Boatwright later explained her position, "I was simply looking after Edward's business interests in my capacity as president of Tempo Music. Billy worked for Edward. Therefore, his work was rightfully Edward's."*

Ellington himself, his veneer of insouciance scraped thin by grief, appeared more deeply affected by the loss of his longtime artistic companion than by any setback since his mother's death thirty-two years earlier. "It was a big blow to the old man," said Mercer Ellington. "He couldn't accept any kind of misfortune—that was one of the secrets of his success. He couldn't accept that Strayhorn really wasn't there anymore. It was too huge a shock to his system." A famous insomniac who rested with occasional catnaps, Ellington started heading to bed earlier (that is, around two or three in the morning, rather than five or six) and sleeping straight through to the next afternoon; yet he appeared more listless and, to some, detached. "Arthur told Edward he was depressed," said Marian Logan. "He told him he had to do something to come out of it." Within the first few months following Strayhorn's death, Ellington decided to release his grief musically, much as he had by composing his seminal long-form work "Reminiscing in Tempo" after losing his mother. To start, he began arrangements for an all-star concert in tribute to Strayhorn (eventually held on October 6, 1968, at New York's Philharmonic Hall and featuring Lena Horne, Tony Bennett, Joe Williams, and Lou Rawls, as well as Duke Ellington and His Orchestra); the proceeds would be donated to the Juilliard School of Music as seed money for an annual scholarship in Billy Strayhorn's name. Joe Morgen handled publicity for the event, a task that he took to include responsibility for ensuring that Ellington's public remorse would not be interpreted as anything other than collegial and purely fraternal affection. For an article on Ellington's

* After Strayhorn's death, members of his family assumed stewardship of the contents of his apartment, including scores of approximately twelve hundred works of music and more than five hundred other papers, photographs, and artifacts. These materials were unexamined until the Strayhorn estate granted this author, Loren Schoenberg, and Walter van de Leur access to them.

initiation of the Strayhorn scholarship in the black digest *Jet*, Morgen provided what he said was material from an unpublished exclusive interview in which Strayhorn defended his bachelorhood. "Look, I'm an individualist. The rugged kind. I don't bat an eye when the fellows in the band call me a character," he has Strayhorn blustering. "Love or not, I wouldn't subject a wife to the road. It's punishment. Often I work around the clock scoring the exacting music for Ellington. I've gone days without shaving. Kept awake with coffee, cigarettes and chewed pencil tips. I snarl at little children. I'm not fit company for man nor beast. The chosen Eve of my life surely has no reason to put up with that cross-section." Morgen sent the "interview" to Leonard Feather, who commented, "It was quite accurate—as a description of Joe Morgen. Ellington, to his credit, grieved terribly for Billy because he loved him. Unfortunately, some people couldn't accept that any better than they accepted Billy when he was alive."

At the same time Ellington was putting together the Philharmonic benefit, he was preparing to record a musical tribute to Strayhorn: an album of new renditions of Strayhorn and Ellington-Strayhorn compositions. Made in the RCA Records studios in New York three months after Strayhorn's death, the record included both well-known Strayhorn pieces ("Rain Check," "Day Dream," "My Little Brown Book") and rarities ("Snibor" and "Boo-Dah," the latter title derived from his friends' nickname for him). The sessions were shaded gray by Strayhorn's shadow. "You kept expecting to turn your head and see him," said Jimmy Hamilton. "You knew all the guys was thinking about Swee' Pea." They played like it: the album is full of trenchant solos, particularly by Johnny Hodges (and especially on "Day Dream," the first song he and Strayhorn recorded together, nearly forty years earlier). As one session ended, the band members packed up and talked a bit while Ellington sat alone at the piano, as he had done at the conclusion of so many performances, and played "Lotus Blossom" for himself. This time, however, one of the studio tape recorders hadn't been turned off, and the performance—solemn, tormented, unnervingly intimate—was captured. At the urging of the producer, Brad McCuen, Ellington agreed to use it as the album's final track, the flubbed notes and ambient studio noises only enhancing the dramatic reality of the moment, a coda of closure.

Having paid musical tribute to Strayhorn, Ellington soon recovered his ardent regality and resumed his traditional schedule of touring and composing; indeed, he seemed to dedicate himself to his music with relentless drive. "I'm writing more than ever now," Ellington told an interviewer. "I have to. Billy Strayhorn left that big, yawning void."

A year after Strayhorn's death, on the last Sunday morning in May 1968, Marian and Arthur Logan led a few of Strayhorn's friends back to the 79th Street boat basin, where they had watched Strayhorn's ashes blow away. "We said a few prayers, and a boatkeeper came up and asked what we were doing there," said Marian Logan. "I told him a friend of ours died a year ago today and we came here to remember him. He said, 'I was just curious, because another fellow had been here a little while ago.' We looked down the walkway, and there was Duke, all alone in the distance, slowly walking along the river." Ellington honored Strayhorn aptly, in the eloquence of anonymity.

ACKNOWLEDGMENTS

My thanks to:

Aaron Bridgers, Gil Evans, and Gary Giddins for their support early on and when it mattered most.

Editors Jonathan Galassi and Paul Elie of Farrar, Straus and Giroux, whose patient nurturing and clear-eyed guidance made this book this book.

Walter van de Leur, the musicologist I met trying to map the same twisting and sometimes dark road that I was, who soon became my companion in research, my most trusted counselor, and my dear friend.

Chris Calhoun, agent and more.

Stanley Crouch, Karla Eoff, Robert Frenay, Krin Gabbard, Roy Hemming, Fred Hersch, Mary Makarushka, Dan Morgenstern, Albert Murray, Loren Schoenberg, Roslyn Schloss, Mark Tucker, Jerry Valburn, Michele Wallace, and, again, Walter van de Leur, for reading the manuscript and galleys in various stages and providing invaluable advice on matters large and small.

Barbara Lea, Mary Cleere Haran, and, again, Loren Schoenberg and Fred Hersch, for musical aid.

Strayhorn family members: Cheryll Chakrabarti, Adrienne Alyce Claerbaut, Michael Conaway, Robert Conaway, Donna Strayhorn Davis, Leslie Demus, Lillian Strayhorn Dicks, Creola Grady, Thelma Morris, Carole Strayhorn, Darryl A. Strayhorn, Deborah Strayhorn, James Strayhorn, Larry Strayhorn, William Strayhorn, and especially Gregory Morris, executor of the Billy Strayhorn estate.

Ellington family members: Ruth Ellington Boatwright, Mercedes Ellington, Mercer Ellington, and Michael James.

My good friends at the New York arm of the Duke Ellington Society (TDES, Inc.), especially presidents Douglas Bray, Tom Detienne, Tom Harris, Morris Hodara, and Lynne Mueller, as well as Rich Ehrenzeller, Bruce Kennan, and all my fellow members.

Those I interviewed and quoted in this book: Lionel Abel, Muriel Boyd Albitz, Sally Amato, Edmund Anderson, Louis Applebaum, Svend Asmussen, Cholly Atkins, George Avakian, Dave Bailey, Harold Belcher, Louie Bellson, Sathima Bea Benjamin, Jean Berdin, Abba Bogin, Claude Bolling, Frederick Brewington, Clyde Broadus, Ernest Brown, William Brown, Perry Bruskin, Ralph Burns, Diahann Carroll, Benny Carter, Billy Catizone, Dini Clarke, Rosemary Clooney, Maria Ellington Cole, Bill Coleman, Willie Cook, Buster Cooper, Maurice Cullaz, Helen Oakley Dance, Stanley Dance, Blossom Dearie, Carmen DeLavallade, Alan Douglas, Miriam Machiz Dworkin, Jerome Eisner, Rolf Ericson, Merlie Evers, Bill Finegan, Dorothy Ford Gardin, Linton Garner, Michel Gaudry, Pastor John Garcia Gensel, Frank Goldberg, Claire Gordon, Norman Granz, Stephane Grappelli, George Greenlee, Dick Gregory, Johnny Griffin, Chico Hamilton, Slide Hampton, Luther Henderson, Jon Hendricks, Harry Herforth, Al Hibbler, Kenneth Hill, Lois Hill, Lena Horne, Dr. Orva Lee Ice, Phoebe Jacobs, Ahmad Jamal, Marshall Jamison, Herb Jeffries, Mary Joliffe, Herbie Jones, Orrin Keepnews, Eartha Kitt, Ralph Kroger, John Lamb, Irwin Landau, Ray Leavy, Henry Lee, Gerhart Lehner, Alfred Leslie, Willard Levitas, John Lewis, Teo Macero, Marian McPartland, Jimmy McPhail, Christopher Manos, Mildred Dixon Manos, Wendell Marshall, Herbert Martin, Samuel Matlovsky, Peter Matz, Jimmy Maxwell, Billy May, James Minor, Dwike Mitchell, Jimmy Monici, Joyce Mordecai, LeRoy Myers, Dorcas Neal, Paul Newman, Bernard Oshei, Gustava Goldberg Pagan, Gordon Parks, Bill Patterson, Thomas Patterson, Mimi Perrin, Brock Peters, Michael Phelan, Marie Pleasant, Albert Popwell, Hope Preminger, Jack Purcell, Frank Raucci, Helen Reis, Larry Rivers, Max Roach, Henry "Phace" Roberts, Rachel Robinson, Timmie Rogers, Jimmy Rowles, Willie Ruff, Pete Rugolo, Bruno Salvaterra, Michael Scrima, Sam Shaw, Joya Sherrill, Roy Shoemaker, Bobby Short, Silvestri Silvestri, Art Simmons, Alice Babs Sjoblom, Wonderful Smith, Frank Spangler, Thelma Spangler, Fred Staton, James Stevens, James Stewart, John Stitt, Harold Strange, Creed Taylor, Clark Terry, Rudy Van Gelder, Royce Wallace, George Wein, Beatrice W. Westbrooks, Randy Weston, Fred Whitlinger, Bob Wilber, Haywood Williams, Madeline Grove Williams, Gerald Wilson, John S. Wilson, Kay Davis Wimp, Janet Wolfe, Jimmy Woode, Britt Woodman, Leo Yagella, and Lee Young.

Those interviewed and not quoted directly: George Arthur, Harold Ashby, Charles Austin, Jean Bach, Butch Ballard, "Peg-Leg" Bates, Nanette Beardon, Aaron Bell, David Berger, Betty Berry, Bill Berry, Dottie Bigard, George Birt, Leona Bishop, Johnny Blowers, Larry Buster, Kenny Cannon, Claude Carriere, Irma Smith Crippen, Maurice Cullaz, Yvonette Cullaz, Jimmy Davis, Dr. Nathan Davis, Pat D'Emilio, Ilene Denver, Mario DiLeo, Alice Eisner, Karen Esch, Ray Esch, Art Farmer, Tommy Flanagan, Robert E. Furgeson, Bubba Gaines, Olive Douglas Gambrell, Herb Gentry, Milt Grayson, Nazeh Islam Hameed, Lionel Hampton, Herbie Hancock, Cleo Hayes, Jimmy Heath, Joe Henderson, Henri, Milt Hinton, Nancy Holloway, Hildred Humphries, Ilene Boyd Hutchinson, Eddie Johnson, Quincy Jones, Dick Katz, Michael Langham, Milton Larkin, Anna Lescsak, Irving Machiz, Junior Mance, Johnny Mandel, Sarah Marks, Jean Mayer, Joe Merenda, Louise Michelle, Grover Mitchell, James Moody, Joyce S. Moore, Gloria Nance, Harold Nicholas, Larry O'Leno, Stewart Prager, "Red" Press, Alexandre Rado, Henri Renaud, Betty Roche, Annie Ross, Nipsy Russell, Monsignor John Sanders, Mary Sanford, Hal Schaeffer, Artie Shaw, George Shearing, Dr. Donald Shirley, Walt Silver, Stanley Silverman, Robert Spatafore, Dakota Staton, Delores Gomez Stevens, Grady Tate, Dr.

Billy Taylor, Joe Temperley, Teri Thornton, Norris Turney, Leslie Uggams, George Van Eps, Benny Waters, Hamilton Whitlinger, Geneva Wood, and Marie Pleasant Woods.

Chip Deffaa for his answers to countless questions, usually before I had to ask.

James W. Seymore, managing editor of *Entertainment Weekly*, for support above and beyond the call.

Brooks Kerr for his passionate interest in this and all things Ellingtonian.

Nisid Hajari and Chris Nashawaty, for innumerable assists.

The many people who helped in my research, most importantly Deirdre Cossman, James Wardrop, and Marge Wardrop; John Edward Hasse and the staff at the Duke Ellington Collection of the Smithsonian Institution, the Institute of Jazz Studies at Rutgers University, Will Friedwald, the Yale Music Library, the Lincoln Center Library for the Performing Arts, the Schomburg Center for Black Culture, Tom McNulty of the Bobst Library at New York University, Stephen Novak of the Juilliard School Archives, Joan Anderson and the staff of the Pittsburgh Public Library, Steve Doell and the Western Pennsylvania Historical Society, Mary Sanford of the Hillsborough Historical Society, Richard Wang of the Jazz Institute of Chicago, Charles Silver of the Museum of Modern Art research department, Sedge Clark, Stacie Fenster, Tawanda Williams, Jeff Austin, Gretchen Haller, Kipp Cheng, the administration of Westinghouse High School, Irene Dee, Christopher Beall, and members of the Duke Ellington Internet list-serve.

The staff of Solway House, where I wrote.

Some conscientious readers of the first hardcover edition, who recommended additions, changes, and corrections: Lucille Orr Crooks, David Fleming, Claire Gordon, George F. Murray, Art Pilkington, and Terry Teachout.

Those I interviewed who are now gone, including George Abbott, Ted Allen, Talley Beatty, Henry Blankfort, Billy Byers, Sammy Cahn, Cab Calloway, Honi Coles, Chuck Connors, "Wild Bill" Davis, Tibor de Nagy, Bill Dillard, Billy Eckstine, Mercer Ellington, Ray Esch, Veronica Esch, Gil Evans, Leonard Feather, Oliver Fowler, Dizzy Gillespie, Jimmy Hamilton, Roy Hemming, Felrath Hines, Edith "Cue" Hodges, Fran Hunter, Oliver Jackson, Sid

Kuller, Marian Logan, Jimmy Lyons, Carmen McRae, Carl Mc-Vicker, Dr. Jake Milliones, Gerry Mulligan, Mitchell Parrish, Leslie Peacock, Lee Remick, Marshall Royal, Oliver Smith, Sylvia Syms, Bob Thiele, and Lana Turner.

And the vital helpmates dearest to me: most of all, Karen Oberlin, my parents, and my brother Chuck, Seth Fahey, Jeff Menell, Anna Kula—and, of course, my children, Victoria and Jacob, and their mother, Joanne.

NOTES

Unless cited below or attributed to other sources in the text, all quotations in this book are from the author's interviews. Musical descriptions and analyses are based on the author's study of music and recordings at the Duke Ellington Archives of the Smithsonian Institution; the Institute for Jazz Studies at Rutgers University; the Yale Music Library; and private sources, most significantly the papers of the Billy Strayhorn estate and the personal collections of Aaron Bridgers, Lena Horne, Honi Coles, Marian Logan, Jerome Eisner, Oliver Fowler, and Jean Mayer.

PREFACE

ix–x Duke Ellington and Billy Strayhorn, interview by Paul Worth, KBCA radio, Los Angeles, 1962 (month and day unknown).

1. SOMETHING TO LIVE FOR

10   My grandmother . . . to me: Strayhorn, interview by Duke Ellington on the radio program *Jazz Casual*, date unknown.

11   During grade . . . got one: Sinclair Traill and Gerald Lascelles, *Just Jazz 3* (London: Four Square Books, 1959).

11   I started . . . like that: Ibid.

11–12   Well, eventually . . . that piano: Ibid.

14   She did . . . invaluable training: Strayhorn interviewed for the Duke Ellington Jazz Society, New York, March 1962 (unpublished).

2. PASSION FLOWER

24   I was . . . a success: Sinclair Traill and Gerald Lascelles, *Just Jazz 3* (London: Four Square Books, 1959).

28   We were . . . really something: Strayhorn interviewed for the Duke Ellington Jazz Society, New York, March 1962.

30   I went . . . didn't stay: Ibid.

32   He was . . . from him: Bill Coss, "Ellington & Strayhorn, Inc.," *Down Beat*, June 7, 1962.

34   I had . . . it was done: Strayhorn, Duke Ellington Jazz Society interview.

34   It's a . . . it's about: "New Hit, 'Lush Life,' Is Not New," *Down Beat*, August 12, 1949.

43   One of . . . "Smoky City": Walter van de Leur research.

44   Whether . . . repertoire: Ibid.

3. OVERTURE TO A JAM SESSION

51   When Stray . . . got me: Sinclair Traill and Gerald Lascelles, *Just Jazz 3* (London: Four Square Books, 1959).

51   I know . . . this lyric: Strayhorn interviewed for the Duke Ellington Jazz Society, New York, March 1962.

51   Everybody was . . . little peaked: Ibid.

52   He said . . . all right: Ibid.

53   They were . . . the drugstore: Ibid.

54   As the band . . . well organized: Harry Carney interviewed for the Duke Ellington Jazz Society, New York, December 1960 (unpublished).

55   Every day . . . from Duke: Strayhorn, Duke Ellington Jazz Society.

55   Bill Esch . . . he did: Ibid.

55–56   "A" Train . . . like that: "Mi Dica, Mister Strayhorn," *Musica Jazz* (Italy), May 1964, translated from the Italian by Antonio Monda.

56   I said . . . of Pittsburgh: Strayhorn, Duke Ellington Jazz Society.

56–57   [In the] morning . . . send for you: Ibid.

57   You don't . . . I am: Traill and Lascelles, *Just Jazz 3*.

57   I don't . . . like doing: John S. Wilson, "Billy Strayhorn: Alter Ego for the Duke," *New York Times*, June 6, 1965.

60   Arrange these . . . ten o'clock: Strayhorn, Duke Ellington Jazz Society.

60   What could . . . did it: Ibid.

60   He left . . . find it: Ibid.

60–61 From then . . . organization: Bill Coss, "Ellington & Strayhorn, Inc.," *Down Beat*, June 7, 1962.

61   I stayed . . . "Day Dream": Ibid.

61   The guys . . . flattered: Strayhorn, Duke Ellington Jazz Society.

62   Tizol refused . . . the scores: Ibid.

62   I walked . . . all right: Ibid.

62   Though . . . chord effects: Walter van de Leur.

62   So I . . . arrangements: Strayhorn, Duke Ellington Jazz Society.

63   I was . . . in Pittsburgh: Ellington quoted by George Greenlee, interview with the author, November 7, 1993.

63   I got . . . embarrass him: Strayhorn, Duke Ellington Jazz Society.

4. SO THIS IS LOVE

71   He used to come . . . in his hand: Mary Lou Williams interviewed for The Ellington Project, Oral History, Yale School of Music, March 16, 1981.

5. BEYOND CATEGORY

81–82 Ellington's . . . observe: Billy Strayhorn, "The Ellington Effect," *Down Beat*, November 5, 1952.

82   Strayhorn also . . . didn't record: Walter van de Leur.

82   Duke originally . . . Blanton's bass: "Swee' Pea Is Still Amazed at Freedom Allowed in Writing for Ellington Orchestra," *Down Beat*, May 30, 1956.

82   As long . . . doesn't matter: John S. Wilson, "Busy Duke Likes It That Way," *New York Times*, August 7, 1963.

84   There was . . . of things: Strayhorn interviewed for the Duke Ellington Jazz Society, New York, March 1962.

86   The renaissance . . . the band: Duke Ellington and Billy Strayhorn, interview by Paul Worth, KBCA radio, Los Angeles, 1962 (month and day unknown).

88   Pres: Lester Young, the "President."

92   As the manuscript . . . Mercer Ellington: Van de Leur.

98   Although . . . the project: Ibid.

101   I realized . . . very much: Perry Watkins interviewed for the Duke Ellington Jazz Society, New York, March 1966 (unpublished).

104   Mr. Ellington's . . . modern harmonies: Robert Bagar, " 'Beggar's Holiday' a Brilliant Musical," *New York World-Telegram*, December 27, 1946.

104   Mr. Ellington . . . modern setting: Brooks Atkinson, "The Play in Review: Beggar's Holiday," *New York Times*, December 27, 1946.

6. I'M CHECKIN' OUT, GOOM BYE

110   I never . . . at parties: Strayhorn, interviewed for the Duke Ellington Jazz Society, New York, March 1962.

110   At that . . . whatsoever: Ibid.

121   As a result . . . his name: Walter van de Leur.

125   Song and . . . incredible: "Cabin in the Sky," *Variety*, August 12, 1953.

7. ALL ROADS LEAD BACK TO YOU

140   "Things Ain't What They Ought to Be with Ellington's Band": Ted Hallock, "Duke Lays an Egg," *Down Beat*, May 21, 1952.

148   I have . . . the fingers: Bill Coss, "Ellington & Strayhorn, Inc.," *Down Beat*, June 7, 1962.

156   Ellington has . . . to jazz: Sinclair Traill and Gerald Lascelles, *Just Jazz 3* (London: Four Square Books, 1959).

157–58 It will . . . a man has: Duke Ellington, interview by Ted Allen, Paris, January 1961 (unpublished).

158   I suppose . . . I arranged: Duke Ellington and Billy Strayhorn, interview by Paul Worth, KBCA radio, Los Angeles, 1962 (month and day unknown).

159–60 We were . . . rushed: Traill and Lascelles, *Just Jazz 3*.

160   That night . . . very well: Ibid.

8. THERE WAS NOBODY LOOKIN'

167   Today's . . . at Birdland: Earl Wilson, "It Happened Last Night," *New York Post*, November 13, 1956.

169   "Duke Bounces Back with Provocative New Work": John S. Wilson, *New York Times*, October 15, 1957; "A Living Legend Swings On": *Look*, August 20, 1957.

170   Entitled . . . jazz spectacular: " 'Crazy Little Story,' " *Newsweek*, May 6, 1957.

170   This is . . . extended works: John S. Wilson, "Duke Bounces Back."

172   Harlem society . . . great difference: Jesse DeVore, "Article on Homosexuals Drew Fire," *Amsterdam News*, October 12, 1957.

179   Such as . . . "Come Sunday": Walter van de Leur.

179–80 I was . . . year later: Duke Ellington and Billy Strayhorn, interview by Paul Worth, KBCA radio, Los Angeles, 1962 (month and day unknown).

180   Though . . . of jazz: Beatrice Washburn, "The Duke—I Hear Music All the Time," *Miami Herald*, January 12, 1958.

186   Extensive revisions . . . patron pull: Lary Solloway, "Florida's Boxoffice 'Bests,' " *Variety*, March 11, 1959.

190   This is . . . one man: Nat Hentoff, "The Well-Constructed Anatomy," *Hi Fi Review*, September 1959.

190   Music in . . . show them: Ellington, in *American Weekly Entertainment Guide*, August 1, 1959.

9. UP AND DOWN, UP AND DOWN

197   Mr. Strayhorn . . . that matters: Stanley Dance, *Jazz Music*, no volume number, 1943.

204   It was a . . . already was: Strayhorn interviewed for the Duke Ellington Jazz Society, New York, March 1962.

211   Most of . . . *a Murder*: John Tynan, "Paris Blues," *Down Beat*, November 23, 1961.

213   In Paris . . . sound like: Strayhorn, Duke Ellington Jazz Society.

213   After more . . . low-keyed set: John S. Wilson, "The Peaceful Side," *Down Beat*, March 31, 1963.

218   Ellington will . . . he desires: "Duke Signs with Reprise, Will Supervise Sessions," *Down Beat*, January 3, 1963.

10. BLOOD COUNT

230   I found . . . depressed: Arthur Logan interviewed for the Duke Ellington Jazz Society, New York, March 1964 (unpublished).

233   I think . . . to me: Perry Watkins interviewed for the Duke Ellington Jazz Society, New York, March 1966 (unpublished).

234   If you . . . true art: Dan Morgenstern, "Spotlight Review: *Far East Suite*," *Down Beat*, July 1967.

240   Mr. Strayhorn . . . mocking wit: John S. Wilson, "Jazz: The Ellingtonian Billy Strayhorn," *New York Times*, June 7, 1965.

240   This concert . . . lesser hands: Dan Morgenstern, "Billy Strayhorn," *Down Beat*, July 29, 1965.

245   The suite . . . categorization: Dan Morgenstern, "Caught in the Act: Duke Ellington at Philharmonic Hall," *Down Beat*, January 27, 1966.

261   I'm writing . . . yawning void: Mary Campbell, "Ellington's Newest Album Tribute to Billy Strayhorn," *The White Plains Reporter Dispatch*, June 28, 1968.

In response to inquiries filed by the author under the provisions of the Freedom of Information Act, the Federal Bureau of Investigation says the U.S. Government's internal intelligence files on Billy Strayhorn were destroyed after his death. The author is appealing this position.

Note on music research:
For some of Billy Strayhorn's music, the history of authorship detailed in this book differs from the information on record labels and in various published sources. Primary research resources used by the author follow, for other authors' reference and future scholarship.

"All Heart" (from *Portrait of Ella Fitzgerald*)—autograph score, The Duke Ellington Collection, Smithsonian Institution.

"Brown Penny"—autograph score (untitled), Bridgers collection.

"The 'C' Jam Blues"—autograph score, Billy Strayhorn estate; Walter van de Leur research.

"Day Dream"—published interview with Strayhorn; corroboration, author's interviews.

"Grievin' "—autograph score, Billy Strayhorn estate.

"I'm Checkin' Out, Goom Bye"—autograph score, Billy Strayhorn estate.

"The Mood to Be Wooed"—autograph score, The Duke Ellington Collection, Smithsonian Institution; van de Leur research.

"Northern Lights" (from *The Queen's Suite*)—copyright registration, Library of Congress.

"Orson"—autograph score, Aaron Bridgers collection.

"Something to Live For"—autograph score for the Mad Hatters, Jerome Eisner collection, Jean Mayer collection; corroboration, author's interviews.

"The Star-Crossed Lovers"—autograph score (entitled "Pretty Girl"), Aaron Bridgers collection.

"Sugar Hill Penthouse" (from *Black, Brown and Beige*)—autograph score, The Duke Ellington Collection, Smithsonian Institution; van de Leur research.

"A Tone Parallel to Harlem"—autograph score, The Duke Ellington Collection, Smithsonian Institution.

"Tonight I Shall Sleep (With a Smile on My Face)"—autograph score, The Duke Ellington Collection, Smithsonian Institution; van de Leur research.

"Tonk"—autograph score, Billy Strayhorn estate; van de Leur research.

"Your Love Has Faded"—autograph score for the Mad Hatters, Jerome Eisner collection; corroboration, author's interviews.

Beggar's Holiday: the "Boll Weevil Ballet," "Girls Want a Hero," "I'm Afraid," "Maybe I Should Change My Ways," "Women, Women,

Women," "The Wrong Side of the Railroad Tracks"—The Duke Ellington Collection, Smithsonian Institution; van de Leur research; corroboration, author's interviews.

The Blessed and the Damned—author's interviews.

Jump for Joy: "Cindy with the Two Left Feet," "Flame Indigo," "Rocks in My Bed," "Uncle Tom's Cabin Is a Drive-In Now"—The Duke Ellington Collection, Smithsonian Institution; van de Leur research; corroboration, author's interviews.

BIBLIOGRAPHY

A selected listing of books drawn on in this work follows. Magazine, newspaper, and newsletter articles, too numerous to list, are not included.

Abrahams, Peter. *Mine Boy*. Portsmouth, England: Heinemann, 1985.

Baldwin, Leland. *Pittsburgh: Story of a City*. Pittsburgh: University of Pittsburgh Press, 1938.

Bigard, Barney. *With Louis and the Duke: The Autobiography of a Jazz Clarinetist*. New York: Oxford University Press, 1985.

Bridgers, Aaron. "Piano in the Background: The Life of a Bar Pianist," 1973.

Buckley, Gail Lumet. *The Hornes: An American Family*. New York: Alfred A. Knopf, 1986.

Chauncey, George. *Gay New York*. New York: Basic, 1994.

Collier, James Lincoln. *Duke Ellington*. New York: Oxford University Press, 1987.

Dance, Stanley. *The World of Duke Ellington*. New York: Charles Scribner's Sons, 1970.

Davis, Ursala Brozhke. *Paris without Regrets*. Iowa City: University of Iowa Press, 1986.

Ellington, Duke. *Duke Ellington Piano Method for Blues.* New York: Robbins Music Corp., 1943.

———. *Music Is My Mistress.* Garden City: Doubleday, 1973.

Ellington, Mercer, with Stanley Dance. *Duke Ellington in Person: An Intimate Memoir.* Boston: Houghton Mifflin, 1978.

Fabre, Michel. *From Harlem to Paris: Black American Writers in France, 1840–1980.* Chicago: University of Illinois Press, 1991.

Feather, Leonard. *The Jazz Years: Earwitness to an Era.* New York: Da Capo, 1987.

Flender, Harold. *Paris Blues.* New York: Ballantine, 1957.

Frank, Rusty M. *Tap! The Greatest Tap Dance Stars and Their Stories, 1900–1955.* New York: William Morrow, 1990.

Gabbard, Krin. *Jammin' at the Margins: Jazz and the American Cinema.* Chicago: University of Chicago Press, 1996.

Gammond, Peter. *Duke Ellington.* London: Apollo Press, 1987.

———, ed. *Duke Ellington: His Life and Music.* London: Dent, 1958.

George, Don. *Sweet Man: The Real Duke Ellington.* New York: G. P. Putnam's Sons, 1981.

Gleason, Ralph J. *Celebrating the Duke, and Louis, Bessie, Billie, Bird, Carmen, Miles, Dizzy, and Other Heroes.* Boston: Little, Brown, 1975.

Griffith, Richard. *Anatomy of a Motion Picture.* New York: St. Martin's Press, 1959.

Haskins, James S., and Kathleen Benson. *A Biography of Lena Horne.* Lanham, Maryland: Madison Books/UPA, 1991.

Hasse, John Edward. *Beyond Category: The Life and Genius of Duke Ellington.* New York: Simon & Schuster, 1993.

Hawkeswood, William G. *One of the Children: Gay Black Men in Harlem.* Berkeley: University of California Press, 1995.

Hayes, Samuel. *City at the Point: Essays on the Social History of Pittsburgh.* Pittsburgh: University of Pittsburgh Press, 1989.

Hentoff, Nat. *Jazz Is.* New York: Random House, 1976.

Holway, John B. *Blackball Stars.* New York: Carroll & Graf, 1992.

Horne, Lena, and Richard Schickel. *Lena.* New York: Limelight, 1986.

Houseman, John. *Unfinished Business: A Memoir.* London: Chatto & Windus, 1986.

Howard, Brett. *Lena Horne.* Los Angeles: Holloway, 1991.

Jewell, Derek. *Duke: A Portrait of Duke Ellington.* New York: W. W. Norton, 1977.

Lambert, G. E. *Duke Ellington.* London: Cassill, 1959.

Leaming, Barbara. *Orson Welles: A Biography.* New York: Viking, 1986.

Lord, Tom. *The Jazz Discography.* 9 vols. West Vancouver, B.C.: Lord Music Reference and Redwood, New York: Cadence Jazz Books, 1992–94.

Machiz, Herbert. *The Artists Theatre.* New York: Grove Press, 1960.

Massagli, Luciano, Liborio Pusateri, and Giovanni M. Volonte. *Duke Ellington's Story on Records.* 16 vols. Milan: Raretone, 1966–83.

Morgenstern, Dan, and Ole Brask. *Jazz People.* Englewood Cliffs, New Jersey: Prentice-Hall, 1976.

Moule, François-Xavier, comp. *Concerts, Radio Broadcasts, Television Shows, Radio*

Transcriptions, V-Discs, Film Soundtracks. Vol. 1 of A Guide to the Duke Ellington Recorded Legacy on LPs and CDs. Le Mans: A Madly Production, 1992.

Myers, John Bernard. Tracking the Marvelous: A Life in the New York Art World. New York: Random House, 1983.

Nielsen, Ole J., comp. Ellington. Vol. 6 of Jazz Records, 1942–1980. Copenhagen: JazzMedia, 1991.

Preminger, Otto. Preminger—An Autobiography. New York: Doubleday, 1977.

Rattenbury, Ken. Duke Ellington: Jazz Composer. New Haven: Yale University Press, 1990.

Ruff, Willie. A Call to Assembly: The Autobiography of a Musical Storyteller. New York: Viking, 1991.

Schuller, Gunther. Early Jazz. New York: Oxford University Press, 1968.

———. The Swing Era. New York: Oxford University Press, 1989.

Stewart, Rex, and Claire P. Gordon, eds. Boy Meets Horn. Ann Arbor: University of Michigan Press, 1991.

Stratemann, Klaus. Ellington Day by Day and Film by Film. Copenhagen: JazzMedia, 1992.

Timner, W. E., comp. Ellingtonia: The Recorded Music of Duke Ellington and His Sidemen. 3rd ed. Metuchen, New Jersey: Institute of Jazz Studies and Scarecrow Press, 1988.

Traill, Sinclair, and Gerald Lascelles. Just Jazz 3. London: Four Square Books, 1959.

Tucker, Mark. Ellington: The Early Years. Urbana: University of Illinois Press, 1991.

———, ed. The Duke Ellington Reader. New York: Oxford University Press, 1993.

Ulanov, Barry. Duke Ellington. New York: Creative Age Press, 1946.

Valburn, Jerry. The Directory of Duke Ellington's Recordings. Hicksville, New York: Marlor Productions, 1986.

———. Duke Ellington on Compact Disc. Hicksville, New York: Marlor Productions, 1993.

Van de Leur, Walter. "Duke Ellington and Billy Strayhorn: Their Collaboration for the 'Blanton-Webster Band,' 1939–1941." Master's thesis, Department of Musicology, University of Amsterdam, 1993.

Welles, Orson, and Peter Bogdanovich. This Is Orson Welles. New York: Harper-Collins, 1992.

Williams, Martin. The Jazz Tradition. 2nd rev. ed. New York: Oxford University Press, 1983.

DISCOGRAPHY

The following is a list of Billy Strayhorn's compositions and collaborations issued on records and CDs. The credits listed for composers and lyricists reflect copyright registrations as filed by Tempo Music and other publishers, and they may differ from the authorship history described in this book; the dates cited represent the earliest listing with the Library of Congress or ASCAP. (Title spellings used here correspond with copyright registrations and sometimes differ from popular usage. No dates are listed for songs not copyrighted or registered with ASCAP.) The recordings noted are exemplary performances; where possible, Strayhorn's own performances have been chosen. All are available on CD except where noted. Music not recorded, arrangements by Strayhorn of other composers' work, adaptations of his music by others, and lyrics added to Strayhorn's music after his death are not included.

SONGS

"Absinthe" (1963) Registered composer: Strayhorn. Recommended recording: *Afro-Bossa* (Discovery), Duke Ellington and His Orchestra. Strayhorn's original title was "Lament for an Orchid." The piece was alternately entitled "Fluid Jive" and "Water Lily" in its early performances; a later working title was "Ricard," after a French brand of absinthe.

"After All" (1942) Registered composer: Strayhorn. Recommended recording: *The Blanton-Webster Band* (RCA), Duke Ellington and His Orchestra.

"Allah-Bye" (1957) Registered composer: Strayhorn. Recommended recording: *Duke '56–'62, Volume 1* (CBS 2-LP set), Duke Ellington and His Orchestra.

"All Day Long" (1951) Registered composer: Strayhorn. Recommended recording: *. . . And His Mother Called Him Bill* (RCA), Duke Ellington and His Orchestra.

"All Heart" *See* Suites: *Portrait of Ella Fitzgerald.*

"Baby Clementine" *See* "Clementine."

"Bagatelle" (1995) Registered composer: Strayhorn. Recommended recording: *Portrait of a Silk Thread: Newly Discovered Works of Billy Strayhorn* (Dutch Jazz), The Dutch Jazz Orchestra. This vintage Strayhorn piece was copyrighted and recorded under the stewardship of the composer's estate.

"Ballad for Very Tired and Very Sad Lotus Eaters" (1957) Registered composer: Strayhorn. Recommended recording: *Duke's in Bed* (Verve LP), Johnny Hodges. Released as "Ballade for Very Tired and Very Sad Lotus Eaters."

"Barefoot Stomper" (1965) Registered composers and lyricists: Ellington–Strayhorn. Recommended recording: *Concert in the Virgin Islands* (Reprise), Duke Ellington and His Orchestra.

"Barney Goin' Easy" *See* "I'm Checkin' Out, Goom Bye."

"BDB" (1962) Registered composers: Ellington–Strayhorn. Recommended recording: *First Time! The Count Meets the Duke* (Columbia), the Duke Ellington and Count Basie orchestras performing together.

"Big Fat Alice's Blues" (1965) Registered composers and lyricists: Ellington–Strayhorn. Recommended recording: *Concert in the Virgin Islands* (Reprise), Duke Ellington and His Orchestra.

"Blood Count" (1967) Registered composer: Strayhorn. Recommended recording: *. . . And His Mother Called Him Bill* (RCA), Duke Ellington and His Orchestra. The piece was intended to be the first movement of a three-part Strayhorn composition, *The North by Southwest Suite* ("Blue Cloud," "Pavane," "Up There").

"Blossom" (1954) Registered composers: Ellington–Strayhorn. Lyricist: Johnny Mercer. Recommended recording: *The Complete Capitol Recordings of Duke Ellington* (Mosaic), Duke Ellington and His Orchestra.

"Blues in Orbit" (1958) Registered composers: Ellington–Strayhorn. Recommended recording: *Blues in Orbit* (Columbia), Duke Ellington and His Orchestra.

"Blue Star" (1995) Registered composer: Strayhorn. Recommended recording: *Portrait of a Silk Thread: Newly Discovered Works of Billy Strayhorn* (Dutch Jazz), The Dutch Jazz Orchestra. Copyrighted and recorded after Strayhorn's death, through his estate.

"Boo-Dah" (1953) Registered composer and lyricist: Strayhorn. Recommended recording: *Lush Life* (Red Baron), Billy Strayhorn. On this CD, the only release of a Strayhorn performance of this composition, it is misidentified as another Strayhorn piece, "Smada."

"Brown Betty" (1948) Registered composers: Ellington–Strayhorn. Recommended recording: *Carnegie Hall, November 13, 1948* (VJC), Duke Ellington and His Orchestra. Although Ellington described the piece as Strayhorn's work in his comments at Carnegie Hall on November 11, 1948, Tempo Music's copyright was registered in the names of Ellington and Strayhorn on November 7, 1951.

"Bugle Breaks" (1945) Registered composers: Strayhorn–Duke Ellington–Mercer Ellington. Recommended recording: *Take the "A" Train: The Blanton-Webster Transcriptions* (VJC), Duke Ellington and His Orchestra. The Ellington Orchestra occasionally performed a concert version of this piece as "Bugle Breaks Extended."

"Cafe au Lait" (1962) Registered composer: Strayhorn. Recommended recording: *Duke '56–'62, Volume 1* (CBS 2-LP set), Duke Ellington and His Orchestra.

"Cashmere Cutie" (1957) Registered composer: Strayhorn. Recommended recording: *Portrait of a Silk Thread: Newly Discovered Works of Billy Strayhorn* (Dutch Jazz), The Dutch Jazz Orchestra.

"Chalmeau" (1946) Registered composers: Strayhorn–Harry Carney. Recommended recording: *Music for Loving: Ben Webster with Strings* (Verve), Ben Webster. This CD incorporates the LP *Harry Carney with Strings*, which includes this song.

"Charpoy" (1946) Registered composer: Strayhorn. Recommended recording: *. . . And His Mother Called Him Bill* (RCA), Duke Ellington and His Orchestra. Composed in the mid-1940s, the piece was originally entitled "Lana Turner"; on some music for the Ellington Orchestra, the title was inverted as "Anal Renrut." In its first copyright, the piece was entitled "Francesca."

"Chelsea Bridge" (1941) Registered composer: Strayhorn. Recommended recording: *The Peaceful Side* (United Artists LP), Billy Strayhorn.

"Clementine" (1942) Registered composer: Strayhorn. Lyricists: Stanley Clayton–Ruth Roberts–Bill Katz. Recommended recording: *The Blanton-Webster Band* (RCA), Duke Ellington and His Orchestra. On some later recordings of the vocal version of this song, entitled "Baby Clementine," the record producer Bob Thiele is credited as a fourth lyricist.

"Cue's Blue Now" (1960) Registered composers: Strayhorn–Johnny Hodges. Recommended recording: *Cue for Saxophone* (London), Billy Strayhorn's Septet.

"Day Dream" (1940) Registered composers: Ellington–Strayhorn. Lyricist: John

Latouche. Recommended recording: *The Peaceful Side* (United Artists LP), Billy Strayhorn.

"Dirge" Registered composer: none. Recommended recording: *The Duke Ellington Carnegie Hall Concerts, January 1943* (Prestige), Duke Ellington and His Orchestra. Although Strayhorn is credited as composer on the record and in various accounts of this performance, no copyright registration has been filed for the song.

"Double Ruff" (1946) Registered composer: Strayhorn. Recommended recording: *The "Collection": '46–'57 Recordings* (Hindsight), Duke Ellington and His Orchestra.

"Drawing Room Blues" (1947) Registered composer: Strayhorn. Recommended recording: *Duke Ellington at the Blue Note, 1959* (Roulette), Duke Ellington and His Orchestra. This CD is a live recording featuring Strayhorn in a solo piano performance.

"E and D Blues" (1958) Registered composers: Ellington–John Sanders. Recommended recording: *Ella Fitzgerald Sings the Duke Ellington Songbook* (Verve), Ella Fitzgerald with Duke Ellington and His Orchestra. Strayhorn is credited as co-composer (with Ellington and Sanders) on LP and CD releases. In Tempo Music's first copyright, registered on September 10, 1958, Ellington is cited as sole composer; in the publisher's second registration, filed on March 2, 1959, both Ellington and Sanders are cited as the composers.

"Eighth Veil" (1946) Registered composers: Ellington–Strayhorn. Recommended recording: *Afro-Bossa* (Discovery), Duke Ellington and His Orchestra. Some releases credit Ellington and Strayhorn as co-composers, some cite Strayhorn alone.

"Elysee" (1964) Registered composer: Strayhorn. Recommended recording: *Duke Ellington: The Private Collection, Volume Four* (SAJA), Duke Ellington and His Orchestra.

"Far-Eastern Weekend" (1957) Registered composers: Strayhorn–Louie Bellson–Seymour Press. Recommended recording: *Drummerama* (Verve LP), Louie Bellson.

"Feather Roll Blues" Registered composer: none. Recommended recording: 78 rpm single (Sunrise), Billy Strayhorn Orchestra. Although Strayhorn is credited as composer on the record, no copyright registration has been filed for the song.

"Flippant Flurry" (1947) Registered composer: Ellington. Recommended recording: *The "Collection": '46–'57 Recordings* (Hindsight), Duke Ellington and His Orchestra. ASCAP, Tempo Music catalogs, and recordings cite Billy Strayhorn as composer of this piece. In Tempo Music's copyright, registered on January 14, 1947, Duke Ellington is cited as sole composer.

"A Flower Is a Lovesome Thing" (1941) Registered composer and lyricist: Strayhorn. Recommended recording: *The Peaceful Side* (United Artists LP), Billy Strayhorn. The title was inspired by the poem "My Garden" by Thomas Edward Brown (1830–97): "A Garden is a lovesome thing, God wot!" Released as "Passion" on Johnny Hodges's *Creamy* LP.

"Frou-Frou" (1965) Registered composer: Lil Young. Recommended recording: *The Duke's DJ Special, March 27, 1959* (Fresh Sound), Duke Ellington and His Orchestra. Composed by Strayhorn under his mother's maiden name. He received the song's royalties, by contract with the publishing organization SESAC. Also known as "So Easy."

"Gonna Tan Your Hide" (1957) Registered composers: Ellington–Strayhorn. Recommended recording: *The Complete Capitol Recordings of Duke Ellington* (Mosaic), Duke Ellington and His Orchestra. On record labels and in the song index to Ellington's memoirs, *Music Is My Mistress*, Ellington and Strayhorn are credited as co-composers of this piece. In Tempo Music's first copyright, registered on March 1, 1957, Strayhorn is cited as sole composer; in the publisher's second copyright, filed on March 1, 1962, Ellington is named as composer.

"Grievin' " (1939) Registered composers and lyricists: Ellington–Strayhorn. Recommended recording: *The Chronological Duke Ellington and His Orchestra, 1939, Volume 2* (Classics), Duke Ellington and His Orchestra.

"Happy-Go-Lucky Local" *See* Suites: *The Deep South Suite*.

"Hark for Duke's Trumpets" (1956) Registered composer: none. Recommended recording: *Duke Ellington at the 1957 Stratford Festival* (Music and Arts), Duke Ellington and His Orchestra. Ellington and Strayhorn are credited as co-composers on recordings of the piece. This CD, erroneously titled, documents a performance from 1956.

"Hear Say" *See* Suites: *The Deep South Suite*.

"The History of Jazz in Three Minutes" Registered composer: none. Recommended recording: Short film of the same title. Concert programs for live performances credited Ellington and Strayhorn as co-composers.

"Hi-Ya" (1957) Registered composer: Johnny Hodges. Recommended recording: *Ellingtonia '56* (Verve LP), Johnny Hodges. Although Strayhorn and Hodges are credited jointly on the recording, Hodges alone is cited in the copyright registration filed on March 11, 1957.

"The Hues" (1995) Registered composer: Strayhorn. Recommended recording: *Portrait of a Silk Thread: Newly Discovered Works of Billy Strayhorn* (Dutch Jazz), The Dutch Jazz Orchestra. Copyrighted and recorded after Strayhorn's death, through his estate.

"I Don't Mind" (1942) Registered composer: Ellington. Lyricist: Strayhorn. Recommended recording: *The Blanton-Webster Band* (RCA), Duke Ellington and His Orchestra.

"Imagine My Frustration" (1966) Registered composer and lyricist: Ellington. Recommended recording: *Ella at Duke's Place* (Verve), Ella Fitzgerald with Duke Ellington and His Orchestra. The music for this song, originally entitled "When I'm Feeling Kinda Blue," was composed by Gerald Wilson and credited to his wife, Jo Villasenor; Wilson performed the song with his big band and recorded it prior to introducing it to Ellington. On Ellington Orchestra recordings of the retitled lyric version, Wilson is credited jointly with Ellington and Strayhorn. Tempo Music's copyrights, filed on February 11, 1966 (as "Imagine"), and April 9, 1970 (as "Imagine My Frustration"), cite Ellington as sole author of both words and music.

"I'm Checkin' Out, Goom Bye" (1939) Registered composers and lyricists: Ellington–Strayhorn. Recommended recording: *The Chronological Duke Ellington and His Orchestra, 1939, Volume 2* (Classics), Duke Ellington and His Orchestra. Also recorded as an instrumental entitled "Barney Goin' Easy."

"In a Blue Summer Garden" Registered composer: none. Recommended recording: *Great Times* (Riverside), Duke Ellington and Billy Strayhorn. Ellington and Strayhorn are credited as co-composers on recordings of the piece.

"The Intimacy of the Blues" (1968) Registered composer: Strayhorn. Recommended recording: *. . . And His Mother Called Him Bill* (RCA), Duke Ellington and His Orchestra.

"Isfahan" *See* Suites: *The Far East Suite.*

"Jazz Festival Jazz" (1958) Registered composers: Ellington–Dick Vance. Recommended recording: *Live from Newport* (Columbia), Duke Ellington and His Orchestra. ASCAP, Tempo Music catalogs, and recordings cite Ellington and Strayhorn as co-composers. In Tempo Music's copyright, filed on November 4, 1958, Duke Ellington and Dick Vance are registered as co-composers.

"Johnny Come Lately" (1942) Registered composer: Strayhorn. Recommended recording: *Just Jazz All-Stars* (Capitol LP), various artists, including Strayhorn. Also performed by the Ellington Orchestra as "Stomp."

"Just A-Sittin' and A-Rockin' " (1941) Registered composers: Ellington–Strayhorn. Lyricist: Lee Gaines. Recommended recording: *Lush Life* (Red Baron), Billy Strayhorn.

"Kissing Bug" (1945) Registered composers: Strayhorn–Rex Stewart. Lyricist: Joya Sherrill. Recommended recording: *Black, Brown and Beige* (RCA), Duke Ellington and His Orchestra.

"Lament for Javanette" (1941) Registered composers: Strayhorn–Barney Bigard. Recommended recording: *The Great Ellington Units* (RCA), various artists. Copyrighted in the names of Strayhorn and Bigard on April 5, 1941, and released on a recording featuring Bigard and a small band, the song is credited to Ellington on its CD release.

"Lonely Co-ed" (1939) Registered composers and lyricists: Ellington–Strayhorn–Edgar Leslie. Recommended recording: *Ivie Anderson with the Duke Ellington Orchestra* (Jazz Archives), Duke Ellington and His Orchestra.

"Lost in Two Flats" (1940) Registered composer: Strayhorn. Recommended recording: *The Chronological Duke Ellington and His Orchestra, 1939–1940* (Classics), Barney Bigard and His Orchestra.

"Lotus Blossom" (1946) Registered composer: Strayhorn. Recommended recording: *. . . And His Mother Called Him Bill* (RCA), Duke Ellington and His Orchestra. Originally recorded by Johnny Hodges and a small band as "Charlotte Russe."

"Love Came" (1965) Registered composer: Strayhorn. Lyricist: Ellington. Recommended recording: *Lush Life* (Red Baron), Billy Strayhorn. Strayhorn is cited as composer in the copyright registration filed on August 18, 1965. Ellington is credited as composer on this CD, released posthumously under Strayhorn's name.

"Love Has Passed Me By, Again" Registered composer and lyricist: none. Recommended recording: *Lush Life* (Red Baron), Billy Strayhorn. On the Strayhorn CD, the song is erroneously listed as "Pass Me By," a different composition by Mercer Ellington and Hillis Walters (misspelled Waiters).

"Love Like This Can't Last" (1945) Registered composer and lyricist: Strayhorn. Recommended recording: *Take the "A" Train: The Blanton-Webster Transcriptions* (VJC), Duke Ellington and His Orchestra.

"Lovelinessence" Registered composer: none. Recommended recording: *Ellingtonia* (Strand LP), Cat Anderson and the Ellington All-Stars. No copyright registration has been filed for this composition.

"Lush Life" (1949) Registered composer and lyricist: Strayhorn. Recommended recording: *Lush Life* (Red Baron), Billy Strayhorn. Composed by Strayhorn before he met Ellington, the piece was never performed by the Duke Ellington Orchestra. It is featured on several CDs of "the music of Duke Ellington," including releases by Sarah Vaughan and Ella Fitzgerald.

"Malletoba Spank" (1959) Registered composers: Ellington–Strayhorn. Recommended recording: *Jazz Party* (Columbia), Duke Ellington and His Orchestra. Released as "Spank" in an edited version on 45 rpm record.

"Maybe" (1961) Registered composer and lyricist: Strayhorn. Recommended recording: *Lena at the Sands* (RCA LP), Lena Horne.

"Metronome All-Out" (1945) Registered composers: Ellington–Strayhorn. Recommended recording: *The Metronome All-Star Bands* (RCA), Metronome All-Stars.

"M.H. & R." (1962) Registered composers: Strayhorn–Johnny Hodges. Recommended recording: *Not So Dukish* (Verve LP), Johnny Hodges. Released as "M.H.R."

"A Midnight in Paris" (1963) Registered composer: Strayhorn. Recommended recording: *Midnight in Paris* (Columbia), Duke Ellington and His Orchestra.

"Mid-Riff" (1944) Registered composer: Strayhorn. Recommended recording: *Black, Brown and Beige* (RCA), Duke Ellington and His Orchestra. The piece's original title was "Raindrop Stomp."

"Minuet in Blues" (1940) Registered composer: Barney Bigard. Recommended recording: *Ellington Sidekicks* (Epic/Sony), various groups of Ellingtonians. Originally released as "Minuet in Blue" on a 78 rpm single by Barney Bigard and His Orchestra (Vocalion). Although Strayhorn is credited as composer on the recording and the song's original music manuscript is in his hand, the song was copyrighted in Bigard's name.

"Multicolored Blue" *See* "Violet Blue."

"My Little Brown Book" (1944) Registered composer and lyricist: Strayhorn.

Recommended recording: *The Blanton-Webster Band* (RCA), Duke Ellington and His Orchestra.

"Mysterious Chick" (1965) Registered composers: Ellington–Strayhorn. Recommended recording: *Concert in the Virgin Islands* (Reprise), Duke Ellington and His Orchestra.

"Night Time" (1954) Registered composers: Ellington–Strayhorn. Lyricist: Doris Julian. Recommended recording: *The Complete Capitol Recordings of Duke Ellington* (Mosaic), Duke Ellington and His Orchestra.

"Noir Bleu" (1947) Registered composer: Strayhorn. Recommended recording: *The Chronological Duke Ellington and His Orchestra, 1941, Volume 2* (Classics), Barney Bigard and His Orchestra.

"Once upon a Dream" (1949) Registered composer: Strayhorn. Lyricists: Bill Contrell–T. Hee. Recommended recording: *The Complete Duke Ellington, 1947–1952, Volume 2* (CBS), Duke Ellington and His Orchestra.

"Orson" (1955) Registered composers: Ellington–Strayhorn. Recommended recording: *The Complete Capitol Recordings of Duke Ellington* (Mosaic), Duke Ellington and His Orchestra.

"Overture to a Jam Session" (1947) Registered composer: Ellington. Recommended recording: *The "Collection": '46–'57 Recordings* (Hindsight), Duke Ellington and His Orchestra. ASCAP, Tempo Music catalogs, and recordings cite Billy Strayhorn as sole composer of this piece. In Tempo Music's copyright, filed on March 12, 1947, Duke Ellington is registered as composer.

"Paradise" (1948) Registered composer: Strayhorn. Recommended recording: *Carnegie Hall, November 13, 1948* (VJC), Duke Ellington and His Orchestra.

"Paris Blues" (1962) Registered composer: Ellington. Lyricists: Strayhorn–Harold Flender. Recommended recording: *Featuring Paul Gonsalves* (Fantasy), Duke Ellington and His Orchestra.

"Passion Flower" (1944) Registered composer: Strayhorn. Lyricist: Milton Raskin. Recommended recording: *Lush Life* (Red Baron), Billy Strayhorn.

"Pentonsilic" (1995) Registered composer: Strayhorn. Recommended recording: *Portrait of a Silk Thread: Newly Discovered Works of Billy Strayhorn* (Dutch Jazz), The Dutch Jazz Orchestra. Copyrighted and recorded after Strayhorn's death, through his estate. Part of this work is related to "Sonata" (also known as "Love," "Under the Balcony," and "Balcony Serenade") from the Ellington-Strayhorn *Perfume Suite*.

"Pomegranate" (1957) Registered composer: Ellington. Lyricist: Strayhorn. Recommended recording: *A Drum Is a Woman* (Columbia LP), Duke Ellington and His Orchestra. The song was included in the television version of *A Drum Is a Woman*, though it is not included on the CD release.

"Portrait of a Silk Thread" (1995) Registered composer: Strayhorn. Recommended recording: *Portrait of a Silk Thread: Newly Discovered Works of Billy Strayhorn* (Dutch Jazz), The Dutch Jazz Orchestra. Copyrighted and recorded after Strayhorn's death, through his estate.

"Pretty Girl" (1956) Registered composer and lyricist: Strayhorn. Recommended recording: *Creamy* (Verve LP), Johnny Hodges. Originally recorded, released, and copyrighted (in Strayhorn's name) under this title (or "Pretty Little Girl"), the song was later retitled "The Star-Crossed Lovers" for use in the suite *Such Sweet Thunder* and copyrighted again under the names of both Ellington and Strayhorn.

"Pretty Little One" Registered composer: none. Recommended recording: *Duke Ellington's Jazz Violin Session* (Atlantic LP), Duke Ellington. Although Strayhorn is credited as composer on the record, no copyright registration has been filed for the song.

"Prima Bara Dubla" (1958) Registered composers: Ellington–Strayhorn. Recommended recording: *Newport, 1958* (Columbia), Duke Ellington and His Orchestra.

"Progressive Gavotte" (1948) Registered composer: Strayhorn. Recommended recording: *The Complete Duke Ellington, 1947–1952, Volume 2* (CBS), Duke Ellington and His Orchestra.

"Put-Tin" (1964) Registered composers: Ellington–Strayhorn. Recommended recording: *Yale Concert* (Fantasy), Duke Ellington and His Orchestra.

"Rain Check" (1942) Registered composer: Strayhorn. Recommended recording: *The Blanton-Webster Band* (RCA), Duke Ellington and His Orchestra.

"Rock Skippin' " (1952) Registered composers: Ellington–Strayhorn. Recommended recording: *. . . And His Mother Called Him Bill* (RCA), Duke Ellington and His Orchestra. Released as "Rock Skippin' at the Blue Note."

"Le Sacre Supreme" (1995) Registered composer: Strayhorn. Recommended recording: *Portrait of a Silk Thread: Newly Discovered Works of Billy Strayhorn* (Dutch Jazz), The Dutch Jazz Orchestra. Copyrighted and recorded after Strayhorn's death, through his estate.

"Satin Doll" (1954) Registered composers: Ellington–Strayhorn. Lyricist: Johnny Mercer. Recommended recording: *The Soul of Ben Webster* (Verve), Ben Webster, Johnny Hodges, Harry Edison. This CD includes the contents of the Hodges LP *Blues A-Plenty*.

"Smada" (1952) Registered composers: Ellington–Strayhorn. Recommended recording: *. . . And His Mother Called Him Bill* (RCA), Duke Ellington and His Orchestra. Strayhorn's original version of this composition, composed while he was in Pittsburgh, was alternately entitled "Ugly Ducklin' " and "Smoky City."

"Snibor" (1956) Registered composer: Strayhorn. Recommended recording: *. . . And His Mother Called Him Bill* (RCA), Duke Ellington and His Orchestra.

"Something to Live For" (1939) Registered composers and lyricists: Ellington–Strayhorn. Recommended recording: *The Peaceful Side* (United Artists LP), Billy Strayhorn.

"The Star-Crossed Lovers" *See:* "Pretty Girl"; *see also* Suites: *Such Sweet Thunder*.

"Strange Feeling" *See* Suites: *The Perfume Suite*.

"Swamp Drum" (1951) Registered composer: Strayhorn. Recommended recording: *The Johnny Hodges All-Stars with the Duke Ellington All-Stars and the Billy Strayhorn All-Stars* (Prestige), various groups of Ellingtonians.

"Sweet and Pungent" (1960) Registered composer: Strayhorn. Recommended recording: *Blues in Orbit* (Columbia), Duke Ellington and His Orchestra.

"Take It Slow" (1942) Registered composer: Strayhorn. Recommended recording: *The Private Collection, Volume 3* (SAJA), Duke Ellington and His Orchestra. Composed by Strayhorn and copyrighted in his name, the song was performed by Ellington as "Self Portrait" in a WNBC radio broadcast from New York's Waldorf-Astoria Hotel on April 26, 1957.

"Take the 'A' Train" (1941) Registered composer and lyricist: Strayhorn. Recommended recording: *Lush Life* (Red Baron), Billy Strayhorn. The Ellington Orchestra performed an extended version of "Take the 'A' Train," entitled "Manhattan Murals," at Carnegie Hall on November 13, 1948; in its release on CD, the adaptation was credited jointly to Ellington and Strayhorn.

"Tapioca" Registered composer: none. Recommended recording: *Ellington Sidekicks* (Epic/Sony), various groups of Ellingtonians. Although Strayhorn is credited on recordings as its composer, no copyright registration has been filed for the piece.

"Three and Six" (1962) Registered composer: Strayhorn. Recommended recording: *Not So Dukish* (Verve LP), Johnny Hodges. The piece is derived from "Wounded Love," a song from Strayhorn's score for the Federico García Lorca play *The Love of Dom Perlimplín for Belisa in Their Garden.*

"3:10 Blues" (1963) Registered composer: Strayhorn. Recommended recording: *Everybody Knows* (Verve LP), Johnny Hodges. Released as "310 Blues."

"Tigress" (1963) Registered composer: Strayhorn. Recommended recording: *Afro-Bossa* (Discovery), Duke Ellington and His Orchestra.

"Tonk" (1940) Registered composers: Ellington–Strayhorn. Recommended recording: *Great Times* (Riverside), Duke Ellington and Billy Strayhorn. Best known as a four-hand piano duet, the piece was originally composed for jazz orchestra. Ellington and Strayhorn also released the piano version as "Pianistically Allied."

"Triple Play" (1948) Registered composer: Strayhorn. Recommended recording: 78 rpm single (Wax), no artist credited on the label.

"Tymperturbably Blue" (1959) Registered composers: Ellington–Strayhorn. Recommended recording: *Jazz Party* (Columbia), Duke Ellington and His Orchestra.

"Upper Manhattan Medical Group" ("U.M.M.G.") (1956) Registered composer: Strayhorn. Recommended recording: *Lush Life* (Red Baron), Billy Strayhorn. The piece is named after a New York medical institution where Arthur Logan practiced.

"Violet Blue" (1947) Registered composer and lyricist: Strayhorn. Recommended recording: *The Peaceful Side* (United Artists LP), Billy Strayhorn. Also released as "Multicolored Blue."

"Watch Your Cue" (1960) Registered composers and lyricists: Strayhorn–Johnny Hodges. Recommended recording: *Cue for Saxophone* (London), Billy Strayhorn's Septet.

"Wounded Love" *See:* "Three and Six."

"You Better Know It" *See* Suites: *A Drum Is a Woman.*

"You're the One" (1955) Registered composer and lyricist: Strayhorn. Recommended recording: *It's Love* (RCA), Lena Horne with Lennie Hayton and His Orchestra.

"Your Love Has Faded" Registered composer and lyricist: Ellington. Recommended recording: *Billy Strayhorn and the Orchestra* (Verve LP), with Johnny Hodges, soloist. Composed and performed by Strayhorn during his Pittsburgh years, the song was not copyrighted until June 2, 1960, when Robbins Music filed a registration citing Ellington as composer and lyricist.

SUITES

The Deep South Suite (1947) Registered composers: Ellington, Ellington–Strayhorn. Movements: "Happy-Go-Lucky Local," "Sultry Sunset," "Hear Say," "There Was Nobody Lookin'," "Magnolias Dripping with Honey." Recommended recording: *The Great Chicago Concerts* (Music Masters), Duke Ellington and His Orchestra. The copyright registrations for "Happy-Go-Lucky Local," "Hear Say," and "There Was Nobody Lookin' " cite Ellington and Strayhorn as joint composers; the filings for "Sultry Sunset" and "Magnolias Dripping with Honey" credit Ellington alone. Strayhorn performed "Hear Say" at his New York solo concert in 1965 and recorded the piece in a demonstration record (unissued). The entire suite has been credited to Ellington in performances by the Lincoln Center Jazz Orchestra. "There Was Nobody Lookin' " is sometimes referred to as "Nobody Was Looking."

A Drum Is a Woman (1957) Registered composers and lyricists: Ellington–Strayhorn. Movements: "A Drum Is a Woman," "Rhythm Pum Te Dum," "What Else Can You Do with a Drum," "New Orleans," "Hey, Buddy Bolden," "Carribe Joe," "Congo Square," "You Better Know It," "Madam Zajj," "Ballet of the Flying Saucers," "Zajj's Dream," "Rhumbop," "Finale." Recommended recording: *A Drum Is a Woman* (Columbia), Duke Ellington and His Orchestra. The television production, which has some different music, is not available on video but can be seen at New York's Museum of Television and Radio and some other institutions.

The Far East Suite (1964) Registered composers: Ellington–Strayhorn. Movements: "Tourist Point of View," "Bluebird of Delhi (Mynah Bird)," "Isfahan," "Depk," "Mount Harissa," "Blue Pepper (Far East of the Blues)," "Agra," "Amad." Recommended recording: *The Far East Suite* (RCA), Duke Ellington and His Orchestra. "Isfahan" was originally entitled "Elf." An Ellington composition (inspired in part by a theme by Jimmy Hamilton), "Ad Lib on Nippon," has been added to commercial releases of the suite.

The Newport Jazz Festival Suite (1956) Registered composers: Ellington–Strayhorn. Movements: "Festival Junction," "Blues to Be There," "Newport Up."

Recommended recording: *At Newport* (Columbia), Duke Ellington and His Orchestra.

The Perfume Suite (1945) Registered composers and lyricists: Ellington–Strayhorn. Movements: "Sonata" (also known as "Love," "Under the Balcony," and "Balcony Serenade"), "Strange Feeling" (also known as "Violence"), "Dancers in Love" (also known as "Naivete" and "Stomp for Beginners"), "Coloratura" (also known as "Sophistication"). Recommended recording: *The Duke Ellington Carnegie Hall Concerts, December 1944* (Prestige), Duke Ellington and His Orchestra. "Sonata" was copyrighted in the name of Strayhorn alone on April 13, 1945. "Strange Feeling," copyrighted in the names of both Ellington and Strayhorn on the same date, was included on Strayhorn's solo record *The Peaceful Side* and was used in the theatrical presentation *My People*, in the latter case attributed to Ellington. Tempo Music cited Ellington as sole composer of both "Dancers in Love" and "Coloratura" in its registrations filed on January 4, 1945, and April 18, 1945, respectively.

Portrait of Ella Fitzgerald (1957) Registered composers: Ellington–Strayhorn. Movements: "Royal Ancestry," "All Heart," "Beyond Category," "Total Jazz." Recommended recording: *Ella Fitzgerald Sings the Duke Ellington Songbook* (Verve), Ella Fitzgerald with Duke Ellington and His Orchestra. Copyrighted jointly in the names of Ellington and Strayhorn, the work has been credited to Ellington in performances by the Duke Ellington Orchestra under Mercer Ellington's direction. One of the suite's movements, "All Heart," was performed by the Ellington Orchestra at Carnegie Hall on December 27, 1947, as "Entrance of Youth."

The Queen's Suite (1959) Registered composers: Ellington–Strayhorn. Movements: "Sunset and the Mockingbird," "Lightning Bugs and Frogs," "Le Sucrier Velours," "Northern Lights," "The Single Petal of a Rose," "Apes and Peacocks." Recommended recording: *The Queen's Suite* (Pablo), Duke Ellington and His Orchestra. "Northern Lights" was copyrighted in the name of Strayhorn alone on April 16, 1959. All other sections have been copyrighted in Ellington's name. In its LP release, the suite was credited jointly to Ellington and Strayhorn. On CD, the suite is credited solely to Ellington.

Such Sweet Thunder (1957) Registered composers: Ellington–Strayhorn. Movements: "Such Sweet Thunder," "Sonnet for Caesar," "Sonnet to Hank Cinq," "Lady Mac," "Sonnet in Search of a Moor," "The Telecasters," "Up and Down, Up and Down," "Sonnet for Sister Kate," "The Star-Crossed Lovers," "Madness in Great Ones," "Half the Fun," "Circle of Fourths." Recommended recording: *Such Sweet Thunder* (Columbia), Duke Ellington and His Orchestra. See Songs: "Pretty Girl."

Suite for the Duo Registered composers: none. Movements are untitled. Recommended recording: *Strayhorn* (Mainstream LP), the Dwike Mitchell–Willie Ruff Duo. Also known as *Suite for Piano and French Horn*. No copyright registration has been filed for this piece.

Suite Thursday (1961) Registered composer: Ellington. Movements: "Misfit

Blues," "Schwiphtiey," "Zweet Zurzday," "Lay-By." Recommended recording: *Three Suites* (Columbia), Duke Ellington and His Orchestra. Although Strayhorn is credited as co-composer on the suite's recordings, Tempo Music copyrighted all four movements in Ellington's name. "Schwiphtiey" has been released as "Schwiphti."

Symphomaniac (1949) Registered composer: Ellington. Movements: "Symphonic or Bust," "How You Sound." Recommended recording: *Carnegie Hall, November 13, 1948* (VJC), Duke Ellington and His Orchestra. The piece is attributed to Ellington and Strayhorn on recordings. No copyright has been filed for its first movement, "Symphonic or Bust." Ellington was cited as sole composer of the second movement, "How You Sound," in Tempo Music's registration, filed on April 28, 1949.

Toot Suite (1962) Registered composers: Ellington–Strayhorn. Movements: "Red Garter," "Red Shoes," "Red Carpet," "Ready Go." Recommended recording: *Jazz Party* (Columbia), Duke Ellington and His Orchestra.

The Virgin Islands Suite (1965) Registered composers: Ellington–Strayhorn. Movements: "Island Virgin," "Virgin Jungle," "Fiddler on the Diddle," "Jungle Kitty." Recommended recording: *Concert in the Virgin Islands* (Reprise), Duke Ellington and His Orchestra.

Note on unrecorded music:

More than 160 known compositions by Billy Strayhorn remain unrecorded, including his earliest music in a classical vein ("Valse" and "Concerto for Piano and Percussion"); his first copyrighted songs ("You Lovely Little Devil" and "I'm Still Begging You," both written with John Raymond Wood); unpublished work for the Mad Hatters ("If You Were There") and pieces for various orchestras in Pittsburgh; dozens of his compositions for the Copasetics; virtually all of the scores for his produced theatrical projects (*Fantastic Rhythm* and *The Love of Don Perlimplín for Belisa in Their Garden*); most of his music for unproduced plays (*Rose-Colored Glasses* and *Saturday Laughter*, the former a collaboration with Luther Henderson, the latter primarily an Ellington project); Strayhorn compositions (and collaborations with Ellington and others) copyrighted but not recorded ("All Roads Lead Back to You," "Boo-Lose," "Christmas Surprise," "So This Is Love," others); and several dozen jazz pieces and songs whose music is currently in repository at the Smithsonian Institution or under stewardship of the Billy Strayhorn estate ("Just in Case," "South Wind," "What Else Can I Do," "Wish I Knew What Happened," others).

Illustration Credits

Frontispiece: Portrait of Billy Strayhorn by Duke Ellington, 1973.

Illustrations following page 148:

Strayhorn in Montclair and the Strayhorn house in Homewood, courtesy of Lillian Strayhorn Dicks. The Strayhorns in Hillsborough, courtesy of the Hillsborough Historical Society. Manuscript of "Something to Live For," courtesy of Jerome Eisner. Strayhorn in Pittsburgh, courtesy of the Smithsonian Institution. Strayhorn at the piano, courtesy of the Institute of Jazz Studies, Rutgers University. Strayhorn with Aaron Bridgers and Billie Holiday, courtesy of Aaron Bridgers.

Illustrations following page 244:

Strayhorn with Lena Horne, courtesy of Aaron Bridgers. Strayhorn with Horne and Lennie Hayton, courtesy of Cholly Atkins. Strayhorn and Ellington in Paris, by Sam Shaw, copyright © by Sam Shaw; used by permission. Strayhorn and Ellington, 1957, courtesy of the Institute of Jazz Studies, Rutgers University. Strayhorn and Ellington, early 1960s, courtesy of the Schomburg Center for Research in Black Culture. The Copasetics, courtesy of Frank Goldberg. Strayhorn family reunion, courtesy of Lillian Strayhorn Dicks. Strayhorn with the Logans et al., courtesy of Marian Logan. Strayhorn and Bill Grove, courtesy of Frank Goldberg. Strayhorn and Ellington kissing, courtesy of the Schomburg Center for Research in Black Culture.

All other photographs, records, and memorabilia are from the author's collection.

Index

estate of, 258–59; family background of, 4–5; family ties of, 74–76, 201–2, 208, 214–17; and film scores, 188–90, 206–8, 211; Fitzgerald and, 167–69; gains reputation as arranger, 43–45; Gershwin's influence on, 21–22; Goldberg and, 172–74, 182–83, 187–88, 200–1; Grove and, 235–36, 247–49; Henderson's proposed collaboration with, 137–38, 141–42; at Hickory House, 165–67; hired by Ellington, 51–55; and Hodges's recordings, 122–23, 176–79, 197–99, 217; in Hollywood, 90–92; homosexuality of, 20, 33–34, 79–80, 149, 172; Horne and, 94–97, 108–10; independent theater projects of, 124–33; interview with Ellington and, ix–x; introduced to Ellington, 49–51; at jazz festivals, 151–53, 202; in Logans' social circle, 191–96; as lyricist, 134–36; and Mahalia Jackson recording, 179–80; memorial service for, 255–58; on Middle East tour, 230–31; and Mine Boy project, 180–81, 183–85; in mixed-race trio, 36–43; moves to New York, 56–59; mugging of, 149–50; and musical revues, 22–29, 91–94, 185–87; nature of collaboration with Ellington, 81–83; in Neal Salon, 114–18; negotiates new relationship with Ellington, 153–54; nickname of, 89; in Paris, 108, 111–14, 142–45, 208–14, 219–21; philosophy of life of, 76–77; plays piano with Ellington Orchestra, 61; publication of works by, 120–22; and Shakespeare project, 154–57, 159–61, 163–64; shopping by, 33, 143–44; Sinatra and, 218–19; singers influenced by, 97–99; and small bands, 60–61; solo album of, 211–14; and Steinbeck project, 202–3, 208; as studio musician, 136–37; Tchaikovsky and, 203–6; and television special, 157–63; Welles and, 112–13; Wood in composing partnership with, 20–21; during World War II, 99–100

Strayhorn, Georgia (aunt), 4
Strayhorn, Georgia (sister), see Conaway, Georgia Strayhorn
Strayhorn, Harry (brother), 8
Strayhorn, James (father), 4–10, 30–31, 55, 75, 173, 202, 225–26
Strayhorn, James, Jr. "Jimmy" (brother), 3, 5, 10, 19, 202, 226, 248
Strayhorn, Jobe (grandfather), 4, 10–11
Strayhorn, John (brother), 8, 9, 31, 202
Strayhorn, Joseph (uncle), 4
Strayhorn, Julia (aunt), 4, 5, 55, 75
Strayhorn, Larry (nephew), 247–48
Strayhorn, Leslie (brother), 3

Strayhorn, Lillian (sister), see Dicks, Lillian Strayhorn
Strayhorn, Lillian Young (mother), 3–12, 31, 55, 57, 58, 74–75, 195, 202, 226, 249
Strayhorn, Lizzie (grandmother), 4, 10–11
Strayhorn, Sadie (sister), 3
Strayhorn, Samuel (brother), 8
Strayhorn, Theodore (brother), 8, 202
Strayhorn, William (uncle), 4, 5
Studio One (television program), 157
Stump and Stumpy, 186
"Subtle Slough," 91
Such Sweet Thunder (Ellington and Strayhorn), 156–57, 160–61, 163, 164, 169, 170
Sudan nightclub (Harlem), 174
"Sugar Hill Penthouse," 121
Suite for the Duo (Strayhorn), 251
Suite Thursday (Ellington and Strayhorn), 203, 205n, 208
Sullivan, Ed, 167
"Sunday Morning," 246
"Sun-Tanned Tenth of the Nation, " 91
"Sweet Sue," 42, 109
Sweet Thursday (Steinbeck), 202
Syms, Sylvia, 256

"Take It Away," 82
"Take the 'A' Train," xi, 55–57, 84–86, 93, 97, 133, 167, 176, 211, 212, 219, 258
"Tapioca," 121
"Tattooed Bride, The," 140
Tatum, Art, 32, 50, 53, 66, 136, 154
Taylor, Billy, 60, 258
Taylor, Creed, 217–18
Tchaikovsky, Peter Ilych, 203–7
"Telecasters, The," 161
Temperley, Joe, 183–84
Tempo Music, Inc., 121–22, 133, 134, 175, 240–41, 258–59
temps court, Le (Time Runs) (Welles), 112–13
Terry, Clark, 147, 148, 159, 176, 191, 238, 240–41
"That's the Blues, Old Man," 83
Theater Guild (New York), 157, 159
"There'll Be Some Changes Made," 96
Thomas, Dylan, 235
Thomas, Johnny, 117
Thornhill, Claude, 87
Threepenny Opera, The (Weill and Brecht), 101
"Three Shows Nightly," 185–86
Time magazine, 152
Tizol, Juan, 62, 88, 123, 140, 205
Todd, Michael, 166
Tone Parallel to Harlem, A (Ellington and Strayhorn), 140, 246